ON GROUP ANALYSIS
AND BEYOND

ON GROUP ANALYSIS AND BEYOND

Group Analysis as Meta-theory, Clinical Social Practice, and Art

Anastassios Koukis

Routledge
Taylor & Francis Group
LONDON AND NEW YORK

First published 2016 by Karnac Books Ltd.

Published 2018 by Routledge
2 Park Square, Milton Park, Abingdon, Oxon OX14 4RN
711 Third Avenue, New York, NY 10017, USA

Routledge is an imprint of the Taylor & Francis Group, an informa business

Copyright © 2016 to Anastassios Koukis

The right of Anastassios Koukis to be identified as the author of this work has been asserted in accordance with §§77 and 78 of the Copyright Design and Patents Act 1988.

All rights reserved. No part of this book may be reprinted or reproduced or utilised in any form or by any electronic, mechanical, or other means, now known or hereafter invented, including photocopying and recording, or in any information storage or retrieval system, without permission in writing from the publishers.

Notice:
Product or corporate names may be trademarks or registered trademarks, and are used only for identification and explanation without intent to infringe.

British Library Cataloguing in Publication Data

A C.I.P. for this book is available from the British Library

ISBN 9781782203612 (pbk)

Edited, designed and produced by The Studio Publishing Services Ltd
www.publishingservicesuk.co.uk
email: studio@publishingservicesuk.co.uk

CONTENTS

ACKNOWLEDGEMENTS viii

ABOUT THE AUTHOR x

SERIES EDITOR'S FOREWORD xi

INTRODUCTION xiv

PART I
IN SEARCH OF A THEORY AND
META-THEORY OF GROUP ANALYSIS

CHAPTER ONE
Principles of the group-analytic group: 3
towards a meta-theory

CHAPTER TWO
Paternal function and group analysis as a reverse 23
symmetry of conductor (father) and group
(mother): the prospects after Foulkes and Bion

PART II
GROUP ANALYSIS IN OPERATION: SOME FUNDAMENTAL ASPECTS AND PHENOMENA

CHAPTER THREE
Money: from the "thing" itself to its symbolic death 47
and to recognition of the symbolic father. A group-
analytic approach with a transcultural dimension

CHAPTER FOUR
Envy in group analysis 63

CHAPTER FIVE
Spaltpilz: a case of self-destructive projective 77
identification and scapegoating in the early phase
of a transcultural group-analytic group

CHAPTER SIX
Early ending in group analysis and borderline conditions 95

CHAPTER SEVEN
Ending in group analysis and neurosis: from 107
pathological narcissism to social consciousness

PART III
GROUP ANALYTIC PSYCHOTHERAPY AS A TREATMENT OF MAJOR DISORDERS

CHAPTER EIGHT
Group analysis and eating disorders: a study of 121
the therapeutic impact of group-analytic psychotherapy
on women suffering from anorexia and bulimia nervosa

CHAPTER NINE
Depression in schizophrenia and the therapeutic impact 135
of the group-analytic group

CHAPTER TEN
Dreaming and psychosis: coping with hearing 149
voices in group analysis

CHAPTER ELEVEN
The ontology and phenomenology of dreaming 163
in psychosis: a group-analytic approach with a
neuropsychological perspective

PART IV
GROUP ANALYSIS AND ITS RELATIONSHIP
WITH THE SOCIAL UNCONSCIOUS AND ART

CHAPTER TWELVE
Desire and despair in postmodern times: aspects 177
of the social unconscious in a declining world and
the significance of group analysis for future prosperity

CHAPTER THIRTEEN
Group analysis and music: similarities and 199
differences between conducting a group-analytic
group and conducting an orchestra

EPILOGUE 221

REFERENCES 227

INDEX 247

ACKNOWLEDGEMENTS

This book covers a broad spectrum of psychoanalytic and group analytic issues with an inter-disciplinary perspective, and was written successively over the past twenty years or so. Thus, it is obviously indebted to a great many colleagues and people, in Greece and abroad, and in other domains, from science and philosophy to music. It would be hazardous to try and enumerate them all here, with a high risk of inadvertently leaving someone out. A large number of colleagues, among whom special mention should be made of Malcolm Pines, the patriarch of group analysis after Foulkes, are properly cited in the book as sources. They all know how much I appreciate their contribution to the preparation of this book through our discussions and communications or collaborations over the years and, above all, I thank them wholeheartedly for their encouragement in my effort to investigate further subtle and perplexed issues in group analytic theory, meta-theory, and clinical practice that remained as yet unexplored.

Special thanks are due to the Karnac editors—and in particular to my colleague Earl Hopper—who not only read the manuscript and supported its publication, but also expressed their continuous and mindful concern for it during the editorial processes. I also express my thanks to the editors of the journals referred to in this book for their permission to allow chapters that were initially published as articles in their journals to be reprinted here.

My warmest thanks to all the members of my group-analytic groups, past and present. Nobody has taught me as much as they have, or has given me the strength to continue at times when the desire to deepen the understanding of the human soul seemed to be dwindling rapidly under the burden of what appeared to be impenetrable or inconceivable, an obstacle with which all psychological researchers are known to struggle ceaselessly.

ABOUT THE AUTHOR

Anastassios Koukis, PhD, BSc (Hons) in Psychology, MBPsS, is a psychologist, group analyst and psychoanalyst; a full member of the Group Analytic Society International (GASI) and a member of the International Association for Group Psychotherapy and Group Processes (IAGP); and also the founder of the International Society for Psychological and Social Approaches to Psychosis (ISPS) Hellas, the Greek branch of ISPS. He is the author of two books in Greek, *Dreams in Group Analysis*, and *The Decline of Paternity*, and has written many papers on group analysis and psychoanalysis, especially on group psychotherapy of psychoses. He is also a musician and clarinet player.

SERIES EDITOR'S FOREWORD

Privileged, is what I felt when reading and studying this intelligent and erudite selection of mostly previously published articles that the author has integrated into an extended essay conveying a broad and deep understanding of the meta-theory of group analysis as the product of psychoanalysis, sociology, and the study of group dynamics. Dr Anastassios Koukis, PhD draws upon the ideas of Freud, Klein, and Lacan, as well as those of Bion and Foulkes in order to explain clinical and empirical data. And vice-versa, he presents data in order to illustrate general ideas and hypotheses about fundamental group and personal processes. Although informed by the ideas of Schopenhauer, Nietzsche, and Heidegger as well as those of Sartre, Merleau-Ponty, Levi-Strauss, and other secular priests from within this broad church of the *condition humaine*, this book is concerned primarily with therapeutic work in groups, often with difficult patients in difficult circumstances.

It is obvious to me that Dr Koukis is an "Independent", non-aligned to any particular school of thought and practice. This is not an easy achievement in the context of the development of group analysis and psychoanalysis, especially in Greece where there have been many attempts to integrate intellectual and clinical influences from Germany, Britain, France, and even the US. Perhaps, however, only a modern Greek who understands the mercurial nature of Hermes can find comfort within this conflicted space.

This tension between the fluid and the solid within time and social space can be seen most clearly in Anastassios Koukis' ability to maintain his identity as a musician who is sensitive to both classical music and jazz, and to grow his identity as a psychoanalyst and group analyst, who is sensitive to non-verbal communication in dyads and in larger group ensemble. He understands the music of the group within its social context, and gives due weight to the importance of political struggles in which all attempts to balance human expectations and human achievements are embedded. For example, the tension between the universal and local appeal of forms of musical art can be compared to the tension between the universal archetypes and their local representations, both collective and personal, which is why it has been necessary to develop a field theory of the social unconscious. Foundation matrices and dynamic matrices always have a species based biological and physiological dimension, and, hence, must be understood both in terms of the universality of the "collective unconscious", in the classical Jungian sense of the term, and in terms of the specificity and particularity of the "social unconscious" in the modern group analytical sense of the term.

I am particularly interested in Koukis' work on the Freudian and later Kleinian understanding of expectations and desires, of frustrations and *ennuie*. Although the study of such topics benefits from familiarity with some of the biggest ideas of twentieth century philosophy, especially before the advent of modern linguistic philosophy, they also require the study of psychoanalysis and group analysis, and I would suggest clinical experience in each. Anastassios has studied psychology, pedagogy, and philosophy in Greece and in the UK. He was awarded a PhD in philosophy in 1988 (University of Ioannina) and in 1992–1993 prepared his post-doctoral thesis *Heidegger et l'historialité: Aspects de l'inconscient pré-ontologique* (University of Warsaw). Following his initial career as a philosopher at the Research Center for Philosophy at the Academy of Athens, he trained in Group Analysis at the Institute of Group Analysis (IGA) in Athens, and subsequently at the Hellenic Association of Group Analysis and Psychotherapy, where he was a training analyst. During 1988–1995 he also trained in Lacanian psychoanalysis. He is well known to group analysts throughout Europe where he participates in various international congresses in philosophy, psychoanalysis, group analysis, and psychodrama. He is a member of the International Association for Group Psychotherapy and Group Process (IAGP) and a full member of the Group Analytic Society International (GASI). In 2007 he founded ISPS Hellas, the Greek branch of the International Society for Psychological and Social Approaches to Psychosis (ISPS), and he is the current President of it.

I am pleased to recommend this book to colleagues in group analysis and psychoanalysis in Europe and the US. It is especially relevant to those who are training as group analysts.

Earl Hopper
Series Editor

Introduction

The existence of this book seems to have been pre-determined, fatalistic though this might sound. Some of its chapters were partially presented as papers at European or international conferences or published as articles in learned journals, or were prepared as introductory lessons for relevant seminars in reflection of my theoretical and clinical involvement in group-analytic psychotherapy over the past two decades. However, the evolution of my observations and research on many aspects of group analysis, as seen in the chapter titles, supports the view that they were written step by step, consciously or unconsciously, with the intention of being presented together eventually in book form. The book has thus been written and rewritten over a considerable period of time, since each chapter has been revised and adapted as required by its publication in a single volume. At the same time, as the book evolved, it utilised the main bibliographical sources that that were current throughout the period.

These chapters, although interrelated and overlapping, are organised into four parts, according to the axes around which my theoretical understanding and clinical approach to group-analytic themes have always revolved, as also reflected in each title.

Part I is made up of two chapters that aim to open new pathways in the formulation of group-analytic theory and meta-theory by combining and extending the views of Bion, Klein, and Foulkes. Since its initial formulation by Foulkes (1948, 1964) and Foulkes and Anthony (1957), group analysis is known to lack a systematic theory. It was originally based on the views of Bion (1961) regarding the function of groups, views that were then modified, extended, and transcended by the theoretical, socio-psychoanalytical, and practical views of Foulkes regarding the function of small group-analytic groups as therapeutic tools. By reabsorbing and reprocessing the views of Freud and, above all, those of Bion, a pioneer in the theoretical and clinical approach to groups, especially large groups, as to whether or not they required a father/leader, and by avoiding the well-known contemporary dilemma of whether Foulkes was more orthodox (psychoanalytic) than radical (social) in his approach or *vice versa* (Dalal, 1998), Chapters One and Two endeavour to draw the outline of a group-analytic theory and meta-theory by linking the paternal and the maternal functions as expressed by the conductor and the small group, respectively, and extending them to the psychoanalytic and psycho-linguistic aspects of Lacan, the dialectic of Kant's philosophy, and the structuralism of Levi-Strauss's anthropological views. In Chapter One, the idea of the circle (signifying maternity on the pre-oedipal level), expressed by group analysis as encompassing the triangle (symbol of the oedipal situation and paternity), according to Foulkes and Bion, and the idea of the oedipal triangle or paternity, contributed principally by psychoanalysis, as taking precedence over the circle (Freud) have been founded on a new epistemological model that combines both perspectives with the circle and the triangle touching externally as two autonomous entities. In Chapter Two, an effort has been made to supplement the proposed new model by conceiving the role of father and mother as parts of a kaleidoscope rather than as triangle and circle, respectively. Paternity and maternity, or psychoanalysis and group analysis, ceased to be registered on the triangle and circle, respectively, that represent static and self-restricting schemata, and are instead conceived in terms of a kind of mental and psychological kaleidoscope that combines both circular and triangular dimensions in a highly flexible way. The role of father (triangle) and mother (circle) as symbolic, imaginary, and real, following Lacan's views, are conceived in their kaleidoscopic dimension as autonomous and interchangeable positions, "languages" or "mythemes" that rotate freely and uninterruptedly in a dynamic way based on the "reverse symmetry" of the parental functions as expressed by Lévi-Strauss (1958, 1973).

Part II comprises five chapters and aims to provide substantial evidence of the new theoretical and meta-theoretical perspectives on group analysis outlined in Part I by further exploring a set of major group-analytic factors and phenomena. In Chapter Three, we investigate the role of money in group analysis by indicating the ways in which the members' payment for their therapy expresses the different levels of their therapeutic development, as long as they re-experience the pre-oedipal and oedipal phases, together with the evolution and development of the group as a whole. In Chapters Four and Five, an effort is made to shed light on scapegoating and envy, two extremely strong and complicated phenomena linked with projection and projective identification processes, as revealed mainly during the earliest or regressed phases of the group-analytic situation, and exhibiting the features of a malignant symbiosis syndrome. Chapter Six is devoted to studying the ways in which people with borderline personality disorder terminate their group-analytic therapy early. Early termination is related to some alterations of the patients' ego linked with introjections of a mothering object, which happens in a cataclysmic way in psychosis (Bion, 1992), so this ego is, to some extent, psychically dead. Part II concludes with Chapter Seven on normal ending in the group-analytic psychotherapy of people suffering mainly from neurosis, and is conceptualised as the result of their transcendence of the inverted oedipal situation and adequate resolution of their Oedipus complex.

In Part III, we investigate the crucial issue of whether and to what extent group analysis can be effective in treating severe mental disturbances such as eating disorders and psychosis. Chapter Eight explores the treatment of women suffering from anorexia nervosa and bulimia nervosa and Chapter Nine that of patients with depression in schizophrenia by using a modified version of group analysis. In Chapter Ten, we approach the phenomenon of the inability of patients who hear voices to dream, and conclude that dreaming proper in these patients can also be considerably reconstituted using a modified form of group-analytic psychotherapy. In Chapter Eleven, we further support the idea that group analysis helps patients with psychosis to reconstruct their ability to dream and initiate the discussion of ways in which neuropsychological research could further investigate this concept in the future.

Part IV considers two major domains into which group analysis could be expanded and used effectively, while at the same time deriving great benefits from them, by transcending its psychoanalytic roots and broadening its inherent social perspective. One domain is that of the social unconscious, the study of which was initiated by Foulkes (1948, 1990) and by de Maré and colleagues (1991) and is currently being explored and deepened by group analysts and theorists such as Earl Hopper (2001) and Haim Weinberg (2007). On this topic, Chapter Twelve is devoted to the dialectic of desire and despair in the postmodern world as one aspect of the socio-political decline of the social unconscious leading to the "deadening" of desire and the arousal of psychotic anxiety due to instant gratification of the subject's needs provided by postmodern consumer capitalism. The other domain is that of art, and the book ends with Chapter Thirteen, based on my dual identity as psychoanalyst and musician. It investigates the essential similarities between the act of conducting a group-analytic group and the art of conducting an orchestra, a comparison that Foulkes (1964, 1990) first observed in the guise of a metaphor. Utilising the theory and history of classical music in its more sophisticated dimensions as presented in the literature, not only by expert researchers but also by major composers such as Wagner (1887) and Berlioz (1902), and reinforced by rich clinical material, the final chapter concludes that there are significant and real, not just metaphorical, similarities between the art of the maestro and that of the group-analytic conductor, despite their differences. This is because the group-analytic group, owing to the evolution of its free-floating discussions as expressed by related musical scales and seen in human speech and prosody, bears a strong resemblance to a baroque orchestra in particular, as distinct from a classical one.

Despite its ambitious objectives, this book has at least three limitations, about which I should like to warn the reader. The first limitation concerns the heterogeneity in its style and in the elaboration of content that characterises the various chapters. Some articles were written many years ago and might require updating, while others are much more recent. Notwithstanding this discrepancy, it was decided to publish the earliest articles in their initial form (very few modifications have been made, either to provide new data from more recent literature or to better reformulate some sentences), as they express the evolution of ideas over time on matters such as analysands' anxieties, needs, and wishes as well as those of the analyst. Other articles have already been published in journals. They are republished here in their original form, with some slight modifications either in content or in the use of some patients' names (pseudonyms), in order to give logical coherence and continuity to the clinical material used in the book.

The second limitation is more serious and has to do with the idea of formulating a group-analytic theory, which was declared above to be one of the aims of this book. It should be noted that my efforts are intended to indicate the directions that our thinking should take in building a group-analytic theory and meta-theory, rather than to present a coherent theoretical structure.

The third limitation has to do with the scientific validity of the results. The fact is that research on group-analytic issues cannot be evidence-based in a strictly scientific way. The strongest evidence in the group-analytic material presented in this book is founded on a more or less linear symmetry between the clinical material and the relevant theoretical constructs proposed, both of which have been influenced by the subjectivity of the writer. It is hoped that evidence of this kind will be further reinforced by the accumulation of analogous research by other colleagues. In some cases, however, the investigation of group-analytic issues could be further supported by using scientific tools such as experiments on the basis of which one could verify the interrelation between the reconstitution of dreaming in psychosis through the group and its neuronal correlates, or the systematic description, categorisation, and evaluation of musical scales as used in the speech rhythms of group-analytic group members as a further verification of the similarities between the art of group analysis and the art of music. I wholeheartedly support such a future collaboration between group analysis and scientific research in connection with the former conceived as an art closer to music, and it is with the hope that I will take part in it by seeking to validate the results presented here to the reader.

In conclusion, I would like to say a few words about the clinical material presented here, and about my patients who, as group members, are the real actors in this book, which owes a great deal to them. Although all group members are designated here by pseudonyms, the clinical material related to them is real. I would like once more to express my deepest thanks to them all for consenting to have their stories published here.

PART I
IN SEARCH OF A THEORY AND META-THEORY OF GROUP ANALYSIS

CHAPTER ONE

Principles of the group-analytic group: towards a meta-theory

Introduction

The establishment of group-analytic group therapy on the principles of a meta-theory and epistemology, implying a coherent theory that is differentiated from the principles on which psychoanalysis is based, has constituted a major quest in group analysis and psychotherapy since the era of Bion (1946, 1961, 1962, 1963, 1970, 1992), Foulkes (1948, 1964, 1990), and Foulkes and Anthony (1957), to whom we owe the first attempts in this regard. The reason is obvious. Whereas, on the one hand, the theoretical and epistemological approach to clinical experience frequently alludes to some distancing from the latter, on the other hand—as is obvious particularly in an age characterised by rapid advances in science and knowledge—clinical experience cannot be utilised effectively in treatment unless it is founded on a credible epistemological paradigm (Lo Verso, 1996). In this chapter, an attempt is made to indicate the direction our thinking should take in the search for principles on which to build a meta-theory of group analysis. And, paradoxical though this may sound, it does not seem to be heading in the direction of contemporary post-modern group-analytic thought, but, rather, towards the thinking of

Bion, Foulkes, and even Freud (1900a, 1912–1913, 1914c, 1915e, 1921c, 1930a, 1937c), many of whose valuable writings remain unutilised. In other words, we are heading towards a positive re-engagement of psychoanalysis, and even of group analysis, as established by Foulkes. This re-engagement, in correlation with the re-evaluation and re-establishment of the main axes of the paternal function as expressed in psychoanalysis and particularly in group analysis, which will be the theme of the second chapter of this book, constitute, in our view, the two major cornerstones on the basis of which an epistemological group-analytic paradigm could begin to be constructed.

Sociality as a common denominator in group analysis and psychoanalysis

A thorough search of the literature leads directly to the realisation that many modern theoreticians and clinicians in group analysis are seeking this foundation through a new epistemological model that is radically distanced from the psychoanalytic model, which still provides it fundamental support, despite the equally radical change brought to the psychoanalytic process by group analysis, in terms of both context and therapy direction. The theoreticians and clinicians in question seek to establish a radical differentiation between the group-analytic epistemological model and the psychoanalytic one, mainly in the difference between psychoanalysis and group analysis as a distinction between intrapsychic individualism and a transpersonal or intersubjective field, or between the individual and the social, the person and the group (Brown, 1994; Cohn, 1993; Dalal, 1998; Lo Verso & Profita, 1991; Schulte, 2000; Stacey, 2000, 2001; Weegmann, 2001). Psychoanalysis thus takes on the spurious nature of a limited and diminished form of reality, in that it dwells upon psychic conflicts of an intrasubjective nature, which are, at most, reduced to a personal Other, maternal (pre-oedipal level) or paternal (oedipal level). On the contrary, group analysis constitutes a much richer and more fertile means of approaching and decoding reality, as it reduces psychic conflict to psycho-social and socio-political conflict in the creation of which an important role is played by the social Other.

Accordingly, the distinction in question is between the intrapersonal and social Other, between the psycho-biological, psychophysical and psycho-social, between the unconscious and conscious, or the Freudian unconscious, and, at most, the social unconscious, between pre-oedipal and oedipal relations (transference) and interrelations or relatedness (Brown, 2001; Dalal, 1998; Hopper, 2001; Lo Verso, 1996). This leads people whose thinking ranges within the framework in question to seek the epistemological foundation of group analysis in long-term borrowings of principles from across virtually the entire spectrum of philosophy, sociology, and neurology (Brown, 1994; Cohn, 1993; Dalal, 1998; Karterud, 1998; Powell, 1991; Schulte, 2000; Stacey, 2000, 2001), since the biological factor never ceases to allude with certainty to a "scientific" foundation. It is characteristic that an effort has recently been made to base the social nature of the person on an ambivalent and nebulous semi-social and semi-biological notion of a social function that is considered to be a kind of social instinct (Ormay, 2012). For the present, all these borrowings enter and remain in the field of group-analytic thought as metaphors (Stacey, 2000).

It is true that Foulkes and many other contemporary group analysts (Brown, 2001; Hopper, 2001) do not present this distinction in a disjunctive (either/or) manner, but in a supplementary (both–and) one, a manner which, as Stacey (2001) points out, originates from Kant's thought. The difference is that in Foulkes, supplementarity serves continuity in a centripetal way: despite the clear precedence of the social over the individual and the concomitant establishment of new semantics and a new therapeutic framework, group analysis remains within the epistemological universe of psychoanalysis. However, among the theoreticians who follow a post-Foulkesian perspective, and frequently adopt a dividing line between the orthodox and radical Foulkes (Dalal, 1998), disjunction or supplementarity serves continuity in a centrifugal way, that is, in a new epistemological plan beyond the psychoanalytic. Despite which, there are no grounds for this distinction, because it rests on the unstable base of an epistemological vacuum, which is suppression of the fact (in the sense of "I don't want to know") that psychoanalysis, from Freud's founding act (to which the influence of Kant's critical idealism undoubtedly contributed), far from being an intrasubjective and non-social activity, constitutes a social and political achievement of major importance. Thanks to psychoanalysis, the subject ceased to be the metaphysical and psychological abstraction to which he had been reduced in the centuries-old metaphysical tradition and ideology, as a result of which, through the philosophy and ideology of western liberalism, he was shown for the first time to be a specific psycho-biological, psycho-mental and psycho-social being. As crystallised in the ontogenetic unconscious, this subject constitutes a cross-fertilisation of the complex mechanisms, conscious and unconscious, created by the interweaving of the phylogenetic unconscious (which is primarily determined by the interrelation of the paternal and maternal imago) with the life of the subject in the group, as the latter evolved from pre-history through history, from the primal horde (first "family" group), to the totemic group and the fraternal clan, to the modern society and family (Freud, 1912–1913, 1921c).

Under these conditions, the distinction between psychoanalysis and group analysis is ultimately reduced to a distinction between two different versions of the social, or of groupishness. As recorded in modern group-analytic thought, the social appears to betray the idea of the unconscious interweaving of the maternal and paternal imago or, in Freud's (1921c) terms, the "ideal ego" and the "ego ideal", especially as they are represented by the group and the leader on the social level, respectively, with which the canvas of the social is woven in both Freud and Foulkes to a high degree. In essence, it betrays the Oedipus myth on which psychoanalytic thought is essentially founded and which, according to Bion, constitutes the cornerstone of *"socialism"*, or genuine sociability, conceived as the other pole of narcissism (Bion, 1992, pp. 105–106, my italics). Thus, it is in danger of being a philosophical idea whose epistemological validity could be seriously disputed. The idea that man, from an existential, anthropological, and political viewpoint, is a social being determined intrapsychically by a total of intersubjective relations with which his existence is involved constitutes, to use Kant's (2004[1783]) terms, an *a priori* "analytic judgement", that is, a tautological judgement whose predicate concept adds nothing new to our knowledge, in contrast to an *a priori* "synthetic judgement" whose predicate concept does add something new to our knowledge. A new epistemological group-analytic model, founded on the idea of intersubjectivity (interpersonal, transpersonal, social, intercultural, and intergenerational relations, etc.), by adding something new to our knowledge about the nature of sociality, in other words, by using sociality as a synthetic judgement instead of considering it a tautological analytic judgement, would have to discuss and overcome the tautological gaps inherent in the thinking of Freud, Foulkes, and Bion.

The unresolved Kantian antinomies of psychoanalysis and the Oedipus myth

The above analysis has indicated that the psychoanalytic (Freudian) epistemological universe is fundamentally a social one. It is also, despite its antinomies (in the Kantian sense) and its inherent indeterminacy, or, rather, because of them, a universe structured and unequivocal. More precisely, although it mainly constitutes a psychological theory, psychoanalysis is, from a philosophical viewpoint, an epistemological universe disposed *mutatis mutandis* chiefly towards the principles of Kant's epistemological universe.

1. As in Kant (2004[1783]), there are boundaries between the finite and the infinite beyond which we cannot see things without the intermediation of the human eye, that is "noumena", so, in Freud, there is a limit to knowledge of the unconscious ("the dream's navel") which we cannot unravel because it coincides with the "unknown" (Freud, 1900a, p. 525).
2. In Kant (2004[1783]) psychological, cosmological, and theological ideas are interwoven with a number of antinomies (thesis–antithesis) that are ultimately resolved in the *a priori* synthetic judgement, whose predicate concept confers something new to our knowledge. The two major synthetic judgements are those of God and of moral freedom (autonomy of the will). Similarly, in Freud (1912–1913, 1921c), post-psychological (ontogenetic unconscious), historical, anthropological (phylogenetic unconscious), and social (social unconscious) ideas are interwoven in the antimony that fundamentally characterises paternity and maternity:
   - *Thesis*: the father (totemism, paternal imago, ego ideal, social group, leader of the group, oedipal level) takes precedence over the mother (exogamy, maternal imago, ideal ego, natural and social group, pre-oedipal level);
   - *Antithesis*: the mother takes precedence over the father.

The antinomy to which this relationship is subject is partially resolved through what could constitute an *a priori* synthetic judgement, that is, through the Oedipus myth in the light of which the maternal and paternal imagos create a relationship of equality and self-rule on the prehistoric (pre-oedipal) level, in the sense of the common wellspring of totemism (civilisation, social group) and exogamy (nature, natural/social group), identification of the primal father/leader with the archaic mother/group (Freud, 1912–1913), and on the historical (oedipal) level in the sense that, on this level, the father and mother have differentiated themselves in terms of their gender and contribute self-sufficiently to the subject's access to the situation and to resolution of the Oedipus complex, but with the catalytic triumph of the father/leader, since the nature of the mother/group is chiefly pre-oedipal (Freud, 1921c, 1926d, 1933a). The idea that the Oedipus myth is an *a priori* synthetic judgement whereas sociability is an *a priori* analytic judgement, although implied in Freud, is mine. Freud attributes to the Oedipus myth the place that Kant attributes to the categories as well as to the *a priori* representations of space and time. Through them, perceptions, as daily subjective experience, which is personal clinical experience in this case, take on a sensible character in the form of a "schema" and are transformed into an objective experience (Kant, 2004[1783]). More precisely, Freud maintains that the Oedipus complex "relates to the phylogenetically inherited schemata, which, like the categories of philosophy, are concerned with the business of 'placing' the impressions derived from actual experience" (Freud, 1918b, p. 119).

Despite the solid and mostly valid theoretical knowledge and anthropological foundation of Freud's principles, the Freudian psychoanalytic epistemological model, as we will see more analytically in the next chapter, has always presented two main weak points in the context referred to here.

1. The special dimension taken on by the Oedipus myth weakens its pre-oedipal prerequisites in such a way that the ideal of the father or the leader of the group ("ego ideal") displaces that of the mother or the group ("ideal ego") (Freud, 1921c) and does not take advantage of the latter's nature as a "container" of the infant's or the member's psychic, mainly unwanted, reactions as projected to her or the group (Bion, 1962, 1963, 1970). In other terms, on the group level, the group/mother is not considered as a mothering soil based on the intercommunication of the group members in the context of the group matrix conceived as a highly

social network in which the individual, including the leader/ father, is simply a nodal point (Foulkes, 1964). As a result, oedipal relationships as expressed on either an individual or group level cannot be unravelled in such a way as to avoid splitting the cohesion of the group and wasting its emotional richness, and, thus, lead to an imaginary/archaic re-experience of the oedipal situation. The group's emotional richness is spent on the idea of an archaic father/leader who is considered as the main cause of the formation of the group and society. The leader of the group is an outstanding, "absolutely narcissistic" and "self-confident" personality and, as such, he "himself need love no one else". The group's and society's members, on the contrary, "stand in the need of the illusion that they are equally and justly loved by their leader" (Freud, 1921c, pp. 123–124). This is the reason why they give up their "ego ideal", by separating it temporarily from their ego, and substitute for it "the group ideal as embodied in the leader" (Freud, 1921c, p. 129). By putting *one and the same object in the place of their ego ideal*" they can then identify themselves "*with one another in their ego*" (Freud, 1921c, p. 116, original italics) by reinserting the "ego ideal" as paternal (leader) or maternal (group) ideal in their ego, and, consequently, with the leader/ father as a common shared "ego ideal" on an archaic imaginary level. In this sense, the leader/father of the group ("ego ideal"), who is nothing but a version of the father of the primal horde, remains an illusion of the group on the imaginary level, and the group/mother ("group ideal"), which is conceived as "a revival of the primal horde" and as a narcissistic extension of the primal father (Freud, 1921c, p. 123), represents an imaginary and hallucinatory entity.

2. The fundamental idea on which the Oedipus myth rests is that the primal father, the father of the primitive horde, who is first introjected by infants or primitive men in their imagination as an omnipotent and permanently "living" (immortal) father, or, in Lacan's terms, as an imaginary father, returns, cleansed of his primality, in the form of what Lacan (1981, 1994, 1998) calls a symbolic father in his archaic dimension because the child "kills" him by internalising him as a "dead" father. Thus, the sons of the father of the primal horde reach a resolution of the oedipal complex and later become the new fathers themselves (Freud,

1912–1913). However, this idea seems to refer to a closed and self-sufficient, psychotic-like system of paternity, which turns into a vicious circle. More specifically, Freud's idea of the oedipal myth further weakens the strength of the mother/group on the symbolic or imaginary level, while paving the way for the high-handedness of the idea of a leader/father who, even though he is conceived as more symbolic and less archaic than his predecessors due to his stronger identification with the idea of a "dead" father, and a better resolution of the oedipal complex, risks being no more than a continuation of the primal father as imaginary father (Freud, 1912–1913).

With these premises, the need is to further extend and enrich the oedipal myth, which remains a very useful tool in psychoanalysis and group analysis, by exploiting the ideas of Foulkes and Bion regarding a group-analytic frame of reference with the aim of starting to construct a new, more integrated epistemological paradigm of group analysis.

Group analysis and the antinomies of the Oedipus myth

It is obvious at this point how valuable Foulkes' effort has been—and that of group analysis in general—in giving paternity, or, more precisely, the Oedipus myth, a container, by reintroducing the more general (mainly pre-oedipal) concept of the matrix, that is, of the hypothetical network of all possible intercommunications and mental processes between the members of a group or society, conceived as the nucleus of sociality, the origin of which is the «Image of the "Mother"» (Foulkes, 1964, p. 289). Through a simple *a priori* analytic judgement based on the idea of the matrix (man is a social animal) (Foulkes, 1964; Foulkes & Anthony, 1957), Foulkes referred to and covered the epistemological vacuum on which the *a priori* synthetic judgement (Oedipus myth) of Freudian theory was fundamentally based. Foulkes emphasises that although, according to Freud, the oedipal conflict and the family conflict more generally is inevitable, on the basis of an "organic inheritance", "in terms of direct, inherited, archaic repetition", for him, the oedipal/family conflict "is rather in the nature of a living *transmission* of the whole previous cultural and biological experience"

(Foulkes, 1990, p. 238, original italics). Nevertheless, the idea of the "transmission of the cultural and biological experience", apart from the fact that it is not radically differentiated from the idea of the "inherited repetition", is also in the nature of *a priori* synthetic judgement.

But this reopens the epistemological vacuum that Freud was trying to cover, and constitutes the weak point of Foulkes' theory, since:

- despite the fact that the group is constituted on the basis of a triangular relationship (the conductor, the group and its members), it is doubtful whether the Oedipus myth can be fully unfolded in such a context because, on the one hand, personal transference is weakened through interpersonal relations (Foulkes, 1964) and on the other, because the group on the post-oedipal level (as "progression beyond the oedipal stage") (Foulkes, 1990, p. 241) becomes no more than an abstraction. The assumption of the Oedipus myth seems to be condensed and undermined in the group in a regressive rather than progressive schema (Foulkes, 1990), which is why Foulkes, too, regards it as *a priori* given—harking back to Freud's *a priori* synthetic judgement—that the conductor, when establishing the group as analyst/conductor, "must have solved his own Oedipus conflict satisfactorily" (Foulkes, 1964, p. 65).
- it appears that, in a thoroughly paradoxical and contradictory way, the Oedipus myth can somehow be developed on the group's primary level (initial phase) when the conductor carries all the authority of the leader conceived as a representation of the primal father, who, on this level, "corresponds to the early pre-oedipal phallic mother" (Foulkes, 1990, p. 242), without whose "sanction", though, the formation of the group remains ontologically inconceivable (Foulkes, 1964, pp. 62–63). On the secondary level, the Oedipus complex will be resolved on the initiative of the conductor/primal father who, it is hoped, will "dig his own grave" in the sense described above (Foulkes, 1964, p. 62), which remains a largely illusory idea, since no father/conductor is expected to be able to favour his own symbolic death. But even if this could happen, it would be an act preventing members from experiencing the frustration of being less strong than the father/conductor and, thus, being led to "killing" by their own

hand. Normally, we would expect that such an act of protecting the members/children derives from the maternal attitude of the mother/group on the pre-oedipal level rather than from the conductor/father on the oedipal level. In any case, the vicious epistemological circle of the Oedipus myth is also reproduced here on other premises.

The views of Foulkes, as we will see more concretely in the next chapter, seem to legalise Lacan's position, which, in essence, reproduces that of Freud, but on a new epistemological and mathematical foundation, according to which groupishness (the idea of the whole or the circle) can be created only within the bonds of paternal kinship and in fact, contrary to what Freud believed, under the unifying principle of the primal father. According to Lacan, the whole (circle) can be constituted only by men—given that, owing to their limited phallic enjoyment, they are in their totality subject to symbolic castration—on condition, however, that at least one of them is not subject to this castration; he, as we can conclude indirectly, can be none other than the primal father. On the contrary, the whole cannot be constituted by women, since, owing to their excessive phallic enjoyment, women are not subject in their totality to symbolic castration (some are and others are not, so that you have to enumerate them one by one) (Lacan, 1998a). For Lacan, as we can likewise conclude indirectly, only psychoanalysis can restrict the role and function of the primal father to that which he really represents: a tough but simple and useful version of the imaginary father, he who, by depriving the mother of her imaginary possession of a penis, is obliged to urge castration of the boy to the point of (imaginary) deprivation of his penis as real (and potentially symbolic) object, which later will lead the boy to a stronger claim and possession of the penis in the sense of the penis as phallus on the symbolic level (Lacan, 1994).

In these terms, we can assume that within the group, even if it is conducted according to the conditions set out by Foulkes, the concept and function of the primal father, as represented by the conductor, is in danger of taking on an excessive and unrealistic dimension beyond its lawful limits and, since the group moves on a very fragile line between the psychotic (pre-oedipal) and neurotic (oedipal) level (Foulkes & Anthony, 1957), can lead to destructive results. On the one hand, the primal father, who is represented over a long period of time by the conductor conceived as a leader of the group, is possessed by excessive narcissism (Freud, 1921c) that does not permit him to accept symbolic castration, and seems to become even more inflated as the primal horde is somehow brought back to the initial cradle in which it was hatched. The horde is for a long time represented by the group. As a result, it is by no means certain that the primal father/conductor will prefer gradually to become "dead" (i.e., to favour the reshaping of personal transferences to interpersonal and transpersonal relations) instead of remaining constantly "alive" and diverting group relations into a somewhat particular kind of inter-transference towards him. On the other hand, the group, given that it is always under the influence of a "living" father, leans towards a long-term regression to its initial phase, that is, the primordial or archaic level, long before the level of projection and transference or the phase of bodily and mental images, thus avoiding a full entrance into the group's final and mature level of a good enough contact with everyday reality (Foulkes, 1964). As a result, therapy in the group-analytic group is quite often in danger of:

- favouring fixation of the member who suffers from psychosis at the primary level and intensifying it. This person is at risk of being in absolute fusion with the mother/group and being devoured by it;
- leading the member who is suffering from a borderline personality disorder to a constant regression to the same primary level or to the intermediate level of bodily and mental images, in which issues of the patient's mirroring by others and their body and self images as based on relative projective group processes are continuously fought for and negotiated;
- causing the fixation of the patient with neurosis at the intermediate level, conceived as a level of re-handling transference rather than projections or mirroring. This fixation is in danger of being reinforced by the fact that the patient is unable to distinguish whether his transference should or can be resolved either by returning to the primordial level or through a stable transition at the current level, where transference is converted to relatedness. The neurotic patient is, thus, in danger of finding himself in a state of immobilisation which eventually leads to the inherent antinomy which the Oedipus myth seems to take on in the group, which is to be favoured on the primordial/archaic level, during

which, as happens in the earliest phases of the infant's development, the Oedipus conflict risks leading the member/child to "a dread of being devoured and destroyed" (Klein, 1928, p. 187), and suppressed on the current level, which is the level of mature experiencing of the Oedipus complex without this causing deep psychotic fear. Needless to say that, according to Foulkes, in this case there is no antinomy. For him, the Oedipus complex, as it may appear in the primordial/archaic, projective, and transference levels of the group in the form of the *"transmission"* of a "cultural and biological experience", has the features of an "irrational manifestation" (Foulkes, 1990, pp. 238, 242, original italics) and leads to a dead end. This is because, at these levels, the conductor, as leader of the group, sometimes coincides with the "early pre-oedipal phallic mother" (Sphinx) (Foulkes, 1990, p. 242), and at others—based on a role attributed to him by the group as Sphinx—seems to become an "Oedipus" in the sense of the tragic "hero" who solves the enigma of the Sphinx, kills his father, and marries his mother (Foulkes, 1990, p. 247). This situation can be overcome, according to Foulkes, who does not regard it as "suppression" of the oedipal myth, through the group's utilisation as a "grown-up, mature person" (Foulkes, 1990, p. 242) with whom both the members and the conductor are called upon to identify. In this sense, the conductor ceases to be the "leader *of* the group" and becomes a "leader *in* the group" (Foulkes, 1964, p. 61, my italics), thereby digging his own grave.

These, then, are the thoughts that we must take into account and the antinomies that we must resolve if we are to lay the foundation for the circle created by the group-analytic group as a new epistemological model in comparison to the corresponding psychoanalytic model as expressed by the triangle. This circle does not constitute a new model solely because, in contrast to that of psychoanalysis, it is able to demonstrate the "ontology" of interrelations in the sense of laying the foundation for them on the principle of intersubjectivity (Lo Verso & Profita, 1991). This is not a circle based simply on the principle of intersubjectivity. On the contrary, it is a circle that includes its ontological and epistemological value, and is introduced and constituted as a maternal representation and function with the presence and initiative of a man who is regarded as representing the paternal function (triangle) with a view to promoting the Oedipus myth.

The Oedipus myth as container and Bion's legacy

In this regard, Bion's efforts are of particular importance as he first attempted to establish the Oedipus myth or triangle epistemologically (psychoanalysis level) and then to adapt it epistemologically to the circle (group psychotherapy, society) in such a way that, through a much more flexible and authentic engagement of the myth (linear dimension) by the circle (groupishness, circular dimension) than was attempted by Freud and Foulkes, it led him to the greatest possible effectiveness. We are, of course, referring here to Bion's effort to disengage the oedipal situation from the idea of identification with the father and from its formalist, phylogenetic schematisation, and to correlate it with the idea of the coupling parents (conceived as a mature evolution of the archaic fantasy of the primal scene) in Klein's (1946, 1957) view. According to Bion, the oedipal situation follows the idea of the primal scene as it evolves from an ordinary sensory experience or archaic fantasy (in which parents are fantasised as being constantly in a *coitus a tergo*) to a scene with "the character of a hieroglyph or an ideogram", and from there ultimately to an "abstract" scene (Bion, 1992, p. 203). The oedipal situation unfolds meaningfully only as long as it finds a "container" in the idea of the coupling parents (primary group) as it evolved from its most archaic to its most mature dimension, that is, from the oral–sadistic stage to the successful negotiation between the paranoid–schizoid position and the depressive position.

The depressive position appears to constitute the counterpart of what, on the epistemological level, Poincaré calls a "selected fact" (Bion, 1992, p. 26). It is the supreme "container" by means of which scattered and "dead, unreal objects" or, in Bion's terms, "beta-elements (β-elements)" of the oral–sadistic stage and the paranoid–schizoid position are transformed into "alive, real" objects called "alpha-elements (α-elements)" (Bion, 1992, p. 133) in such a way as to create a "constant conjunction" between them; this is a causal relation, which ceases to be a physiological mechanism, as Hume defined it, and acquires the qualities of an ontological principle (Bion, 1992, pp. 13, 153). Thus, as the transition proceeds gradually from the oral–sadistic stage to the paranoid–schizoid position and from there to the depressive position, a circle is created in the sense that groupishness is cultivated through the transformation of beta-elements to alpha-elements, culminating in the winning of the depressive position (pre-oedipal level). A triangle is also created (oedipal situation, Oedipus myth) which, since its culmination is the result of winning the depressive position, is inscribed in the circle as the latter's maximum unfolding. The oedipal triangle and the circle of groupishness touch at the point that constitutes the highest container of both, that is, the winning of the depressive position. Indeed, they encounter their epistemological cognates in the Pythagorean theorem and in the cosmological course traced by the universe, respectively, as they in turn encounter their mythological and psychological cognates. Theory concurs with myth and *vice versa* (Bion, 1992).

The resulting geometric shape is an isosceles triangle inscribed in a circle touched by its three points. We can infer indirectly that this shape:

- is the reverse of the geometric shape created on the basis of Freud's concept, in which the circle is contained within the isosceles triangle in such a way that it touches its sides. In this concept, the triangle (Oedipus situation) triumphs over the circle (pre-oedipal level) with which, however, it does not lose the point of contact (recognition of the value of the mother's function in promoting resolution of the Oedipus complex);
- is very different from, although related to, the geometric shape created on the basis of Foulkes' viewpoint. According to his concept, access to the oedipal situation and resolution of the Oedipus complex (triangle, father) is advanced through the *a priori* dominance of the circle/group/mother over the triangle, or by ceding of more of the field occupied by the triangle to that occupied by the circle, so that the possibilities of the unfolding of the triangle, which is in danger of losing its contact with the circle, are tangibly reduced (Figure 1).

Finally, based solely on the geometric shape proposed by Bion, it can be said that access to the oedipal situation and resolution of the Oedipus complex is achieved through the equal evolution and dialectical interaction between the paternal and maternal imago. On the level of the chronological and logical container, however, priority is attached to the maternal/female imago, the mother/breast, on either the individual or social level (i.e., the group, which is also a representation of the mother) as the primary container (Bion, 1992).

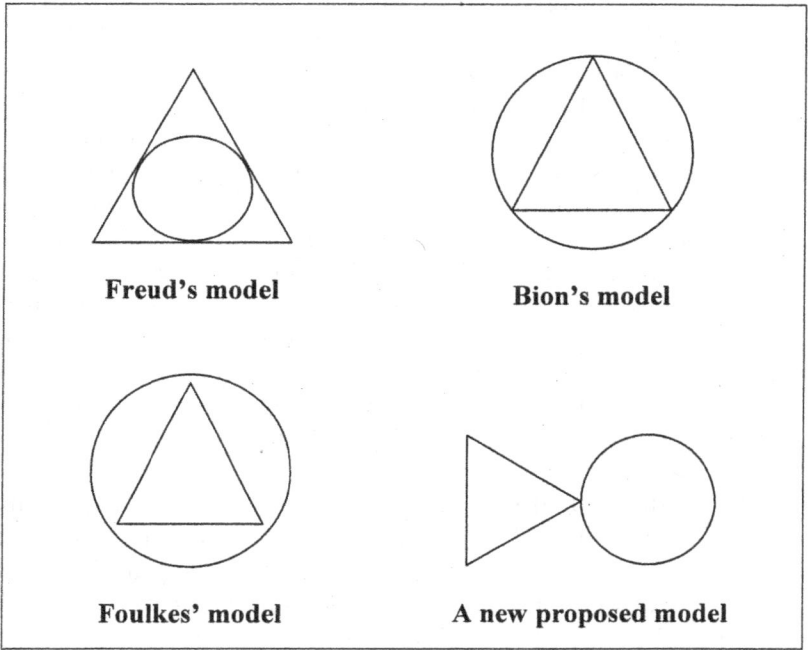

Figure 1. The circle (group analysis) and the triangle (psychoanalysis). Towards a new epistemological model.

Initially, on the proto-real level (Bion, 1992), and despite its ability to supply alpha-elements (i.e., to function as container of the projective identifications and sadistic attacks by the infant/member), the mother/group is deluged with beta-elements, and cannot function as a container in the sense described above (oral–sadistic level) (Bion, 1962). At this level, the father—long before showing himself as a leader—is no more than the breast as equated to the penis. This breast is the "prototype for all the links" and communications (Bion, 1967, p. 93) including the primal scene, which assumes its early form here, not as an archaic fantasy but as the "oral" union of the male (♂) with the female (♀), or that of the nipple with the mouth (♂♀) (Bion, 1962, 1963, 1967).

Then, while the mother/group, always in correlation with the father, passes to the paranoid–schizoid position, when many of the beta-elements start being reshaped into alpha-elements, the father/breast is differentiated from the group/mother for the first time, through the latter's illusion, in order to occupy the position of leader. The father is recognised as leader (meaning a basic-assumption-group leader) (Bion, 1961) in the sense that by means of the projection upon him, the group/mother is called upon to preserve and express a relevant basic assumption to which it is subject (as mother and as basic-assumption group): dependence on an almighty divinity, flight from reality or fight for whatever does not contribute to its acceptance, and the creation of pairing which, as an expression of the type of primal scene that dominates at this level (that of combined parents possessed by the illusion), aim to cultivate the hope that from the union of the combined parents, a new Messiah will be born (deity). However, this hope must not be realised; it must remain an illusion, in order to preserve dependence (Bion, 1961). The following are found at this level, together with their epistemological foundation:

- the myth of Oedipus in the sibyllic, paranoid form initially projected upon him by the Sphinx, a myth which "stimulates curiosity" and whose realisation led to the killing of the father, the suicide of the mother, and the blinding of the son;
- the myths of the Tower of Babel and the Garden of Eden, since this is the level at which discourse unfolds for the first time, in a dimension that is still paranoid and, therefore, arouses powerful forces of envy. This latter myth suggests that the excessive ambition to gain knowledge (curiosity) draws the envy of the god; in other words, it is a form of envy of knowledge, and eventually precipitates the destruction of discourse (Bion, 1963, 1992).

It is, none the less, through the paranoid–schizoid position that the oedipal triangle unfolds for the first time (mother/breast, father/leader, child/Messiah) and conditions are laid down for its more mature development. The father, since he constitutes the mother/group's privileged outstanding person (albeit in the form of an illusion), retains the ability to effect a gradual transformation of beta-elements to alpha-elements or consciousness (in the sense of the conscious or unconscious waking thinking) of the illusory, and of the primitively conscious nature of his relationship with the mother (Bion, 1967, 1992). He is called upon gradually to help the mother acquire the consciousness in question at the group level, to become a "work-group leader", which means the leader of a group that is no longer a "basic-assumption group" or "basic group" but a "work group" (Bion, 1961, p. 178) so that together they can proceed to the depressive position and with it introduce the idea of a mature parental union. It can, in fact, envision the existence of a "leaderless group" (Bion, 1946, 1992, pp. 348–349), which is a mother who can pass to the depressive position without his help, although this is still a utopian concept.

Under these conditions, the Oedipus myth secures a container which is no longer an oral–sadistic stage function but, without losing its maternal dimension, purely genital (the idea of a mature couple). In this way, it can take on the form of a mature Oedipus complex (Bion, 1967) whose resolution does not presuppose the "killing" of the father, "death" of the mother, or "blinding" of the son: in other words, the full splitting of the parental union, which is a purely psychotic mechanism based on the attack on linking, against everything that favours connectivity and communication (Bion, 1967, 1992). According to Bion (1963, 1992), the Oedipus myth can function in an authentic way for the child only to the degree that it is founded on the idea of a unified parental pair, in which the role of the mother proves to be catalytic in the sense that she provides the appropriate container within which the father is revealed as the "intellectual leader" (Bion, 1992, p. 143). He is a leader who, far from constituting the mother's breast/penis (in its oral dimension), represents a breast/penis in the genital sense that he knows, and provides the authentic "interpretation" of things, that is, an interpretation that "must be capable of the functions of the selected fact", leading to a successful negotiation from the paranoid–schizoid to the depressive position with regard to both himself and the mother, and, ultimately, the relationship between the two of them and the child (Bion, 1992, p. 253).

Redefining a new model of sociality and group analysis

It is my belief that Bion's views, which have been briefly sketched above, indicate the direction in which we should be moving in our effort to build group analysis on more solid theoretical and epistemological foundations than it has had to date. According to the above, the solidity of these foundations will depend on shaping the relationship between the circle (groupishness/mother, pre-oedipal level) and the triangle (individual, father, oedipal level) so that this relationship is more harmonious and epistemologically valid than has been the case so far in psychoanalysis and group analysis.

Both psychoanalysis and group analysis are unquestionably based on the view that the circle (social) and the triangle (individual) constitute in essence one and the same shape in the sense that the triangle is already a primitive circle and, however large the circle becomes, the triangle still occupies an essential place in it (father, mother, children). Nevertheless, they both tend to substantiate the view that, of the two shapes in question, at their highest point (as pre-oedipal and oedipal culmination), one had to constitute a prerequisite for the other and to dominate it. The oedipal situation is shown as a prerequisite for sociality (pre-oedipal) (psychoanalysis) and sociality for the oedipal situation (group analysis). This is a shape underlying which is the view that access to the Oedipus complex and its resolution in particular presuppose either transcendence of the maternal object (circle) (psychoanalysis) or the absorption of the father (triangle) by the circle (group analysis).

In both cases, it would appear that the idea of the couple that should be united has been lost, particularly at the culminating point of the resolution of the Oedipus complex. This goes a long way toward explaining why psychoanalysis and group analysis maintain a relationship of malignant symbiosis within which, as shown above, both parties try to elude what they are essentially seeking: the circle that is necessarily intersected by the triangle, or the triangle that is necessarily supported by the circle.

Owing to Bion's concept of the relations between the individual and the group—or between the father and mother, as the relationship of a unified couple—we can argue that the relationship between psychoanalysis and group analysis can become one of (benign) "symbiosis" («"symbiotic"») (Bion, 1970, p. 95). In the light of promoting the idea of the combined parents, which constitutes an "inborn pre-conception" (Bion, 1963, p. 49, n. 1) and is an *a priori* existing triangle (father–mother–child), the latter, unfolding from its most sensual to its most intellectual form, returns to its starting point, the initial container of the unfolding with which it developed in parallel, that is, sociality (circle) in the sense described. From this viewpoint, the triangle is the prerequisite of the circle and *vice versa*.

This concept allows us to place psychoanalysis and group analysis, at least as they have evolved to date, in the initial and intermediate

PRINCIPLES OF THE GROUP-ANALYTIC GROUP: TOWARDS A META-THEORY

phase of development of the idea of the combined parents (primal scene). In these phases, the scene is either a sensory experience or an ideogram (Bion, 1992); it has not yet taken on the intellectual character that constitutes the essential prerequisite for a comprehensive unfolding of the triangle and the circle and for a final concurrence of the two in their diversity.

1. In the first phase (psychoanalysis), sexuality prevails (libidinal bonds), the primal father over the mother, the primary triangle over the circle, which is no more than an illusion of the triangle (illusion of sociality, with sociality as the source of libidinal enjoyment).
2. In the second phase, which supersedes the previous one, in a manner analogous to that in which group analysis tends to supersede psychoanalysis and, at the same time, to contain it, sociality (the circle) prevails which, however, since it relies on love for the society, is interwoven with the countervailing power of self-hatred and, consequently, with narcissistic drives (Bion, 1992). By means of his narcissistic drives, the archaic father/leader is supported anew and his predominance over the mother/group is incited even though, due to the illusion still inherent, it is hoped that he will eventually cede a large part of his authority to the mother/group.

    Both phases presuppose a profound fear, and sometimes envy, of knowledge, a fact that frequently tends to overcompensation through a tendency to omniscience and omnipotence (Bion, 1967). This is undoubtedly the fear and envy of knowledge, the opening to which is directly interwoven with the idea of the combined parents.
3. As the oral–sadistic stage and the paranoid–schizoid position prepare for the depressive position, these two phases seem to be preparing for the third phase, in which we should assume that sociality—which, when based on sexuality, pleasure, and the satisfaction of instincts, is pseudo-sociality—becomes real. Real sociality is founded on the inclination for knowledge and social contact and, at the same time, is differentiated from a mistaken psychoanalytic tendency to frustrate all libidinal instincts, which would also lead to pseudo-sociality (in Bion's terms "social-ism") based on the fear of real sociability, as seen principally in patients

with psychosis. Genuine sociality can only be the group as equal to a breast which, in turn, is conceived by the person as "a gift to him from the family group" (Bion, 1992, pp. 30–31). In this way the primal father/leader becomes not simply an "intellectual leader" but also, one might say, a permanent working hypothesis, and the mother/group becomes the source and nucleus of the social container. The triangle and the circle, by constituting two autonomous entities each of which was produced through the inherent unfolding of the other, touch each other externally rather than internally, as a benign symbiosis, thus rejecting their mutual fear and suspicion (see Figure 1).

However, the above considerations cannot be elucidated without further exploring the function of both of father and mother as seen not only on the individual and family level, but especially on the social level, which is ideally expressed by the union and interrelatedness of the conductor and the group-analytic group. This issue is investigated in the next chapter.

CHAPTER TWO

Paternal function and group analysis as a reverse symmetry of conductor (father) and group (mother): the prospects after Foulkes and Bion*

Paternal and maternal imago: from psychoanalysis to group analysis

The theoretical and clinical foundation for the paternal function, as performed by the therapist of a group-analytic group and—providing he exists and operates as a function of the group (Foulkes, 1964)—by the group itself, is a major issue in group analysis, together with the foundation for the maternal function as performed by the group and alternately by the therapist (Foguel, 1994; Prodgers, 1990). With the exception of the early, basic efforts by Foulkes and Bion to approach this issue, it has not systematically engaged later group analysts, a fact that can be seen in the limited literature on the subject (Conlon, 1991; Horne, 1992; Lear, 1985; Lyndon, 1994; Nitzgen, 2001).

The most important reason for the absence of such an engagement is associated with the more general, and, in other respects, legitimate, trend that developed from the outset within the ranks of group

---

* Part of this chapter was presented as a paper at the Second Regional Mediterranean Conference of IAGP, 1–5 September 2004, Athens, Greece.

analysis with regard to its theoretical, ideological, and clinical differentiation from psychoanalysis. The transition from psychoanalysis to group analysis is known to have been caused by a reversal of the parental imago which had seemed until then to have been dominant. This, in turn, brought about a reversal in the therapeutic framework and in the direction of treatment. Psychoanalysis was based on the precedence of the imago of the father over that of the mother: the paternal imago was a direct function of that of the leader (Freud, 1912–1913, 1921c) as an outstanding individual, and, as a result, lent precedence to individual psychology to the detriment of group psychology, even though the latter was recognised as broader than the former, and established the vertical relationship or transference between analyst and analysand (Freud, 1921c). Reversing the terms, group analysis was founded on the precedence of the maternal imago over that of the father. The imago of the mother, as represented by the group, advocated the precedence of group over individual psychology; as a result, it alluded first of all to the horizontal interpersonal and transpersonal relationship, and only secondarily to the transference relationship between the members of the group, both among themselves, including the leader, and towards the group as a whole (Foulkes, 1964, 1990; Foulkes & Anthony, 1957). This reversal of the imago was undoubtedly influenced by the *Zeitgeist*, since it emerged as the need to disengage groups, and, in particular nations, from the psychotic fascist characteristics they seemed to have acquired owing to their dependence on a leader, a fact made particularly conspicuous by the rise and rule of Nazism, and to demonstrate the deeper democratic spirit with which they are imbued. Under these conditions and under the influence of the Frankfurt School, especially Mannheim, group analysts starting with Foulkes focused on putting forward the maternal imago (groupishness) in its positive aspect, as a new and significant factor and tool in therapy (de Maré, 1983; Nitzgen, 2001; Winship, 2003). It was also an attempt to re-determine the function of the imago of the father/leader as defined by Freud in such a way that it was adaptable to and served the dynamic of the group, until being superseded by it and by the new father model that served it, in the sense described by Foulkes, as we shall see below.

The imago of the father/leader, however, in whatever sense and form we consider it, continues to haunt the group. As Bion's (1946) unsuccessful attempt to create leaderless groups demonstrated, and as

Foulkes (1964) acknowledged, the formation and operation of a therapy group without the sanction of the therapist as representing the father/leader continues for the present to be ontologically unthinkable. No one disputes this. Likewise, no one seems to want to ponder the unthinkable: that is, to discuss afresh the ontological and epistemological foundations for the concept of the father/leader, beyond the discussion and the viewpoint developed by Foulkes and Bion, and to address the contradictions inherent in such a view and possibly to open up new perspectives regarding the determination of paternity. Modern group analysis has certainly not discontinued its efforts to determine paternity. But it seems to be looking for paternity in the various analogies presented by the composition and function of the therapy group based on principles found in physics, biology, neurophysiology, philosophy, and sociology (Brown, 1994; Dalal, 1998; Karterud, 1998; Powell, 1991; Schulte, 2000; Stacey, 2000, 2001). These analogies, however, can only be expressed in group analysis in the form of metaphors (Stacey, 2000) which, apart from the fact that they cannot provide groupishness with the necessary ontological supports, represent, on the unconscious level, fragile substitutes for a paternity whose absence is becoming visible or paternity in the sense of primal leadership which simply returns in modern dress.

In this chapter, we have recorded briefly some of the observations resulting from a long-term study, the aim of which is to encourage fresh discussion and a redefinition of the issue of paternity in group analysis. More precisely, this study attempts to address critically, and to reformulate, the ontological and epistemological principles on the basis of which Bion and Foulkes, through Freud, approach this issue, and, ultimately, to open up a new perspective by taking constructive advantage of similar lines of thought by Lacan and Lévi-Strauss.

Freud's ontology and anthropology of fatherhood

Even though Freud did not deal systematically with the psychology and ontology of groups, he nevertheless deepened his knowledge of their psychological and ontological composition over virtually the entire spectrum of their prehistoric and historic evolution: from the group of the primitive horde (endogamous), to the large group of the fraternal clan (exogamous—maternal bonds) and the tribe or kin (paternal bonds) in the prehistoric period, and all the way up to the modern small family group, the larger social/state group formations, the society, and the state in the historic period. Freud (1912–1913, 1921c) is known to have linked this structure directly with the chronological coincidence of exogamy (motherhood), or natural/social group, and totemism (fatherhood), or social group and with the logical and ontological precedence of the latter, in such a way that, during their evolution, both prehistoric and historic groups (the latter of which appear to constitute a modern restoration of the former) replace the maternal kinship on which they had been initially based with corresponding paternal ones.

The key points in this evolution, as analysed in Chapter One, are:

1. The killing of the "living" (primal) father by his sons, marking the passage from the primitive horde and the self-exiled group of the fraternal clan (first exogamous group) to the group of kin that established the paternal kinship through the totemic meal.
2. The return of the "dead" father as "living" father/leader of the post-totemic groups to the modern family and society, having passed through the intermediate stage of the (still totemic) fraternal clan group within which the return of the father as leader is hatched.

From then on, every group, conceived as a representation of the mother ("ideal ego"), was set up and maintained only as long as it projected on the father/leader:

- its inexhaustible representational richness (its feelings and ability to form libidinal bonds), at the cost of weakening its will and strengthening the will of the leader as a representation of the father who, as a "living" father, reinforces the "illusion" of the group members "that they are equally and justly loved by their leader" (pre-oedipal level) (Freud, 1921c, p. 123). The group/mother can only be formed on the basis of the illusion that its members are loved by the leader/father; thus, it represents an imaginary entity;
- the members' "ego ideal" which thus becomes (after it has been temporarily split off from the members' ego) a common shared "ego ideal" in the form of a "group ideal as embodied in the

leader" (Freud, 1921c, p. 129). This process fosters then the members' identification *"with one another in their ego"* (Freud, 1921c, p. 116, original italics), meaning that the "ego ideal" is reinserted in their ego, and thus with the leader/father as the group's common "ego ideal". It is assumed that through the acceptance of the father as a "dead" father and identification with him, the above evolution contributes to the members' access to the oedipal situation and to resolution of the Oedipus complex (oedipal level), or, in other words, to identification with a strong superego on the imaginary and symbolic level (Freud, 1921c, 1926d, 1933a) (Table 1).

It is clear that, according to Freud, the composition, dynamic, and evolution of groups served primarily the anthropological and historical attestation and evolution of the Oedipus myth. Through these views, and as necessitated by the boy's resolution of the Oedipus complex, Freud was obliged (a) to keep woman/mother constantly repressed (and through her the dynamic of groups), since, in contrast with the father, she never ceased to be an object deeply unknown and difficult to elucidate, and (b) to transfer her cultural contribution to the jurisdiction of the man/father. This is the Achilles' heel of the relevant Freudian view and, by extension, of psychoanalysis in general. It explains the heavy burden shouldered by Bion and Foulkes, despite the difference in their positions, of somehow reversing the concept in question through group psychotherapy and analysis, thereby demonstrating the precedence and therapeutic value of the mother/group, or what Freud called the "ideal ego", over the father, Freud's "ego ideal" or superego (Freud, 1914c, pp. 93–94), and recognising in the father/leader a position that is prominent within this context only as long as he promotes the group's positive re-engagement, from the members' viewpoint and his own as well (Nitzgen, 2001).

Bion: the father as intellectual leader of the working group as mother

More radically opposed to Freud than Foulkes, Bion argued that the group—whether a small group or a social group—takes precedence over the individual both logically and ontologically (even if the

Table 1. Formation and evolution of the group and the father's position according to Freud

Socio-political structure	Kind of group	Group features	Father's position
Primal/patriarchal horde Inheritance through the archaic mother	Patriarchal horde	Endogamy or exogamy Ambivalence towards father (hate–love) Kinship (mother's milk)	Primal father—unrestricted Archaic leader, superego
	Parricide—Totemism—Exogamy		
Institution of matriarchy	Totemic clan (fraternal clan) [Kin]	Exogamy Totemic kinship Original democratic equality	Dead primal father (totem)
	Post-totemic clan	Exogamy Totemic kinship Elevation of the father into a god Veneration for particular individuals Guilt	Revived primal father (unrestricted) God Paternal ideal
Patriarchy Father-deities (the place of mother-goddesses unknown) Divine kings	Society State	Exogamy Love for father increased Kinship (through Christian communion) Inequality Transcendence of guilt	"Dead" primal father (restricted) through Christian communion), New primal fathers (son-religion)
	Family (restoration of the primal horde)	Exogamy Mother (ideal ego) Kinship (through Christian communion), social group Love for father	Revived primal father (restricted) Oedipus complex Ego ideal, superego Leader, illusion of the group

individual is outstanding or a leader) as the whole in relation to the part, since, like the mother on the personal and family level, it constitutes the most primal, "proto-real" (Bion, 1992, p. 133) or "protomental" core of human existence (Bion, 1961, pp. 101–104). Moreover, inspired by Klein, Bion considers that initially, and for a long period in its operation, the group was formed and operated on the basis of the beta-elements that are inherent in the oral–sadistic stage and in the paranoid–schizoid position (Bion, 1962, 1963, 1970, 1992) and which, in the group context, assume the nature of one basic assumption: dependence on a divinity, fight for, and flight from, a reality that is in danger of overthrowing the group's oral–sadistic and paranoid–schizoid status quo, and the pairing through which hope is cultivated—which must remain on the level of illusion and, therefore, unrealised, so that the basic assumption of dependence is preserved—in the birth of a new Messiah (basic-assumption group) (Bion, 1961). Each assumption is entrusted to, or projected upon, the outstanding individual in the group, that is, the individual who, to the degree that he is able to transform many of the beta-elements he has received from the group into alpha-elements (Bion, 1962, 1963, 1970, 1992), achieves the transition of the basic group from the paranoid–schizoid to the depressive position. In this way, the person in question could be regarded, in Freudian terminology, as the "basic-assumption-group leader" (Bion, 1961, pp. 177–178), or as the group illusion. At this stage, the group has not yet perceived that the leader is its own creation. It does not even perceive him as leader, but merely has a suspicion about him (Bion, 1961), since, if the group is taken as the counterpart of the maternal breast, according to the view that seeks to supersede Freud's view of the "living" and "dead" father, he is finally no more than an alternately "good"/"living" and sometimes "bad"/"dead" breast (nipple, to be precise) (Bion, 1963, 1992).

Nevertheless, the group may gradually perceive that the leader is its own creation, to the degree that it begins to rework increasing numbers of beta-elements into alpha-elements: that is, as long as it is moving towards the depressive position and becoming a work group. Then, the "basic-assumption-group leader", who is constantly evolving, changes into a "work-group leader" (Bion, 1961, p. 178) or an "intellectual leader" (Bion, 1992, p. 143), since he can promote a stable link to the alpha-elements. This is a new version of the breast/penis. The father now represents a breast/penis in the (genital) sense that he knows and provides the authentic "interpretation" of things; in other words, the "constantly conjoined" alpha-elements or the successful negotiation of the paranoid–schizoid to the depressive position (Bion, 1992, pp. 250–255). Paternity is correlated with maternity, a correlation that takes on the nature of constant negotiation between the paranoid–schizoid and depressive position (Bion, 1963, 1992). On the basis of the high point created between the two by virtue of access to the depressive position, paternity (intellectual leader) coincides with maternity (work group).

It would, however, be difficult, if not impossible, at present to envisage a leaderless group, since, apart from the fact that the group's traffic lights would disappear in the transformation of beta-elements into alpha-elements, its proto-real element or deepest drives would also surface, about whose nature and dynamic we are ignorant. Bion refers here to the "unconscious emotional impulses" (Bion, 1992, p. 350) which are inherent not only in the individual, but also in the groups, and which constitute an "unknown psychological factor" (x) (Bion, 1992, pp. 346–347), which, without the presence of an intellectual leader, would lead the group to destructive disintegration (Table 2).

Foulkes' ideal father as a conductor leader in the mother group

When Bion's views were first formulated and published, he talked about eliminating the idea of the leader, at least in the Freudian sense of the primal father. These views aroused strong objections on the part of the military and medical leadership, under whose auspices they were initially formulated, causing Bion to back down (Bridger, 1985; Hinshelwood, 1999; Trist, 1985). The *Zeitgeist* more generally demanded the reinstatement of the leader in the game, but in such a way that, although his power was preserved, a large part of it would be ceded gradually to the dynamic of the groups through whose emotional life it would be mitigated even further. This difficult task was assumed by Foulkes, who, even though he believed unwaveringly and sincerely in the profound therapeutic dimension of the group and in its precedence over the leader, nevertheless always remained a Freudian psychoanalyst and, as a result, was still attached to the concept of the primal father (Foulkes, 1990).

Table 2. Formation and evolution of the group and the father's position according to Bion.

Mental-ontological level	Mother's position	Oedipal chain: primal scene	Kind of group	Group features	Father's position
Proto-mental Proto-real Sensual	Proto-real object (breast): good/alive ($\female$) Proto-unreal object (breast): bad/dead Contained in search of a container ($\female$)	Sensory experience	Basic-assumption group (BAG)	BA: dependence Oral-sadistic Beta-elements (Alpha-elements) Pre-conception	Mother's breast (nipple) Deity Hallucination Leader of the basic-assumption group
Real Imaginary (Symbolic, K)	Contained in search of a container	Ideogram// hieroglyph	BAG	BA: fight-flight Paranoid–schizoid position (PS) Beta-elements (Alpha-elements) Pre-conception	Leader of the basic-assumption group
	Contained–container ($\male\female$) [Projective identification] Alpha-function (α-function)	Ideogram// hieroglyph	BAG	BA: pairing Paranoid–schizoid position → depressive position Beta-elements → Alpha-elements Pre-conception → conception	Leader of the basic-assumption group
Symbolic (K) (Real, imaginary)	$\male\female$ Alpha-function Reverie	Ideogram Formularised/ abstract	Work group (WG)	Paranoid–schizoid position ↔ depressive position (PS↔D) Conception	Leader of the work group Intellectual leader Breast = penis = interpretation (Alpha-elements contantly conjoined)
Ultra-real Infra-real Ultra-sensual Infra-sensual Ultimate reality (O)	Restoration of god the Mother) Evolution of god (infinite, ineffable, non-existent)	Euclidean geometry, Algebraic geometry	Leaderless group Unknown factor (x)	Depressive position Alpha-elements Concept Algebraic calculus	
Real Imaginary Symbolic	Contained in search of a container $\male\female$ Alpha-function Reverie	Ideogram (formularised or abstract)	BAG ↔ WG	PS↔D Conception Concept	Leader of basic-assumption group ↔ leader of work group

In introducing group analysis, Foulkes retained in its entirety the Freudian view that the group is created and maintained only with the sanction of the therapist as representing the imago of the primal father (Foulkes, 1964, 1990). This is an imago that co-exists with that of the archaic mother (Foulkes, 1964, 1990), maintaining precedence over it on the level in question, even though this imago, in the sense and form of the matrix, contains the therapist/father. He points out, however, that this refers mainly to the group's primary (primordial) and, by extension, projective and transference level (in Bion's basic-assumption group), a level which it had to retain as long as the group members needed to be dependent on the primal father/mother, who also takes on the form of "leader of the group" (Foulkes, 1964, p. 61). In the secondary or current level of the group (Bion's work group), however, the therapist is presented as the representative of a guiding and mostly friendly authority as exercised within a democratic community, and which, during the period in question, is better expressed by the Anglo-Saxon than by the German model of political governance (Foulkes, 1990), while the group (matrix) at the same time represents reality and adult life.

As a result, the therapist, as per the example of the "musical conductor"—which is why he is called a conductor (Foulkes, 1990, p. 292)—is entrusted with gradually leading the group from the primary to the current level through a "decrescendo" movement of the former and a "crescendo" movement of the latter (Foulkes, 1964, p. 59). He is, in short, entrusted with "digging his own grave" (Foulkes, 1964, p. 62), or, in contrast to Freud's view in which this would require the "killing" of the primal father by his sons, arranging his own symbolic death, in the sense that he is called upon to cede a considerable part of his "anachronistic authority" (Foulkes, 1964, p. 64) to the group and to change it through the group's adult/real dimension, so that he gradually becomes an "instrument of the group" (Foulkes, 1964, p. 57) or, since he retains his authority, but through the intermediation of the group's authority, a "leader in the group" (Foulkes, 1964, p. 61). In this way, he helps the group members to establish a good enough pre-oedipal relationship with the group/mother and, by virtue of this, to address and possibly resolve the Oedipus complex which will not be supported by their "identification" with an "ego ideal" or "superego" (direct result of identification with the Freudian "dead" father or with the living father as ego ideal/superego), but by internalising a superego that ordains current real life, in a paternal and maternal dimension (Foulkes, 1990, p. 293). For Foulkes (1990, p. 293), the person's "inherent need for dependency" on a leader "perhaps repeats the individual's original dependence on the mother" (Table 3).

The clinical data derived from group analytic therapy, as carried out in the light of Foulkes' principles, allow us today to argue that the latter's attempt to abolish the primal father/leader through the group roughly succeeded in both healing the pre-oedipal deficiencies of the subject and, although perhaps less so, resolving his oedipal conflicts. The same data also drew attention to the weak points that can be identified in Foulkes' concept from the epistemological and clinical viewpoint. These points, whose critical refutation and fresh foundation are seen as a prerequisite for the life of group analysis, are linked with Foulkes' three main views, which can be summarised as follows.

1. The view that the group is set up and maintained for a long period (or indefinitely) on the initiative and under the guidance of a therapist (conductor) who represents two diametrically opposed versions of paternity: the primal father (in the members' projections, but not in the opinion of the therapist himself, or on the latent level), and the father as representative of a friendly authority who is regarded as having resolved the conflicts in question (Foulkes, 1964) and whom the conductor is primarily called upon to represent on the manifest level. Of these versions:
(a) The former is in danger of leading the group members and the conductor into regression to an archaic universe in which relations of fusion and a double-bind message prevail from which it is doubtful that they will ever be able to emerge. It is a universe in which the primal father is in absolute fusion with the archaic mother so that—long before reaching the level of oedipal conflict—he is presented simultaneously as not being subject to symbolic castration or, as being subject to a non-symbolic castration by the mother herself;
(b) The latter version seeks to lead the members and the conductor to the level of current reality, but there is no certainty that he will succeed, given that he largely constitutes an abstraction (it is not known how the conductor/father resolved his oedipal conflicts) behind which the primal father is concealed. As a result, the road

Table 3. Formation and evolution of the group and the father's position according to Foulkes.

Mother's imago / Father's position		Level of the group	Group features
Psychoanalysis and group analysis			
Archaic (Great Mother)	Primordial level (Archaic/body/ primary-latent/ lower-psychotic/ immature level	Matrix (mother's womb): "good"/"bad" Collective unconscious Collective images Part(s) of body(-image) "Condenser" phenomena	Primal father (of the primal horde) (Unconscious fantasy of) A godlike father Primordial leader image Leader of the group Superego—ego ideal
Pre-oedipal (Archaic)	Level of bodily and mental images: (projective level) Primary/latent level	Matrix (mother's image): "good"/"bad" Narcissistic "inner" object relations (Klein) Primary narcissism Mirror phenomena/ reactions	Primal father/ leader of the group Personal father (or (mother) Superego—ego ideal
Base line			
Oedipal (pre-oedipal) Personal ideal Ideal ego	Transference level (primary) Secondary/ level	Primary Family relations Transference neurosis Infantile/incestuous Transference Transference situation Transference/ mirroring reactions	Personal father or (mother) Superego—ego
Group analysis			
(Oedipal) Post-oedipal	Current level Transference level Secondary/ manifest level	Interactional matrix (foundation matrix, dynamic matrix, overpersonal matrix) Communication (interpersonal– transpersonal) Adult life/ contemporary reality (community/society Common matrix of interpersonal social reaity Therapeutic situation	Leader in the group Reality-prone "Desirable type of leader in a democratic community Conductor" "Reflection of the group" ("Dead" primal father) "A member of the group" Paternal/maternal ego ideal

is once again opened for regression to the archaic level. This also explains why a group-analytic group is sometimes in danger of becoming a permanent narcissistic reflection of the therapist/primal father: instead of functioning catalytically towards the members' transference to themselves, the multiple transferences conduce to its increasing intensification. Nitzgen (2001, p. 342) also puts forward a similar objection, but in a tougher way, and within a wider context, when he argues that "we might speculate whether in or by group analysis, perhaps more than in psychoanalysis, a transference process is fostered, by which the enigma of the primary other is being transferred to culture and society."

2. The view that the therapist as primal father will effect his own symbolic death, a view which, even though it constitutes a positive step beyond the Freudian view of the "killing" of the father, is in danger of becoming a delusion and of functioning in a castrating way on the group members by removing their incentive in respect of his symbolic death or, on the contrary, of rekindling the need for the return of a "living" primal father. There is a risk here that the idea of the "leader in the group" will turn into an equally good means of retaining the "leader of the group".

3. The view that the matrix, which is initially the counterpart of the primal father (the "good" and the "bad" imago of the Great Mother) (Prodgers, 1990), either by "borrowing" the power of the primal father (Foulkes, 1964, p. 63) or by itself, can introduce a representative of real adult life (current level) independently of the father. This view can be shown to be invalid, given that, for the time being, the creation of a group without the initiative and existence of the therapist/father is still ontologically inconceivable and, in addition, leads to holistic and dangerous views about the whole or the collective taking precedence over the individual and unique. Then, instead of a *decrescendo* movement, there will be a *crescendo* movement at the primary level, a phenomenon frequently observed in analytic groups, even after many years of operation.

In this regard, Bion's concept of paternity as a gradual evolution of maternity, in the sense briefly described, seems more consistent.

Towards a new father–mother epistemological paradigm in groups and society

The deficiencies presented by the ideas of Foulkes and Bion about the concept and function of the father/leader/therapist in the group context must be chiefly attributed to the fact that the clarification of this concept and function is associated with a number of psychoanalytic issues of an ontological and epistemological nature that were to unravel the relationship between the father/man and mother/woman as a relationship of the part to the whole. They are questions that these two authors, who were entrusted to establish group therapy while keeping a safe distance from psychoanalysis, were not obliged to answer. Moreover, Lacan's psychoanalytic thought, which was, at that time, the most competent to shed light on questions of this nature, provided some answers which, despite their new epistemological foundation, indicated a return to Freud and the triumph of psychoanalysis over group psychotherapies. According to Lacan, the function and necessity of the father as the primal, real, imaginary ("living"), and symbolic ("dead") father was overthrown in the new dimension he had acquired as a real, imaginary, and symbolic father ("living father") in the light of managing the significance of the phallus conceived as either the mother's desire, that is, her desire to see the child as the phallic extension of herself (imaginary level), or the father's power to prohibit desire (i.e., incest) as an imaginary process by imposing the law respectively (symbolic level). The primal father was diminished in just one version of the real father (he who castrates the child from being the mother's phallus/desire on the imaginary level) and the imaginary father (he who deprives on the imaginary level the mother and, consequently, the child of the real possession of penis and of its symbolic dimension as phallus in order to help him later acquire it himself). Freud's symbolic father conceived as an ego ideal was completely revised, because his function strongly overlaps with his function as imaginary father, and usually leads to traumatic (unsymbolised) castration of the child and to defective resolution of the oedipal complex. The father was considered as genuinely symbolic (as an ego ideal aiming to castrate desire as the child's desire to be the mother's phallus) solely as long as he is recognised as the real possessor of the phallus as signifying, by its nature as a "signifier" *par excellence* (the Name-of-the-Father), mature desire on the symbolic and social rather than the imaginary and personal level, and favours an effective symbolic castration of the child or patient, which can only take place within a psychoanalytic setting as strictly linked with a successful re-experience and resolution of the Oedipus complex (Lacan, 1994, 1998b).

On the contrary, for Lacan, the function of the primal father in its primordial (Freudian) dimension (real, imaginary, symbolic), since it is linked with the life of groups in their deeper archaic substratum, appears to be logically and ontologically necessary in the case of groups and group psychotherapies, including the family group, as long as they seek to establish themselves as a whole and, indeed, in the form of maternity/female representation: that is, on the basis of pre-oedipal relations (circles) that tend to diminish the relations of the oedipal triangle. This view is founded on Lacan's (1975) concept according to which the idea of the whole (circle, groupishness) cannot be established through women (maternal kinship, according to Freud) since, in their wholeness, they are not susceptible to symbolic castration owing to the increased phallic pleasure with which they are imbued. From this viewpoint, women do not constitute a whole: some parts of them are subject to symbolic castration and others are not, so that we are obliged each time to enumerate them one by one. The idea of the whole can be established through men (paternal kinship according to Freud) since, because of their limited phallic pleasure, they are subject as a whole to symbolic castration, which leads to their identification with the primal father as "dead" (symbolic) father; however, this is valid on condition that at least one man, inevitably referring to the primal father conceived mainly as imaginary father before he is "killed" by his sons (symbolic father), while he is the exclusive agent of symbolic castration, is not himself subject to it (Lacan, 1998a). Thus, Lacan retains the idea of the primal father as a necessary prerequisite for the function of an oedipal triangle within the group as circle.

Lacan's view of symbolic castration remains original and fundamental, so we retain and extend it in order to support the view favourable to group analysis that a group-analytic group can only be established with healthy presuppositions on the basis of a mutual symbolic castration between the therapist/father and group/mother, providing the symbolic castration is a constituent factor in their desire. This view, given that, according to Lacan (1960, 1998b), as we will testify in Chapter Twelve, the desire is on a higher ontological level than that of the sexual drive—which is supported mainly by the need conceived as a need for feeding and the demand for love, which simply constitutes a more developed form of the previous need—carries us beyond the idea of the primal father and the archaic mother. But Lacan bases the idea of symbolic castration on the distinction between the individual and the group, which, in turn, for the opposite reason in Foulkes, and less so in Bion and Freud, is based on a positivist (determinist) reading of the unconscious, both individual and collective, as befits the rationalist Western way of thinking. According to this way of thinking, two psychic or social terms (that is, father and mother, individual and group), whether they are applied to a supplementary (both . . . and) or a disjunctive (and . . . or) relationship, could each claim logical, ontological, and historic precedence, in the sense that one precedes the other (as cause) and determines it, and is, in turn, governed by and subjected to it as a logical effect. This way of thinking has already begun to be rearticulated and re-established by the new findings produced by the anthropological and psychoanalytic investigations of Lévi-Strauss into the functioning of primitive thought, which underlies the unconscious depths of western thought. Lévi-Strauss gave us the valuable realisation that unconscious thought, far from functioning on the basis of the principle of causality, within the context of symmetrical or asymmetrical logic (Matte-Blanco, 1975), is fundamentally supported by the "logic" of inverse symmetry (Lévi-Strauss, 1962). According to this, the two terms of psychic or social reality can be, each on its own side, simultaneously the cause and effect of the other on different levels (differentiating space), in such a way that, precisely because they are thus opposed, they are in harmony in the sense that they secure intertemporaneity (constancy of cause) together with contemporaneity (eventuality of the effect). This logic governs the relationship between totemism (father, man, culture, social composition of groups) and exogamy (mother, woman, nature, constitution of natural and social groups) which has determined the evolution of culture and acquires particular significance in the investigation being undertaken here, since totemism (social group), even though it introduces a difference in terms of exogamy (natural group), never ceases to be its reflection, so that exogamy (cause, intertemporaneity) precedes totemism (effect, contemporaneity). On the other hand, to the degree that it, too, conduces to the formation of social groups, exogamy stems from totemism, so that now the latter (cause, intertemporaneity) takes precedence over the former (effect, contemporaneity) (Lévi-Strauss, 1962). This is a logic that, despite its partial similarities, is opposed to that of Freud, which was partially also that of Foulkes, according to which totemism and exogamy have a common chronological origin in which, based on the causal sequence, the precedence of totemism (father, cause, intertemporaneity) and, ultimately, its predominance over exogamy (mother, effect, contemporaneity) was hatched logically and ontologically.

The combination of this view with that of Lacan regarding symbolic castration leads us to certain discoveries, which should be perceived, in Bion's terms, as "definitory hypotheses" or "selected facts" (Bion, 1992, pp. 250, 275–278), on the basis of which the paternal function, as performed in a group-analytic group, can acquire a more solid inductive–deductive foundation than that presupposed by the views of Foulkes and partially of Bion. These discoveries are:

1. The mother (analytic group) and the father (conductor), from the moment of their "birth", are on a level which, while permitting contemporaneity and change, is intertemporal and constant in a relation of inverse symmetry (Lévi-Strauss, 1962). This is based on the fact that both parties, from their very first meeting, achieve and tacitly (unconsciously) agree on a mutual symbolic castration which sets in motion the will of the conductor/father to establish the group/mother and the desire of the group for him and, of course, their mutual recognition. To be more precise, the analytic group converts its "birth" as group/woman/mother to the decision (manhood) and the thought (maternity, femininity) of the conductor/father who, while "giving birth" to the group, is also simultaneously "born" himself in a relationship of inverse symmetry. The group, accepting its composition (maternity, femininity) by means of the thought (femininity) and decision (manhood) of the conductor/father—in other words, through itself—plugs the hole of its overflowing, potentially uncontrolled, phallic nature (Lacan), which, until now, had made it a mysterious object (Freud), and demonstrates its desire to the conductor/father whom it recognises as such (symbolic). The conductor, on his part, is recognised as such because, as he stands before the desire of the group, he acknowledges that he, as the representation of

his own maternity/femininity and of his desire for it, is the only one who can establish the group. The conductor is recognised as symbolic father only through his own willingness to become the plug for the hole (lack of symbolic castration of both himself and the group/mother), because, if it is left open, it is in danger of making the group/mother an archaic object the nature of which seems difficult to decipher, and himself a primal archaic father who struggles incessantly, like Sisyphus, to prove his prevalence over the mother while, at the same time, he is not very different from her, as Freud notes.

2. Inherent from the outset in the paternal and maternal functions, as they are demonstrated in the analytic group, is a mutual good enough character. Thus, they might be said to create a new archetype which, even though on many points it inevitably contains and condenses the archetype of the archaic mother and the primal father known previously, and the imaginary and symbolic dimension that they have gradually acquired through the evolution of culture, ultimately functions as a catalyst and supersedes it. This is not merely an archetype that is somehow created solely through the oedipalisation of the pre-oedipal mother and the pre-oedipal father, that is, through the symbolic castration (prohibition of incest) imposed on it by the taboo of the symbolic/dead father and, by extension, of social institutions (Freud, 1912–1913), or through a metaphoric replacement of the unknown significance of the mother's desire (signified) for the Name-of-the-Father (signifier) (Lacan, 1998b). It is an archetype that tends continually to take form (without gaining it absolutely) on the basis of the dialectical joining of two, often interchangeable, positions that have no significance or meaning separately or in themselves, but only in their co-articulation. Thus, they resemble the phonemes of a language or meta-language which, as is also the case with myth, draws its meaning from the use proper to it. Yet, they resemble even more closely what Lévi-Strauss (1958, 1973), analogously with phonemes, calls "mythemes", that is, semi-conscious, semi-unconscious structures which, in their conflict or co-mutability, are reproduced in a kind of basic model, infinitely open, with the same number of different perspectives expressing the corresponding technical and economic infrastructure of a society. The difference here is that the paternal and maternal

positions cannot be mythemes in terms solely of their (even potential) structure, but primarily in that of a dynamic process, as mutating or co-mutating and reproducing positions (or "languages") with different levels of prospects. As such, they spring incessantly from the interweaving of the collective/social and the individual unconscious, and, at the same time, open it up in a manner that heals any psychic conflicts only as long as they recognise (symbolic axis) and, therefore, imagine (imaginary axis) and render each other as real (real axis) in a reciprocal self-restriction. This takes place in a context in which maternity, conceived as a contemporaneous (Freud) dimension, or what Lacan called a metonymic/imaginary axis, and paternity conceived as an intertemporaneous (Freud) dimension or as a metaphoric/symbolic axis (Lacan, 1994, 2006), are harmonically conjoined in their interchangeability.

3. Thus, we can understand why, even though Lacan did not identify the dialectic in question as it has been described here, in his terms, when *the mother is symbolic* (frustrates the child from the breast as real), *the father is imaginary* (deprives on the imaginary level the mother and, *par ricochet*, the child of the real possession of penis and of its symbolic dimension as phallus in order to help him later acquire it himself), or when *the mother is imaginary* (sees the child as the phallic extension of herself, which is the cornerstone of her desire), *the father is real* (castrates the child from being the mother's imaginary phallus/desire); when *the mother is real* (does not meet the child's demand for the breast, and then the breast becomes symbolic), *the father is imaginary*; when *the mother is imaginary, the father is symbolic* (real possessor of the phallus as signifying desire on the symbolic rather than the imaginary level, or as an ego ideal aiming to castrate desire as the child's desire to be the mother's phallus) and so on (Lacan, 1994, 1998b). In the terms used by Foulkes (1964) and Bion (1992), we could say that when the father is primal (father/breast/penis, father of the primitive horde) the mother represents the reality principle (mature adult life), or when the mother is archaic (proto-real), the father is the intellectual leader or strongest symbolic representative of the real. In Freud's (1912–1913) terms, when the mother expresses contemporaneity (natural group, exogamy, effect), the father expresses intertemporaneity (social group, totemism, cause), and

vice versa. Since, according to Lacan, the role of the symbolic father usually prevails over the imaginary role of the mother, although both roles are interchangeable, we would assume that, while the mothering soil (the pre-oedipal, metonymic, or contemporaneous dimension) remains stable, despite its continuous movement, a dynamic field (the oedipal, metaphorical, or intertemporaneous dimension) of paternal origin is in constant operation as a result of the interchangeability of the above maternal and paternal positions, leading from contemporaneity (effect) to intertemporaneity (cause) and from the imaginary to the symbolic.

4. Paternity and maternity, the individual and the group, cease to be registered on the triangle and the circle respectively, which are static and self-restricted schemata, and are instead registered on a kind of mental and psychological kaleidoscope that combines the circular and the triangular dimensions in a highly flexible way, with the circle (contemporaneity, imaginary) and the triangle (intertemporaneity, symbolic) being autonomous and interchangeable, either inside or outside the kaleidoscope conceived as a dynamic process that transcends the static dimension of the circle. Consequently, under natural conditions, the kaleidoscope functions by itself on the basis of mental health.

5. Mental illness begins more or less when the maternal (contemporaneous, imaginary) and paternal (intertemporaneous, symbolic) dimensions that simultaneously characterise this kaleidoscope either internally or externally, for reasons of subjective or intersubjective conflicts and traumas, begin to compress in such a way as to become one-dimensional—in one (paternal, symbolic, intertemporaneous, oedipal) or the other (maternal, imaginary, contemporaneous, pre-oedipal) direction, thus leading to a disharmony in the normal interchangeability of the paternal and maternal positions (Figure 2).

6. Since a highly articulated or good enough functioning of the above kaleidoscope remains an ideal and seems utopian, the impact of the everyday interrelation of the paternal and maternal functions as analysed above usually has a traumatic impact on the child's mental development and can be seen in the symptomatology and behaviour of patients in the course of their group-analytic therapy. Evidence for this is provided by the clinical

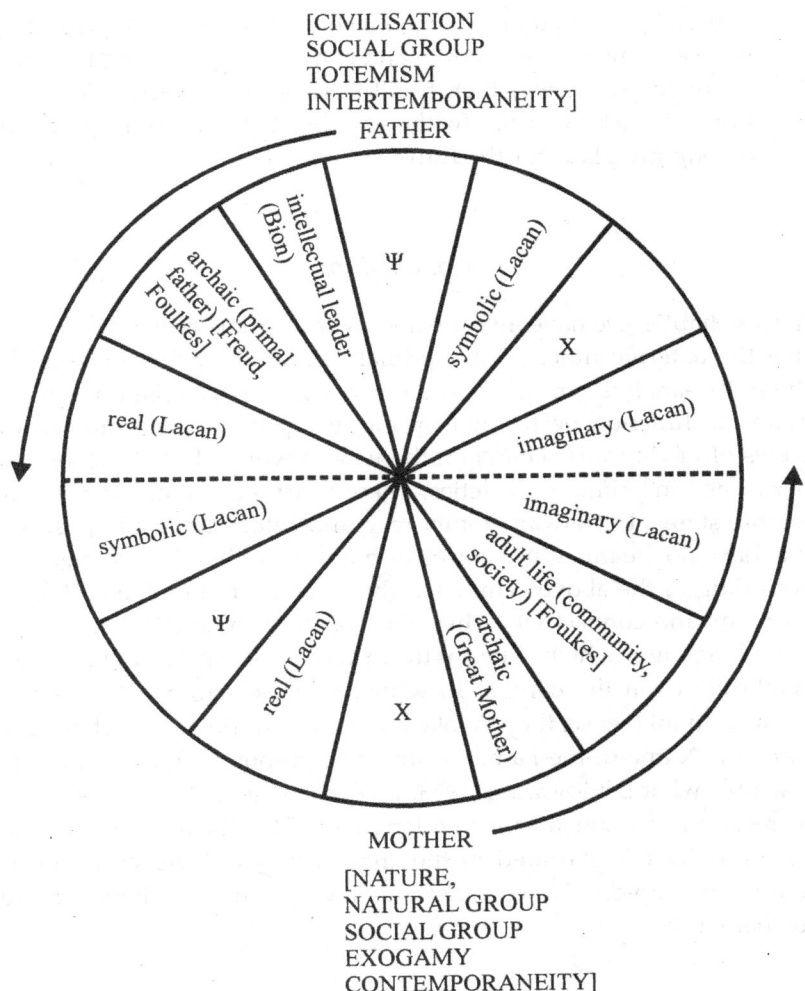

Figure 2. Paternal function and group analysis. The positions (mythemes) of the father and mother in an archetypal mental and psychological kaleidoscope. The Greek letters X and Ψ are primitive symbols used in symbolic logic and mathematics to denote free variables that range over simple or complex propositional functions. Here, they are used to symbolise all possible positions that the paternal and maternal function can assume interchangeably.

material presented in subsequent chapters of this book. However, we are a long way from fully and convincingly proving the validity of the ways in which this kaleidoscopic interrelation functions. To achieve this, further studies are required, which are among my plans for the future.

Conclusions

In this chapter, we have investigated the role of the father by showing that the paternal function, as optimally enacted by the conductor of the group-analytic group, is in a reverse symmetry relation with the maternal function performed by the group itself, according to the views of Lévi-Strauss (1962) on the way in which these functions are performed in primitive societies. These functions are not static, unalterable states, but always temporary and interchangeable positions that have no meaning in themselves but only in their being conjoined, according to the above symmetry, thus leading to familial and social harmony and connectivity. They also constitute a kind of language or meta-language, which, like myth, draws meaning (imaginary, real, symbolic) from the context in which it is used in a kaleidoscopic manner. In this sense, they invoke Lacan's (1994, 1998b) signifier, especially the Name-of-the-Father as the most preponderant signifier, and resemble what Lévi-Strauss (1958, 1976) refers to as mythemes, which correspond to phonemes in the language. The above considerations are partially corroborated in the clinical material presented in the following chapters. However, stronger verification of them requires further study.

PART II

GROUP ANALYSIS IN OPERATION: SOME FUNDAMENTAL ASPECTS AND PHENOMENA

CHAPTER THREE

Money: from the "thing" itself to its symbolic death and to recognition of the symbolic father. A group-analytic approach with a transcultural dimension*

Theoretical and clinical assumptions

Psychoanalysis—and, by extension, any type of individual or group psychotherapy inspired by it—is known to be inextricably interwoven first and foremost with money, in the sense that, in real terms, money reflects and symbolises psychoanalytic therapy, a consumer service with high-level specifications and techniques (Barth, 2001; Borneman, 1976; Dimen, 1994; Herron & Welt, 1994; Krueger, 1986; Myers, 2008). Money is also directly linked to the economy of the subject's drives that determine how the real is fantasised and symbolised. To restore these drives at points where they have been disturbed is the ultimate goal of the psychoanalytic technique. It could even be said that money is one of the most critical internal indicators of the progress of psychoanalytic therapy. This is why studying the ways in which group analysis manages money might perhaps be its most crucial aspect and the one from which we should begin in order to understand the philosophy of group analysis and how it operates, as will be seen in the following chapters of this book.

---

* Part of this study was presented as a poster at the 12th European Symposium on Group Analysis: The Economy of the Group (Bologna, August 2002).

Despite its significance in the practice of psychoanalysis, and especially group analysis in which there is a comparative gap in the literature, the function of money has not been studied in a manner commensurate with its importance (Barth, 2001; Krueger, 1986). Up to now, contemporary research has focused on either the relationship between psychoanalysis and money in general on a social and cultural rather than systematic clinical level (Borneman, 1976; Krueger, 1986) or studied the link between paying in psychoanalysis and the revival of the analysand's specific emotional states during therapy, such as love and hate towards the therapist as a parental figure (Dimen, 1994) or as a tool for renegotiating separation and individuation issues on the basis mainly of the new power relationships as developed between the analyst and the analysand (Barth, 2001) or as a means of managing the resistance that emerges on both sides (Myers, 2008), and so on. A common trend in the above research consists of associating fee payment in psychotherapy with intersubjectivity and the patient–therapist relationship by revising and doubting Freud's (1908b) views about money in psychoanalysis symbolising faeces as fundamentally linked with the patient's difficulties in the anal–sadistic stage of their development (Barth, 2001; Dimen, 1994; Myers, 2008). However, neither the differentiation from the views of Freud nor the study of some partial aspects of the relationship between paying fees for therapy suffices to provide a more substantiated link between psychoanalysis or group analysis and money. While insisting on the association of money with faeces, Freud linked the function of money in psychoanalysis primarily with one of two extreme poles: either on an ideal level, with the subject's access to the genital (phallic) stage (Freud, 1905d, 1923b); that is, to the highest symbolic dimension of the father, which Freud calls the "dead" father, or, on a lower level, with the subject fixated in the anal–sadistic and subsequently in the oral–sadistic stage, that is, to the "living" and castrating/archaic father and, consequently, to the pre-oedipal mother, who is also an archaic and castrating mother (Freud, 1912–1913, 1918b). Of course, according to Freud (1908b, 1916–1917, 1917c, 1918b), money, both in the normal but especially in the inverted oedipal, is permanently dependent on the anal–sadistic dimension. However, this happens in the sense that it is strongly interwoven with a powerful latent and destructive homosexual component, since its higher association with an ideal and unapproachable ("dead") symbolic father seems like an unreachable ideal, which, in turn, frequently proves to be destructive: it reintroduces the "living", castrating father in the guise of a "dead" father. On these premises, the struggle of the child to achieve a successful negotiation between the "living" and the "dead" father by surpassing the anal–sadistic stage and difficulties with managing faeces and, later, money, suppresses a more primary and benevolent link between money and the oral stage, that is, with the mother (breast), and, more precisely, the link that seems to exist between money and the mother's inherent ability to suckle (presence) and wean (absence) the child successfully. This link contributes significantly to the child's normal experience of the anal–sadistic stage and, consequently, to recognition of a genuine symbolic father (genital stage) with whom the correspondingly genuine symbolic value of money is related.

Although Freud (1905d, 1940a) largely recognises this, he seems to estimate that, irrespective of the mother's successful dialectic of suckling–weaning, unless she is enlightened through the father, she remains a relatively archaic (dark) object which promotes the normal homosexual and narcissistic stage of the libido, a stage to which, despite this, the child regresses latently or openly in both the normal and especially in the inverted oedipal (Freud, 1918b, 1940a). In these terms, we can understand why, in Freud's group psychology, the group (as a primal representative of the maternal object) is formed in depth probably as the narcissistic and homosexual alliance of siblings right after the murder of the father (Freud, 1912–12913, 1921c). Such a group, we can easily assume, reminds the siblings of their latent homosexuality; to avoid manifesting it and to surpass the group's power, they try to compensate for their homosexuality by managing the group through strong leadership. This group relies on a family-centred culture (bioculture) which is based on incestuous alliances and extends to broader social groups (de Maré et al., 1991). For Freud, however, the mother always remains a person whose image alone risks leaving the child to be easily fixated on direct memory images of it as a primordial mothering person which is equated to a *"thing"* ("thing-presentations") (Freud, 1915e, pp. 201–202, original italics). So, unless the symbolic father intervenes between the child and the mother, any real separation of the former from the latter is seriously undermined (Freud, 1912–1913). Freud's view has been considerably modified by Bion (1967, 1992), who considers the mother as a thing only to the degree to which she thoroughly fails to contain the infant's beta-elements as projected to her and to transform them into alpha-elements, with the risk of leading the child later to psychosis.

Group-analytic psychotherapy has a substantially different theoretical and therapeutic approach from that of psychoanalysis, though akin to it. It was established on the basis of the group, regarded as a common shared ground and as a "mothering soil" (Foulkes, 1990, p. 212), consisting of "the network of all individual mental processes" and communications between a number of people (Foulkes, 1990, p. 154) and which, on a primordial level (and, eventually, on a transference or projective level), represents a potentially benign «Image of the "Mother"» (matrix) (Foulkes, 1964, p. 289). The group is also regarded, following some of Bion's views, as "breast", which, despite its potentially destructive elements (beta-elements, basic group), can be transformed into a "good" breast (alpha-elements, work group) (Bion, 1961, 1962). This is the breast that is "the prototype for all the links" (Bion, 1967, p. 93); in Klein's terms, the breast "in its good aspect is the prototype of maternal goodness" (Klein, 1957, p. 180), or, as Freud (1940a) described it, the prototype of all later love relations. Such a group is composed and directed by the therapist in the sense that, other than for the immature level of the group and/or for transference reasons, he does not for long assume the role of "leader of the group" "in the image of an omnipotent, godlike father figure", which the group in its immaturity ascribes to him; in other words, he does not assume the role of the castrating father of the primal horde who is simply an archaic symbolic father (and, thus, largely imaginary) whose authoritative guidance panders to the members' infantile neurosis. On the contrary, he conducts the group in the sense that he tries progressively to wean it from its need for a primal father, in order eventually to become himself "a leader in the group" and, in turn, to permit the group to replace his authority with its own (Foulkes, 1964, pp. 60–61). Thus, group-analytic theory and psychotherapy reinstate the primacy of the maternal object (initially regarded by Freud as a "thing") as being at least equal to that of the father. A first perception (proto-anal or oral and pre-genital) of money can be associated with this object in the form initially of suckling or fusion and, gradually, of weaning (separation). Moreover, since group-analytic theory also refers to an adequate confrontation of the castrating father, it contributes definitively to dissociating money (father) from the anal–sadistic stage and is decisive in the subject's successful entry into the Oedipus complex and its successful resolution. Under these conditions, it transcends the group's bioculture (social structure) which it transforms into a culture that, while it might not be the culture of cultures of the larger groups (de Maré et al., 1991), is, nevertheless, a genuine one that helps the group prepare for the culture of the larger groups, especially if the group has a transcultural dimension.

The evolution of the group's payment

More specifically, money in the group-analytic process, that is, the way in which the members/children handle payment to the group/mother for their therapy, follows certain phases that are, to some degree, the phases of the group as well. The duration of all three phases varies according to the level of development of the group as a whole and of each member individually but in both cases they are always interdetermined progressively and in a spiral form. The two first phases are predetermined by the group's pre-oedipal level, the third by its oedipal level. These phases can be described as follows.

- The *money-fusion* or *fixed payment* phase. This is the primary and most decisive phase; it is a psychotic-like phase that corresponds most closely to Freud's (1905d) oral–sadistic stage or, partly, to Bion's (1961) basic group (basic assumption dependence) or to Klein's (1946) oral–sadistic stage and partly to her paranoid–schizoid position, to Mahler's (1968) normal autistic or normal symbiotic phase, or, in more recent terms, to Caparrós' (1999) self-breast < > breast-self step of subjectivity and, according to the pathology, can last anywhere from six months to an average of three to four years, or might never be resolved at all. Briefly, this is a phase during which the mother/group, initially as a part-object representation (breast) (Klein, 1952), tries, according to Winnicott's (1976) view of a good enough mother, to give its members/children good enough "suckling", that is, an analytic and supportive integrative process with pauses, or an ideal mixture of pleasure/presence and frustration/absence represented by money as a genuine sample of reality and as a precursory representative of the symbolic father. However, in this phase the pleasure principle is normally stronger than the reality principle (Freud, 1920g), and the conductor/father, contained (as penis) in the mother/group/breast and in the limits of an early oedipal situation for the members/children (Klein, 1945, 1952), is not yet discernible at all as symbolic father. So, the members, according to their psychopathology and to their level of regression, strongly resist good enough "suckling" and good enough payment. Furthermore, some members express feelings of a primary envy of the mother's/group's (and/or the conductor's) breast. They feel that the group/mother (or the conductor) conceived as a "feeding breast" possesses everything they desire (milk, love) "which the breast keeps for its own gratification" (Klein, 1957, p. 183). Similarly, they might envy the conductor considered as an archaic father figure because he alone "possesses" all the women of the group. With the exception of the members who suffer from certain kinds of severe psychotic, borderline, or even neurotic disturbances, and who might eventually avoid any linking/fusion with the group through irregular payment or a disruption of payment and of therapy, members usually try to make their primary linking with the group/breast through the regular, virtually uninterrupted payment associated with their constant presence in the group, whose meaning is not—as it might appear at first glance—the recognition of the good enough "suckling" they receive, or an extension of the symbolic value of the absence of the breast. It is the illusory hope of retaining the group conceived as breast and ensuring everlasting, uninterrupted "suckling" of it, in the sense that the (imaginary) retention of the group/maternal object as permanently and physically present, or rather as "thing", is sought, which is absolute fusion with it. The group/breast, of course, imposes weaning, its symbolic absence, not only by ending each session but also by means of vacations, during which the member is called upon to pay regularly, even though the group does not meet. The members, in turn, on average, pay regularly during the vacation period, but not in the sense that they recognise the group as an internalised object (present inside them even in its absence) but in the sense that they are still subject to the illusion that they hold it within them as permanently present (incorporation or introjection) or that they deny its absence following the views of Klein (1946). In short, in Klein's (1946) views, it is a kind of identification with the group as absolutely "good" and omnipotent, excluding the group's "badness". In any case, in Caparrós's (1999) terms, the members feel that within the limits of pseudo-separation based on narcissistic symmetry, the breast (really the breast-self) belongs to them as a self-breast.

- The *money-semi-fusion*, or *semi-separation*, or *refusal of fixed payment* phase. This is also a psychotic-like phase which appears to correspond to Mahler's (1968) three sub-phases of the separation–individuation phase, to Freud's (1905d) anal–sadistic stage, to Klein's (1946) paranoid–schizoid position, to Bion's (1961) basic group (basic assumption dependence and fight–flight) or to Caparrós's (1999) self < > breast step of subjectivity. This phase contains many elements of the previous one and is not fully cut off from it, or from the subsequent one that is being worked out. Through the separation/mourning that the group-analytic process presupposes, the members have acquired an initial ability—in terms of benign splitting and disavowal—to symbolise the absence of the group as breast. They are no longer in full fusion with it, as they do not consider that it still belongs to them. Nevertheless, they still refuse to accept such a symbolisation and, thus, to mourn the group/mother as part-object and to see it as a real whole (Klein, 1946, 1952). They feel that they are really (still on a primitive level) separated from the group/breast, but in the sense that they *are* the group/breast (self–breast). Thus, as much as possible, they seek to preserve an illusory retention of the group and a ("good") part-object relationship with it, not by constant payment, as was the case until now, but either by delaying payment or even by openly refusing for a long period to pay, at least for the vacation period. This is, according to Klein (1946), an identification with the "bad" aspect (absence) of the group; it is also a way for the members to accept this "bad" aspect and to test whether or not the group will persecute them. The refusal/delay of payment now becomes an indirect tendency to both fusion and, on the contrary, to autonomy, while payment itself likewise contains the concept of fusion intermingled with feelings of envy. In these terms, the members find themselves in an intermediate state of confusion: they are unable to reply to the essentially spurious question of whether their autonomy/individuation from the group takes place through payment or through refusal to pay.

From the Freudian perspective, this question marks a negative entrance of the members into the anal–sadistic stage and their resulting inability to experience it positively for a long period, and, thus, to pass into the genital stage. This is due first to the fact that they have not yet satisfied their need for "milk" (oral stage) so as to be able to mourn it, and, second, to the fact that for the reasons cited previously, the conductor/father is not yet sufficiently and properly distinguishable. Although he is disassociated from his position as penis/breast, he is now experienced as a father of the primal horde, an omnipotent figure like the omnipotent mother/group. As such, he threatens to castrate the male members by prohibiting their access to the women of the group and the females by submitting them to his omnipotent sexuality.

- The *money-gift, money-competitor-investment*, and generally *symbolic payment* phase. This phase goes hand in hand with a long period of weaning and mourning, which is a necessary consequence of the fact that the members, after satisfying their need for a good enough "suckling", begin to accept their separation from the group as part-object, a fact which is the symbolic death of the "thing", and, by internalising and symbolising it, to recognise it as a whole. It corresponds to the entrance of the members and the group into Freud's (1905d, 1923b) genital–phallic stage, Klein's (1946) depressive position, Bion's (1961) basic group (basic assumption fight-flight and/or pairing) with a tendency to become a work group, and the fourth sub-phase of Mahler's (1968) separation–individuation phase (rapprochement or development of libidinal object constancy) or Caparrós's (1999) self < > other step of subjectivity. This phase certainly contains many elements from previous phases and can only be integrated at the end of the therapy. Nevertheless, the members, after entering this phase, have almost gained the ability to maintain an internal relationship with the group as a whole (Klein, 1946). This relationship is discernible not only during the sessions, but also during the physical absence of the group (vacations). Briefly, the members have gained the ability of attachment, which will later be the prototype of relationships with real people in their per-sonal lives. Envy is considerably diminished and an integration of both the "good" and the "bad" aspects of the group/mother is achieved, leading to feeelings of gratitude for its goodness (Klein, 1957).

They are able subsequently to discern the conductor as he really is, or as he really was from the beginning of the group, as a genuine symbolic father. This is a father whose power lies in recognising the mother/group's real, imaginary, and, above all, symbolic power as being as primeval and definitive as his own, and who, as he was generated by her, needs her symbolic power to shed light on his genuine symbolic value (Lacan, 1994, 1998b). In Foulkes' terms, the members recognise that the conductor is not a "leader of the group", that is, a representative of the primal father of the primal horde, as they imagined, who incited their dependence on the group, but a "leader in the group", who, "as a participant observer" and simultaneously mature observer of the group, "conducts it continuously" in a non-directive way (Foulkes, 1964, pp. 55, 57, 61). His "contribution" is then "similar to that of a conductor" of an orchestra (Foulkes, 1990, p. 292). In this role, he promotes the active participation of the members in order to foster their growth through the group and their independence–individuation from it. In Bion's terms (1961, 1992), it could be said that the members recognise the conductor as an intellectual leader or a leader of the work group in the sense that he is able to show how the members can develop their thinking. As such, he promotes the disengagement of the members (and the group) from a primal psychotic dependence on the mother/group (beta-elements, basic group, thoughts without thinking) and helps them (it) to transform this situation into alpha-elements; in this way, they aspire to reach a high degree of mental and strictly personal individuation (work group, creative/symbolic thinking). In other words, this leader helps the members to negotiate successfully their ongoing transition back and forth from the paranoid–schizoid to the depressive position (Bion, 1992).

We can now see female and male members who have arrived at this level of development, despite the fact that they still "retain" many elements from previous phases, promoting a greater forgetfulness of the oral stage and entering strongly into a normal experience of the anal–sadistic stage and, thus, into the genital stage (oedipal). For the first time, many of the women members begin to feel that the money they pay for therapy actually constitutes a symbolic gift to the group/mother (anal–sadistic stage) and indirectly (at the level of the genital stage in the form of a gift/child) (Freud, 1905d, 1916–1917, 1923b) to the conductor/father (and, potentially, later to a man) with whom they have started feeling more familiar and "playing" with him, even though they still experience him as a mother/breast or as a primal father. At the same time, many male members enter into a more positive competition with the conductor/father: they no longer envy/hate him so strongly or struggle to "murder" him, as was the case in the initial stages, because he has the women in the group, but because he has the power to think and to co-ordinate space–time and money in order to take full advantage of the group as good enough mother, according to Winnicott (1976). Thus, they acknowledge for the first time that: (a) on the level of a normal experience and transcendence of the anal–sadistic stage, the money, as well as the space–time, they pay for their therapy, constitute a symbolic gift to the group/mother, and (b) at the genital stage, which is the level on which the male members identify with the thought of the conductor/father, and strive to exceed it in originality/creativity, it is the surest and *best investment* they have made to date. That is, they have learnt that the mother/group, since it grasps the thinking of the conductor/father, represents the safest bridge for their transition later to the erotic object/woman. On the other hand, the idea of investment described above seems to have at least a double meaning. It signifies not only that the members learn to regulate their psychic energy in a more prolific, non-morbid way, but also to utilise this energy in a way that augments thinking and reinforces productivity and could later lead them to regain the money they paid for therapy through an extension of their professional activities.

Finally, in this phase, the members, males and females alike, either do not pay strictly regularly, or they delay or deny; they simply pay in a relatively normal, mature way, which alludes to an optimistic and happy disposition related to the new symbolic prospects of the group's culture. At the same time, however, it also contains some sadness or mild resentment due to the fact that money reminds them slightly of a "thing" that is on the way to being "buried".

Two clinical vignettes

To substantiate the theory outlined above, the relevant points from two group-analytic sessions are now presented. They have been taken from a slow open group-analytic group with transcultural dimensions conducted by me that meets twice a week in private practice in Athens from 1998 to the present and consists of seven members plus conductor. The first session took place just before the summer vacation of 2001 and generally coincided with the group's effort to pass from the first to the second phase. The second session reported here took place just before the Easter holidays of 2002, about a year after the first. This is a session that shows that the group (most of its old members and those members characterised by an organised neurotic part of their personality and fewer members with a morbid psychotic part of their personality) was experiencing the second phase relatively normally and preparing to pass into the third. Another non-accidental fact is that during the period between the two sessions, the group passed from its fourth to fifth year of life, having been established in January of 1998. Needless to say, for many members of the group, money proved to be one of the most significant factors in shaping their psychopathology and in the conflicts thus caused; its re-handling through the group-analytic process was the cornerstone of their therapy.

Vignette one

Angela: (*A German member, thirty-six years old, entrepreneur. She is married and has two small children. Her personality has a good enough neurotic structure, but with severe difficulties in experiencing an oedipal situation because her mother has the power of money, and her father is seductive.*) On that subject, I want to say that I disagree with paying for the month of August [*month of vacations*]. I don't want to pay for this August and I won't pay. I'm saying that now after three years in the group!

Evangelos: (*A member with a borderline psychopathology, twenty-six years old. He studied law but does not work. For him, paying the group almost uninterruptedly up to the present has been a means of controlling the group/mother so that it does not persecute him; in this way he is controlling his own mother, who has castrated him by giving him a large fortune.*) I haven't paid for April [*last year's Easter holidays*] but I've paid for May. May doesn't create a problem, but April does, and I don't want to pay. I don't know what I'm going to do about August. Probably not much.

Natalia: (*A depressive member, thirty-one years old, private secretary in an international financial company, with a fragile borderline personality* structure and uses the psychotic part of it, from Germany, whose father married for a second time but is now asking his daughter to support him; she is married but is unable to conceive a child, which might be associated with the fact that her mother rejects the idea of her daughter having children.) I've made up my mind. From the beginning I told myself that in August we don't come, so why should we pay?

(*About a minute's silence full of sadness.*)

Alexis: (*A neurotic member, forty-six years old, unmarried mathematics teacher, with great symbiotic needs and in a constant symbiosis with his mother. Even though he has been in the group for three years, he has not been absent even once, despite the urging of other members, and pays uninterruptedly*). I don't know . . . this whole discussion makes me sad . . . It reminds me of my parents who were always fighting about money.

Conductor: (*Addressing the group as a whole.*) Money contains a good deal of sadness.

Alexis: I don't know. Now that I think of it, I associate it with a tendency I have had for years of keeping things from my childhood . . . from elementary school, T-shirts, notebooks, anything you can imagine. I throw nothing away!

(*Half a minute's silence.*)

Grigoris: (*A mildly psychotic member, thirty-year-old man, with studies in electronics, unmarried, whose father, although financially well off, was rejected by his wife, a strong mother figure.*) I think the fact that we pay the group generally has some meaning . . . I don't know . . . I think that when we pay, it's like keeping up our relations with this place . . . but when we don't pay, it's like cutting ourselves off . . .

Angela: (*Angrily.*) What do you mean "cutting ourselves off"? What kind of a word is that? I don't like it at all!

Grigoris: How else can I say it?

Angela: I don't know . . . find another word! I don't understand what "cutting ourselves off" means. You made an assumption, but have you considered that it might work the opposite way?

Grigoris: You mean, when we don't pay . . . we are not cutting ourselves off . . . whereas when we do pay, we are?

Angela: Right! And we're not talking about cutting ourselves off . . .

Alexis: I agree with Grigoris . . . The fact that we pay [*for vacations*] . . . how can I say this? . . . I feel as though we are renting the space . . . like we can reserve this space by paying for August even if we don't have group!

Evangelos: (*As though something stimulated the idea.*) I don't understand this . . . In other words (*turning toward the conductor quizzically*), can we knock on the door in August and come here when we don't have group?

(*Silence of about one minute. The climate starts becoming less heavy and more optimistic. Just before the group's time is up, as though they had the sense that the subject of money as discussed would sometime be solved and that they can pass over to a more advanced stage, they started talking about jealousy, and of course, about the main theme with which the group had started, the conductor.*)

Virginia: (*A thirty-five-year-old member, unmarried, working as counsellor in a private business, with severe psychosomatic disturbances who has great problems with separation mainly due to her strong symbiotic relationship with her mother. She has found a way of mitigating separation from the group by paying every second month.*) Anyway, I think that on this subject, I at least, have found an answer. I'd like to say something to Angela . . . that I was wondering about what you said last time, that you didn't envy me. I can find at least twenty reasons to envy you . . .

Angela: I didn't say I don't envy you, but that "I don't envy you any more"!

Virginia: OK!

Grigoris: I envy the conductor because he's here as a father, and I'm still a child . . . but I'm going to change that, dammit!

Evangelos: Me too, because he has all the women in the group!

Vignette two

Betty: (*A relatively new member from the USA with borderline psychopathology who manages without any financial support from her family. For her, money represents a substitute for mothering care and a way of achieving a normal symbiosis with her mother.*) I want to say something too . . . I don't know if this has any relation to what you've been saying, but I was thinking now . . . Seems to me that the money I give every month for the group is a significant amount . . . and I'm just wondering whether it might be better to pay this money instead on a mortgage, because having a place of my own is very important to me.

(*One minute's silence with contemplation and sadness.*)

Alexis: (*Who has started being absent periodically.*) I don't know . . . what I have to say to you is . . . that in the past I've always been the one to complain about the money I was paying for therapy. But now I can see that it really isn't wasted . . . we need a lot of time and money to understand certain things . . . some things need to be repeated . . .

Angela: (*At this time, she is making an effort to enter into a normal oedipal situation.*) I too want to say that, for the first time now, I feel that the money I pay to the group is truly a gift . . . I don't know . . . I feel strongly that it is a gift I am giving . . . Mind you, I still can't pay for last August because I can't afford to, but I often feel like doing it . . . And one last thing I want to say to the group, is that just lately something's happened that's taken me back . . . Yannis (*her most recent boyfriend, whom she's known for a month*) said he loved me and asked me to marry him and have a child . . . I don't know . . . the next day I went over to another friend's house and we made love . . . I don't know how all these are linked . . .

Grigoris: . . . You couldn't stand it, that's all! . . . (*angrily*)

Angela: Let's not mix everything together . . . one by one.

Natalia: (*Who, in the meantime, has got married and adopted a little boy.*) I also feel that the money I give to the group is like a gift. But a real gift and not like a favour, as I used to believe.

Grigoris: (*In a very serious voice and with a lot of sadness, imitating the tone of some of the conductor's interventions.*) I don't know, you guys. But I really feel that the money I'm paying for therapy is the most important investment that I, at least, have ever made in my life!

Virginia: (*Who has started paying regularly.*) . . . Very important for you to say that, because it has made you less frightened of women!

(*30-second silence with a lot of sadness.*)

Evangelos: It really is like you say. An investment.

Betty: (*With humour and happiness mixed with sadness.*) OK, OK! You've convinced me already! I know what the house I'm looking for means.

Conclusions

Money plays an important role in group-analytic psychotherapy, which also sheds light on the role it plays in psychoanalysis and psychotherapy in general. As seen in the clinical material and its conceptualisation presented in this chapter, money, which is conceived as payment by the patients, is interwoven with the three major developmental phases that every member of the group-analytic group, and the group as a whole, go through as the therapy and the group evolve. Specifically, the payment of money, in either its positive (regular payment) or negative (delay or refusal to pay) form, starts as an expression of the members' fusion with the group, fantasised as an absolutely "good" mother figure or "breast" that provides "suckling", which, thus, engenders envy, and their non-separation from it (oral stage) as part-object relationship (Klein, 1946, 1957) or as a "thing" (Freud, 1900a, 1915e), as well as their refusal to recognise the conductor as an imaginary and, above all, a symbolic father who is different from the group/breast (Freud, 1905d, 1912–1913). The issue of money then passes to the second phase indicating the members' efforts to achieve a semi-separation from the group, which is imagined both as "good" and "bad" object or "breast", through a more systematic negation of payment in the anal–sadistic phase (Freud, 1905d) or the paranoid–schizoid position (Klein, 1946). It is now considered as a refusal to make a gift to the group through payment, thus accepting the group as an entity differentiated from them and recognising the conductor as an archaically imaginary and symbolic father (Freud, 1905d, 1912–1913). The eventual result is the representation and acceptance of payment conceived as expressing gratitude for the "goodness" of the mother/group and the symbolic "death" of the group as a "good" or "bad" feeding object in Klein's (1946, 1957) depressive position or, in Freud's terms, as a "thing". This signifies the members' ability to be separated from the group, and to be identified with the conductor as a mature symbolic father figure and with the group as an integrated whole and as a symbolic mother in the genital/phallic phase (Freud, 1905d), and marks their individuation as adults alluding to a successful ending of their therapy which is ultimately assessed as a highly valuable investment.

CHAPTER FOUR

Envy in group analysis

Introduction

After examining the role of money/payment in group analysis, in particular as it is considered and treated by the patients as a means of "suckling" or denying "suckling" the group/breast, especially during the latter's primordial phase, we can now investigate another crucial phenomenon in the life of group-analytic groups, which is also linked with "suckling" processes and, as already noted, is interrelated with therapy payment: that is, envy. Envy is known to constitute a mental and psychological process, the causes and function of which Freud believed to originate in the triadic infant–mother–father relationship as penis envy (Freud, 1937c). Klein's discoveries, however, proved it to be rooted in the dual relationship between the infant and the mother conceived as a "good" breast/penis, taking the form of breast/penis envy (Klein, 1957). More recent psychoanalytic investigation has verified that the object of envy is not the "good" object, as Klein maintained, but the omnipotent–idealised object that hinders the newborn from mourning it, and leads to envy replacing mourning (Feldman & De Paola, 1994). Other researchers link the phenomenon of envy with the person's enduring fantasies of returning to the womb (Maizels, 1985; Silver, 2007). In any case, the group-analytic group, since it covers all the above levels and relationships due to its multiple dyadic (pre-oedipal) and triangular (oedipal) constellations, as seen in the members' relationships with the group or the conductor or in sibling relationships developed within the group (Wooster, 1998) in the context of a group-analytic situation that strongly favours the members' regression even to the level of the fantasy of returning to the womb, as symbolised by the group, fosters the emergence of envy, according to its stage of development, the psychopathology of its members, and the way in which the group is conducted (Foulkes, 1964). At the same time, owing to its function as container (Bion, 1963, 1967, 1970), the group has the ability not only to manage instances of envy adequately by transforming it into jealousy (Wooster, 1998), even if they are not susceptible to analysis, but also to suggest new dimensions of the ontology and phenomenology of envy that go beyond those suggested by Freud and Klein and were first investigated by Bion.

In this chapter, we shall attempt to demonstrate the manner in which the group copes with instances of envy and to redefine the origins of envy based on the dimensions manifested in the group. In particular, we shall show that envy is less directly linked to an "alteration of the ego" (meaning a character disturbance to some extent) due to "a constitutional strength of instinct", as Freud (1937c, pp. 220–221) and later Klein (1946, 1957) assumed, and more to an "alteration of the ego" which is associated with the incorporation of the mothering object and, by extension, of the group-analytic group, as a "dead" object, according to Bion (1967, 1992).

Theoretical considerations: Freud, Klein, and beyond

The issue of envy in group analysis has rarely, if ever, been an object of systematic study. Investigation of the theme is still a prerogative of psychoanalytic thought, chiefly that of Freud and Klein. Freud (1937c) regarded envy primarily as penis envy, that is, a process attributable to the oedipal state that serves the problem of castration, especially in terms of female sexuality. Klein (1957) assigned envy to the archaic and pre-oedipal level of the patient's development, perceiving it mainly as envy of the maternal breast and, through it, of the paternal penis, as kept inside the maternal body, initially in the form of the fantasy of parental coitus (primal scene) and later as the idea of the parents in an absolutely harmonious union (combined parents). Freud (1915c, 1920g, 1937c) and Klein (1946, 1957) alike, the latter with some variations, believed that the ontological foundations of envy are rooted primarily in the instinctual substratum (life–death instincts, the quality factor), and secondarily in the alteration of the ego, understood as the transformation of a normal ego into a psychotic one through the pathogenic role of the defence mechanisms used as resistance against recovery. Freud, too, placed special emphasis on the pathogenic role of resistance, but always on grounds determined by the "constitutional strength of instinct" (Freud, 1937c, p. 220). Although he recognised that the "alteration of the ego" "has an aetiology of its own" (Freud, 1937c, p. 221), he seems to attribute it ultimately to the "archaic heritage of the id" and especially to the "resistance from the id", and through it to the two primal instincts, Eros and Thanatos, the instincts of life and death, respectively (Freud, 1937c, pp. 240–243). Klein emphasises the same instincts, although with the intermediation of resistance.

However, attributing envy to instincts, and even to resistance, does not explain the phenomenon satisfactorily, at least with regard to the destructiveness entailed in its more extreme forms, which can in no way be linked to the influence of instincts. Even in the case of psychoses, in which there is massive regression to the oral–sadistic stage, and the thrust of the instinctual powers (mainly the death instinct) is shown to be much stronger, the instinct of destruction does not seem to take on any analogous weight (with regard to either the other or the subject). The patient who suffers from psychosis undoubtedly tends toward destruction of the other, and through it, of self (Bion, 1967, 1992). Nevertheless, this presupposes a number of successive failures during the patient's psychic development, the ultimate cause of which does not appear to be attributable to the action of the instincts, but, rather, to the extremely deficient nature of the patient's primal relationship with the other. From this point of view, other, more recent, psychoanalytic perspectives that link envy with the person's overwhelming fantasy of returning to the womb in the sense of womb envy (Maizels, 1985; Silver, 2007) or with the person's fixation on an omnipotent–idealised object (Feldman & De Paola, 1994) sound more convincing. The tendency of some patients, especially patients who suffer from psychosis, to regress so deeply as to fantasise a return to the maternal womb as a representative of a primordial omnipotent and strongly idealised object or to the group conceived as a "womb" has already been reported (Caparrós, 1999; Koukis, 2004). However, the hypothesis that patients who tend to develop strongly emotional states based on envy have introjected aspects of a "dead" mothering object and, by extension, experience the group mostly as a "dead" object, seems more reliable than the hypothesis that they tend to regress to fantasies about returning to the womb. As Bion (1967, 1992) has shown, in the case of patients with severe psychopathology, the other takes the place of the "dead" object almost exclusively, which becomes even more "dead" as the person who suffers from either psychosis or neurosis, whose behaviour is determined mainly by the psychotic part of his/her personality, tends to identify with it in the context of access to the depressive position. This constitutes a factor sufficient to generate envy, and culminates in alteration of the ego.

The hypothesis of the "dead" object, as noted by Bion, could open new paths in the approach to envy with regard to an alteration of the ego, or what might be called character disturbances. Such an alteration, if it is somehow linked to the envious person's tendency to cause moral harm to the other, could, in my opinion, be the primary ontological foundation of envy. Yet, strange as it might seem, the alteration of the ego would not even be worth investigating in cases of psychosis or schizophrenia. In persons suffering from psychosis, the object is certainly "dead", but they have learnt to live with it and to exist without fully identifying with it, which is why they know how to protect themselves from its possible reactivation; it is precisely for this reason that, in their own way, they still keep the object "alive". Moreover, manifestations of envy in people with psychosis are not distinguished by the conscious exaggerated inclination to cause moral harm to the other, perhaps because their conscious part has been fully taken over by their "dead" unconscious (Bion, 1967, 1992). On the contrary, we should seek the alteration of the ego in a broad spectrum of psychopathologies related to borderline or narcissistic personality disorders or transference neurosis. Yet, even in such cases, envy is coloured in such a way that it cannot always be explained by attributing it to the instinctual substratum, much less to patterns of pathological defence mechanisms such as negative transference, negative therapeutic reaction, etc. It appears, rather, to be associated with alterations of the ego that might be due to the fact that the object—the greater part of which is "dead"—is unable to find an outlet through projective identifications, as happens in cases of psychoses or paranoid personality disorders (Bion, 1967, 1992), with the result that it manifests itself through a special form of acting out. In this case, such actions are not of the unconscious nature characteristic of some neuroses and borderline cases, but may actually retain some nuance of consciousness, which is alternately coloured with various features of malignant alterations of the ego.

Forms of envy in the group-analytic group: theory and clinical examples

Envy appears with greater clarity and strength in the group-analytic group for the reasons described above and because the phenomena of multi-mirroring and multi-transference in the group tend inexorably to activate in members a deep regression to primordial/archaic stages of their psychic development, thus fostering malignant dependence on the conductor and the group (Foulkes, 1964, 1990; Foulkes & Anthony, 1957) together with enduring malignant mirroring (Zinkin, 1983). Its timing and intensity are always a function of the person's psychopathology and the stage the group is going through. Phenomena of envy usually appear when the group is making the transition from one phase of its evolution to the next, in accordance with the pattern (initial, intermediate, final) defined by Foulkes (1964). The course of these phases does not, however, determine the force of the envy, which is always a function of the member's regression to the oral–sadistic stage. This regression, even though it is expected to be much more significant in the group's early phase, can, none the less, be quite fierce in the intermediate phase when the patient passes from the paranoid–schizoid position and is preparing to enter the depressive position, but especially in the final phase when the patient is called upon to negotiate the more significant passage from the paranoid–schizoid to the depressive position (Bion, 1992; Klein, 1946) that will allow him to achieve successful access to the individuation—separation phase, following Mahler's (1968) views. Also, both the timing of its appearance and the fierceness of the envy are unrelated to the object at which it is directed. The object can be one or more of the group members at random, the therapist, or the group as a whole, even though the group as a whole remains the ultimate target of envy. The only certainty is that, wherever envy takes on an extreme form, the subject of the envy appears to have lost almost all hope of restoration of the object.

It is also certain that envy tends to appear in three forms or phases: mild, intermediate, and extreme, each of which, as we probe ever more deeply into the unconscious, entails some alteration of the ego. It is worth noting that, in all three cases, the phenomenology of envy remains the same: it differs only in terms of the intensity with which it is manifested. This phenomenology, which needs to be investigated in greater depth, should be characterised, in my opinion, as an amalgam of breast envy and penis envy, but, since penis and breast, according to Klein (1957) and Bion (1992), constitute the idea of combined parents in its rudimentary form, envy in all cases appears to be directed against the idea of the combined parents as personified by the therapist–group union. The ultimate aim of a person subject to this type of envy is always to split the combined parents. Envy is manifested in the three following forms.

Mild form

A close study of relevant clinical data suggests that envy in its mild form appears within the group context mainly through the subject's effort to create pockets of discussion and conflict, usually on trivial matters. The purpose of these is not to clarify or foster awareness of certain psychodynamic aspects of the self or the group, but, rather, to conceal the group dynamics in such a way that the representation of the union between the therapist and the group is not visible. As envy becomes more intense, it takes on the form of acting out and very probably of dropping out, by means of which the ability of the group (as the parental union) to create life is attacked, specifically in its ability to "have children" and to reproduce (e.g., by the entry of new members). In this case, envy can also appear intermixed with jealousy, which, in fact, tends to predominate. However, as it becomes deeper, envy "warns" the patient of the imminent disaster, leading him or her perhaps to drop out or to terminate therapy prematurely. In this way, the patient essentially hastens to sever his symbiotic relationship with the group, for it is a relation that is in danger of becoming malignant, and envy of it seems to be at once the main outcome and means of escape (defence).

The example of Stella is typical. She was a thirty-eight-year-old, unmarried English teacher, who came into therapy to improve her "malignant dependency" on her parents that had created a significant difficulty in her relations with the opposite sex, and an almost insurmountable rejection of marriage and child-bearing. Stella attended ten individual psychotherapy sessions once a week in 2001, and because her continuation caused her many psychodynamic difficulties, she agreed to try group-analytic psychotherapy in a group-analytic group that had been running once a week since 1999 and was conducted by me. After an early period of relatively mild adjustment to the group that lasted about eight months, and on the occasion of the anxiety aroused in her by the arrival of another new member, Stella began to interrupt any deeper analysis by either the group or the conductor and to engage the group constantly in a variety of trite and usually indifferent theoretical or socio-political issues. Any emotionally meaningful communication in the group was slyly interrupted and somewhat "deadened" through Stella's preoccupation with the above issues, behind which it was obvious that her mentally undigested and unverbalised psychic material was projected to the members, the conductor, or the group as a whole. From her brief remarks to the group about her great rage, especially towards her mother, and the latter's indifference to her, it appeared that Stella's projections represented parts of an also undigested and "dead" maternal object (Bion, 1992), owing to which any further relationship with the group/mother and the conductor/father was the object of her envy and eventually suspended. The group kept advising her to relax by just listening to the others so that she would soon have the pleasure of being "nourished" by the group's supportive qualities, such as attention and acceptance, but Stella gave the impression that her ears were closed. Progressively, the group began to take on for her the form of a "bad"/"dead" object ("the group is simply an inert material for me", she said in one session). Under these conditions, and despite the interpretative explanations and support provided to her by the group, Stella decided to terminate her therapy prematurely by dropping out.

Intermediate form

In its intermediate form, envy has much greater depth and intensity than its mild form. It begins to be increasingly differentiated from the jealousy with which it seemed to have been mixed so far and becomes distinct in itself. Then, it emerges not solely as a passive defence process with respect to symbiosis with the group/mother (which has, in this case, also acquired a much greater depth), but also as an active tendency to curtail and "deaden" those relations and behaviours which, on the part of either the group as a whole or its members, suggest mature separation from it as a "live" entity and, by extension, differentiation and individuation. Furthermore, envy seems to draw out characteristics that pertain more to penis envy and less to breast envy, which is why it is frequently directed towards the group therapist, taking the form of a defence mechanism whose aim is to prevent identification of the patient (of both sexes) with the therapist or to favour counter-identification together with a tendency to humiliate him/her and take his/her position. It is implied that the patient's envy also tends to hinder the representation of the therapist and the group as a unified entity, that is, in Klein's (1957) terms, it tends to split off the idea of combined parents. However, since envy of this kind usually emerges in the period when the envious patient is entering the final phase of his or her therapy (separation), it would appear that the ultimate target of envy in this case is to avert separation from an object from which any idea of separation has been excluded because it is preponderantly a "dead" object. In this sense, the development of envy as described by Klein (1957), which is that the infant's envy, which is initially (oral–sadistic stage and paranoid–schizoid position) linked with the latter's attacks on the mother conceived not only as a "bad" but also as a "good" object, could normally be transformed into assimilation of the mothering object as a "good" object, leading to gratitude towards it in the depressive position, cannot be achieved.

The example of Irene, thirty years old, a high school teacher of Greek literature and a married woman, is characteristic. Irene entered a twice-a-week group-analytic group conducted by me that had been running since 1996, after completing two years of individual therapy in once-a-week sessions, in 2001. She mainly complained that she had always felt rejected by her mother and especially her father, with the result that she had great difficulties with marriage and, above all, having children. During her group therapy, even though she had given no previous signs of such behaviour, suddenly one day, as some members reported in one of the group sessions, Irene arranged to meet the new members of the group outside the therapy milieu and suggested to them that it was not worth entering analysis in that particular therapy group and that it would be preferable for them to stop. This happened at a period when, after five years of therapy, Irene had managed to heal her most basic symptom that had sent her into analysis (serious dyspareunia, which was attributable to her parents' neglect and primarily to her father's neglect of her as the third daughter, compared to her two sisters) and was, in fact, preparing her leave-taking from the group, because in the meantime she had married and had a son. In one sense, the envy she showed to the new group members was little more than a shift of the envy she felt toward her own child and aimed through him at her father ("I hate it and I sometimes feel like throwing it out the window", she said about her newborn son at one session. "I hate it like I hate my father, and of course my mother, who is nothing but a lifeless body", she added). The manifestation of envy in this case functioned as a powerful means of preventing a greater internalisation of the parental couple as personified by the union of the therapist and the group. In this sense, the patient was protecting herself—who then proceeded to a hasty and incomplete separation from the group—since, if her therapy had continued, the internalisation in question would have deepened sufficiently to increase the patient's ability to have children, which she would have been unable to bear or, as a reaction to this internalisation, envy would have increased rapidly with the danger of being turned against the patient herself, leading perhaps to auto-destructive behaviour. This is the reason why Irene asked to leave the group. After her behaviour outside the group was revealed, the conductor and the group as a whole helped Irene to elaborate to some extent her feelings of envy and then to prepare a farewell. The positive aspect was that, despite her deeply envious emotional state, Irene was able to listen to others and—due to the relaxation provided by the idea of the farewell and her final disengagement from the "dark and inert lines of the group" (as she usually said)—to accept interventions. She finally arranged a good enough farewell, by means of which a considerable articulation of the group and the conductor as good enough objects and their union as less malevolent and pernicious was achieved.

Extreme form

In the two previous forms of envy, the object as introjected into the personality of the patient possessed by envy appears as an "inert" entity that persecutes it, but not as thoroughly "dead". The opposite, we must assume, is true in the third and most extreme manifestation of envy. Here, the object appears as "dead" on most points, although, as noted earlier, without this indicating a psychotic psychopathology, a fact that permits envy to be manifested in the same undisguised, almost conscious and destructive manner characteristic of the death instincts in their most open expression. Envy appears here encapsulated in the subject's psychic core, in a way that immobilises subject and object alike in a state of war that takes place in the guise of permanent peace. To do this, the envious person strikes out in a fully conscious way against the link between the conductor and the group, not simply to prevent genitality, but to deactivate the very core of human existence and evolution. As a result, envy takes on the nature of calumny or slander with alterations of the ego that approach the limits of character disturbance.

The case of Voula, a member of the twice-a-week group-analytic group previously referred to, is a typical example. Voula was a twenty-seven-year-old psychology student when she came into therapy in 2008, and the first of two children (her brother being a year or two younger) in a family that, according to her own description, was "very troubled". Her demand for therapy consisted of her desire to control her strong homosexual tendencies. Voula maintained sexual relations with other women through which she sought absolute power over the erotic object. This symptom came to the surface gradually in two years of group therapy, in which she entered after about two years of individual psychotherapy.

Even though Voula's transference initially appeared to be proceeding well in her individual therapy, it became increasingly negative after she entered the group, to such a degree that it gradually took on the nature of open belligerence, even when artfully concealed under superficial passivity or politeness. Transference, in this case, is nevertheless not massive, as in psychosis (Bion, 1967). In this sense, the actions of the patient with this type of envy are not in the nature of either acting out—as in cases of borderline personality disorders—or an attack on linking, as mainly expressed in the form of the attack on any idea representing a parental couple in union, as in psychosis (Bion, 1967). They constitute more or less conscious orchestrated efforts by means of which the greatest possible paralysis of the therapy group is sought, in accordance with the model of the "dead" object that the subject carries inside him or her.

After repeated efforts to claim the exclusive attention of the therapist, Voula shifted her stance completely and sought to paralyse the conductor in order to occupy his place and "acquire" his wife, with the latter represented by the group as a whole. The idea of an inverted oedipal complex is surely suggested in this case (Klein, 1957). But it was presented on "dead" ground, since, in essence, it would have conduced to the dispersal of the group (as maternal/female figure) and, as a result, to the idea of the therapist's wife (as Voula imagined her, since they had never met). Against this background, Voula arranged to meet the group members outside the therapy milieu where she spread the rumour that, according to her information, the therapist's wife was unfaithful to him, meaning she had sexual relations with another man, whom Voula knew. In addition to the relevant analyses and interpretations that were provided over a period of about six months from the time this incident took place, the group waited all this time, with the help of the intervening summer vacations, for Voula to become aware of the possible projective or delusory nature of her assertion (paranoid–schizoid position), which would have helped her, gradually perhaps, to apologise, thus achieving access to the depressive position, following Klein's (1946, 1957) views.

However, this matter went far beyond the dialectic of the paranoid–schizoid and depressive position, and perhaps even further back than the oral–sadistic stage. This was not solely a strong attack on the "good" object, but a tendency to what one might call a *de facto* paralysis of the object by means of which the patient's internal object (in this case, her father), which was a "dead" object inside her, was to be legitimised. So, in Freud's (1920g) terms, one could venture to say that this case touched the core in which the life instinct had atrophied to such an extent that it had been fully displaced by the death instinct. The emergence of envy in the sense described here appeared to be connected with the strong agitation of the death instinct that arose from the father's continuous rejection of Voula until his death. Her mother as well always showed feelings of rejection towards her. This is why Voula, who lived alone, had not spoken to her for many years. Voula's stance towards her parents was so rejecting that, when her father died at an early age—Voula was only eighteen years old, and was then writing university entrance exams, which his death caused her to fail—and the other family members were keeping vigil with the body of the dead father, Voula arranged to have intercourse on the parental bed with a random youth whom she called that evening for this precise purpose. This action must have been in the nature of a final and desperate effort to avoid the cataclysmic intrusion of the death instinct into the life instinct with which the act of love is associated. But her effort failed, not to say that it had the opposite effect, leading her to a banquet of the death instinct to the detriment of the life instinct. With regard to identification processes, it was evident that Voula identified with her father as representing a "dead" object and had intercourse with a boy who, in her fantasy, also personified a "dead" mothering object, in the context of an inverted oedipal (Klein, 1957).

Something of this scene, then, must have been repeated in the group context. This was why Voula could allow no room for her assertion that the conductor's wife was unfaithful to be subjected to mental processes, since she continued to perceive it consciously as a true conviction (without being the conviction of persons with psychosis regarding the truth of their delusion). In the context of one of the strongest and most destructive projective identification processes that are assumed to be derived from the hard core of the psychotic part of the personality (Bion, 1967), Voula had "thrown" this assertion to the group. But, despite the fact that her assertion constituted a violation of the therapy contract—since it destroyed any bridge of positive transference to the therapist, the group, and the milieu—Voula did not take responsibility for her own termination. She remained in the group, retaining an openly passive stance (she never spoke). In this sense, and in a way indicating the process of a projective identification in reverse (Bion, 1967), she indirectly drove the group to take the initiative of expelling her, in other words, of paralysing her, precisely as her father had done to her, and as she had done to the group, a fact which appears to have relieved her and to have passed on to her the message that therapy is ultimately nothing but a graveyard.

The group eventually took the initiative, by deciding to provide Voula with perhaps the best possible "maternal" qualities that she could internalise at that point: it proposed to her a brief farewell (i.e., that she should come to the group twice more, and to leave after the second time). This separation, apart from the fact that it would permit Voula to make a small partial introjection of the maternal and paternal object, would keep her far from the field of analysis (at least for a time), a field which, in her case, seemed to lead directly to a fairly malignant and possibly dangerous regression. Voula accepted the group's proposal and made her farewell which, based on the length of time she had been in the group, was judged to be fairly successful. Her farewell gave Voula an opportunity to thank the conductor for liberating her from the group, which she said she experienced as a "prison full of dead objects".

Conclusions

Envy in group-analytic psychotherapy is manifested in three forms: mild, intermediate, and extreme, according to the degree to which the patients have introjected a mothering object (or sometimes also a father figure) that is conceived as emotionally and mentally "dead" (Bion, 1967, 1992). This, according to Freud (1937c), produces severe alterations in the patients' ego, with the result that their feelings of envy towards the inner mother figure or the group conceived as a mainly "good" object, in Klein's view (1957), cannot be activated and are finally resolved by being transformed into gratitude towards the object. The exhibition of envy in the group is strongly correlated with the patients' malignant regression and the related malignant mirroring, leading to destructive attacks against the union of the group and the conductor, considered as representing a harmonious parental couple, according to Klein (1946, 1957). Under these premises, it could be said that, in the cases of people who seem to have all the prerequisites for developing envy, at least in its extreme form, group-analytic psychotherapy is both indicated and counter-indicated and, in any case, remains a very morbid environment. Cases of extreme envy test group-analytic psychotherapy, since they raise many questions about the breadth and scope of its effectiveness. On the other hand, these same cases help group analysis to distance itself from a possible sense of omnipotence towards which it might be heading. Even though it might not offer a full cure or prevent some patients from dropping out, the group-analytic group has an opportunity to protect the patients against an even greater malignant regression and to help them in their wish to terminate their therapy prematurely by permitting them to arrange a good enough farewell.

CHAPTER FIVE

Spaltpilz: a case of self-destructive projective identification and scapegoating in the early phase of a transcultural group-analytic group

Theoretical and clinical considerations

Scapegoating in general

The term "scapegoating", usually linked with envy processes, is known to have originated from an Old Testament ritual of a goat sent into the wilderness on the Day of Atonement, as the symbolic bearer of the sins of the people (Leviticus, 16, 21–22), with Jews being the first sacrificial victims of the modern phenomenon. The term has been progressively expanded to indicate the discharge of psychic material—concepts or ideologies that are unacceptable by a person, group, society, or nation (the agent)—against another person, group, society, or nation conceived as victim (Allport, 1954; Glick, 2005; Glick & Fiske, 2001). The victim, due to its own inner unresolved deficiencies and conflicts, easily becomes the object of scapegoating by accepting the other's negative emotional material as evacuated on it. The full meaning of the phenomenon of scapegoating has not been elaborated systematically and its everyday use remains metaphorical. In psychology and psychoanalysis, scapegoating is the conceptualisation of a complex psychopathological phenomenon that initially results from a malignant (dual) infant–mother relationship, then extends to the family as a primary group (Cornwell, 1967), in the context of which a disturbed child usually becomes the scapegoat to whom unresolved family dynamics are projected (Vogel & Bell, 1960), and from there to the broader socio-political group. Using Klein's (1946, 1957) terms, one could say that the word describes processes of strong projective identification, meaning the act by a person or group of transposing "bad" representations of self and undigested mental material (paranoid–schizoid position), usually interrelated with the envy stemming from their strong dependence on equally strong maternal or paternal "good" representations (oral–sadistic stage), to another person or group who assumes this role. This transposition aspires unsuccessfully to preserve the "good" representations of self by preserving the integrity of the maternal object as "good enough" and of the paternal figure as being in a sufficient union with the former in terms of an evolved form of the primal scene (Bion, 1992). The result is that scapegoating, by its very nature, is a complicated and intoxicating phenomenon of the paranoid–schizoid position (or anal–sadistic stage) in the development of a person or group and serves as a robust defence mechanism against both the separation anxiety linked with the person or group's entrance into the depressive position (or genital stage) and their regression to the oral–sadistic stage of development.

Scapegoating in group-analytic groups

In group-analytic groups, and in small groups in general in which, particularly during the initial stage of their operation, when the members' early intrasubjective and intra-family conflicts are represented and re-enacted, scapegoating is an expected, intrinsic feature (Foulkes, 1964; Gemmill, 1989; Yalom, 1970). Even if it leads to the member's dropping out, it is ultimately expected to be contained by the predominance of the group's "good" image and to contribute to its further maturation (Agazarian & Peters, 1981; Agmon & Schneider, 1998; Yalom, 1970).

More precisely, in the group-analytic context, scapegoating traces its roots to the group's "bad" representations of itself and to the negative feelings that accompany it as long as the members and the group as a whole strive to achieve the passage from the oral–sadistic stage to the paranoid–schizoid position and are preparing to enter the depressive position, following Klein's (1946, 1957) views. The above representations usually stem from the members' fixation on the group as an idealised (archaic) maternal omnipotent "feeding" object and the conductor as an archaic paternal superego (leader) as well as from their frustration by the group (and the conductor) through processes of "weaning", and are mainly linked with envy for the conductor's position whom, in the last resort, they are unconsciously addressing. During the group's oral–dependent or oral–aggressive stage (Agmon & Schneider, 1998), these representations are attributed (usually through one member who expresses the group) either to another member who, because of his/her relative vulnerability, has adopted the unconscious position of the leader's anti-type in the group (Lyndon, 1994) and is ready to accept them by identifying with the role of the group's scapegoat (Agazarian & Peters, 1981; Foulkes, 1964; Horwitz, 1983; Yalom, 1970) or even to the conductor (Agmon & Schneider, 1998). During the anal–expulsive group's stage, the conductor is openly personified as the scapegoat (Agmon & Schneider, 1998). In any event, through this evolution, the group manages to preserve the conductor (and itself) as a benevolent and "good" paternal figure, that is, to pass from incorporating and introjecting him as a destructive superego to interiorising him as a mature superego (Foulkes, 1990), or from its oral–aggressive and anal–expulsive to its anal–retentive stage (Agmon & Schneider, 1998). In other terms, following a modification of Bion's (1961) views, scapegoating is an intrinsic characteristic of the group's second phase, that is, its counterdependence:fight phase, through which its first dependence:flight phase is contained and preparation is made for the third one, the power:authority issue phase (Agazarian & Peters, 1981; Hafsi, 1998). According to Bion (1961), although he is not referring to it, one could say that scapegoating takes place as long as the basic-assumption group oscillates between dependence, fight–flight, and pairing, or between the oral–sadistic stage, the schizoid–paranoid position and the depressive position, as defined by Klein (1946).

Apart from this, the appearance and course of scapegoating in group-analytic groups, since it is based on the projection by the members and the group of their undesired feelings and conflicts to another member or members who become victimised (Kahn, 1980), is unquestionably linked to a series of crucial factors, such as the way in which the group is conducted (Agazarian & Peters, 1981), the conductor's countertransference (Horwitz, 2000), and the dimensions taken on by the members' projective identification. In particular, the role of the latter is catalytic, even though it remains obscure, since it is not certain whether scapegoating is a direct consequence of it, as argued by Scheidlinger (1982), Zender (1991), and, initially, Horwitz (1983), or merely influenced by it, as Horwitz (1983) eventually concludes.

A case of scapegoating in a group-analytic group

General remarks

In the present study, we shall present scapegoating as manifested in one of its strongest forms (when the member who has assumed this role drops out) during the early stage of a twice-a-week group-analytic group conducted by me in private practice. The group was formed in 1996, about two years before the sessions that will be described here with a transcultural dimension, as its founding members included two German women, Katerina and Helka, and three Greeks, Vassilis, Aphrodite, and Angeliki. Katerina was thirty-seven years old, a teacher of Jewish origin, and unmarried mother of two children (two and four years old), characterised by a serious borderline psychopathology with paranoid features. Helka also had a borderline psychopathology, with the prevailing feature of nervous depression, was thirty years old, employed by an advertising firm, and recently married to a Greek. At the period described here, both Helka and Katerina had been living in Greece for about ten years. Vassilis and Angeliki were thirty-eight and thirty-two, respectively, both educators. The former was characterised by phobic neurosis and the latter by neurotic transference on borderline grounds. Aphrodite was forty-five years old, a civil servant, and mother of an adopted daughter of seven years old; she was characterised by a depressive, masochistic psychopathology. In the first two years, the group-analytic group met once a week, and since then, had been meeting twice a week.

Our purpose here is to demonstrate that the scapegoating which appeared in this group derived from the intersection and collision of a set of projective identifications the intensity of which resembles the projective identifications of patients with psychosis (Bion, 1967). Furthermore, scapegoating was linked with the traumatic revival of the fantasy of the primal scene with incestuous components strictly linked with the fantasy of the "anal child", following Klein's (1923) views, and led by what appears to have been established in the group from the outset by the member who assumed the role of scapegoat. These identifications were naturally combined with the corresponding intersection and involvement of a number of malignant mirrorings (Zinkin, 1983) that developed by virtue of the similarity between the maternal and paternal image in many of the members involved and their projection to the group and the conductor. The clinical material I present suggests that conflicts deriving from an inverted oedipal of the members might be also involved (Klein, 1945, 1957). Moreover, the members' projective identifications were intensified, because of a strong splitting that, inevitably and for a long period, led to the intermingling of two or three different cultures, Greek, German, and Jewish (it is not accidental that Katerina, the member who played the role of scapegoat, was simultaneously a German woman of Jewish origin), and, as a result, on the level of the social unconscious (Hopper, 1997, 2001), had two or three different maternal/paternal images (Engels, 2001; Sengun, 2001).

Scapegoating and projective identification based on an incestuous primal scene

More specifically, the dominant projective identification to which we are referring came from Katerina, who also became the scapegoat. It had the sense of "occupying" the position of conductor (as paternal and maternal figure combined) and, through this, "penetration" into the group/mother in such a way as to defuse the incestuous (homosexual and heterosexual) anxiety stemming from the member's imaginary "intercourse" with the conductor/father/mother or with the group/mother as well as that of the conductor/father with the group/mother (primal scene) or with the group/mother, or that of one member with another (pairing), and to control any representation indicative of the product of incest, in this case the birth of children as represented by the arrival of new members conceived as born on the anal or genital level, according to dimensions and alternatives of the above fantasies.

Consequently, we could argue that this was a projective identification stemming from a very tough—and perhaps not susceptible to analysis—layer of the psychotic part of Katerina's personality which should, to use Bion's term (1967), encapsulate the relevant part, in the sense that it foresaw the illusory maintenance of the *status quo* in the group by controlling genitality. In this way, it undoubtedly expressed what was seen later to constitute a fundamental problem among the members of the group as a whole and to the gradual resolution of which she contributed decisively. These problems had their origins in: Helka's inability to conceive, since the words repeated by her mother when she separated from her husband were that "no man is worth it" and "children should not be born" went as far as blocking her tubes; Angeliki's inability to have two and three children, as she would have liked, since she could not find a man who measured up to her "seductive" father, a fact that frequently led her to form parallel relationships with two men; Aphrodite's fear of having children in the natural way, which could possibly be traced to her fear of her "unstable, lady-killer" father, with whom she never had a close relationship, since he rejected her mother, with the result that she was obliged to adopt a child; Vassilis' aversion to the idea of marriage and children, in conjunction with his fixation in an extended adolescence, which can be traced to the fact that his mother, albeit quite "maternal", was "a tough woman" who stressed what one "had" to do in a "male role", and to the fact that his father, in addition to his advanced age, was symbiotic with him, with the result that the confrontation between father and son was inhibited; and, finally, Katerina's own aversion to the idea of giving birth to a third child, since this would have stirred up strongly (a) her incestuous desire for her father (the "schizophrenic professor" who sometimes rejected her and sometimes told her he was "the only man in her life"), a desire that Katerina had suppressed for the present by bearing two children with two different (unknown) men, and (b) the profound guilt created by her own birth, since immediately after she was born her mother "forbade her husband to penetrate her" (or "he couldn't penetrate"), with the result that the marriage dissolved and then the mother placed herself in the position of the child, with Katerina in that of the husband. In essence then, through her "penetration" into the group/mother, Katerina was unconsciously repeating the behavioural pattern that had been established within her in early childhood owing to the attitude of her parents.

To be precise, it was Katerina's identification with the malignant (penetrating, controlling) character that the matrix of the group had begun to take on at this stage through references to analogous traits presented by Helka's mother. These traits alluded to similar traits in Katerina's mother and Katerina herself often compared them to those of the famous fungus *Spaltpilz* that infiltrates plants so deeply that it "eats their innards". In psychoanalytic terms, this was identification with the characteristics of an archaic superego and, simultaneously, with an archaic id (Lyndon, 1994), which, among other things, were inevitably linked to a destructive German culture of the past (Nazism). This identification was initially projected on both the group and the conductor. Then it was extended, leading Katerina to the position of scapegoat, to the degree that she herself began to "penetrate" ever further into Vassilis and Angeliki, and into the pairing (Bion, 1961) that they had created for their own psychodynamic reasons. In other words, to the degree and extent that she, through her "penetration", began to stir up in the two members, especially Angeliki, traits corresponding to those of the father and mother figure, which they in turn projected more weakly to Katerina (as substitute for the conductor) and then to the group as a whole.

Katerina was afraid and defended herself strongly against the incestuous drives by the id (which represented both her mother and her "seducer" father), by projecting them to Angeliki, while increasingly identifying herself with the archaic superego that her parents also represented and, of course, with Nazi Germany, which had obliged parents to raise their children in a harsh, depriving way, similar to what they themselves had known (Sengun, 2001). Angeliki, on her part, began, on the one hand, to become more and more identified with the id, particularly in its incestuous component, which was represented both by her own father and by Katerina's father, and, indeed, to overinvest it by praising the lack of "musts" that characterises the Greek culture, but also to project this, together with the archaic superego (of her mother), to Katerina who, in turn, re-identified with both.

The case history and its phases

From the first to the second phase: control of incest and genitality

Under these conditions, the collision of the two women was inevitable. It happened during the period that can be considered the group's transition from the first to the second stage (early in its operation), which lasted for about four months (fifteenth to twenty-eighth session), and ran through the analytic group between its basic assumption dependence and fight–flight phase (Bion, 1961), or between its oral-dependent and anal-expulsive phase (Agmon & Schneider, 1998), between its dependence:flight and counterdependence:fight phase (Agazarian & Peters, 1981), or between the oral–sadistic stage and the paranoid–schizoid position (Bion, 1992; Klein, 1946, 1957). In contrast to the group's first phase, which also lasted four months (from the first to the fourteenth session), in the second phase, the members began gradually to differentiate the "bad" representation of the group and the conductor from the representations of their parents, that is, to perceive the group/conductor as "good" object, with which they were called upon to form a deeper emotional bond. This did not prove to be free of conflicts, as it appears to have triggered an increase of projective identifications linked with envy processes within the group as well as incidents of acting out in the members' personal lives.

More precisely, the confrontation between Katerina and Angeliki started off in the group's eighteenth session and culminated in the twentieth. It was, of course, already smouldering below the surface from the outset of the group, as was Katerina's assumption of the role of scapegoat. Until the outbreak of the conflict, this fact was primarily expressed in the tension characteristic of their relationship on a nonverbal level and particularly on the level related to the "occupation" of certain positions in the group. From the group's second session until her clash with Angeliki, Katerina would rush in at the beginning to "occupy" the place in which the conductor sat in the first session—a place that was sometimes, in rotation, "occupied" also by Helka and Angeliki—so that she would have control over the Greek section of the group (as expressed characteristically in her phrase "Greece is a country without boundaries and requires state control"). Angeliki constantly avoided sitting beside her, and even more so between her and Helka. These behaviours persisted despite constant interpretations by the conductor.

The second phase: acting out incest and blocking genitality

Angeliki arrived at the group's eighteenth session in a highly nervous state. She was very angry with her mother, with whom she had quarrelled the previous day, since her mother once more had tried to admonish her (through a series of endless "musts") not to be so open in her sexual relations with so many men and to get married. She was also angry with her father because he, even though he had raised her "tenderly" to a point where she was his "beloved", did not, in contrast to her mother, try to dissuade her from having intercourse with men. This led Katerina to argue openly that for her "there are no 'musts', especially in sexual issues". This claim stirred up in Katerina profound fears of incest with her father and, at the same time, harsh punishment by her mother. Thus, from the "conductor's" position that she had once again occupied at the beginning of the session, and with mixed feelings of fear, irony, curiosity, secret nostalgia, and, of course, anger that were barely contained, she addressed the following question to Angeliki: "Would you go so far as to have an affair with someone from here?" And when she received Angeliki's immediate affirmative reply ("Why not?"), fully identified with it and hastened to state in a harsh voice, "In here these things don't happen. Our conductor said so, they just don't happen!" I reassured both of them, reminding them of the terms of operation of the group, and explained the malignant mirroring that had appeared between the two women on the basis of projective identifications. This session, since it focused later on a discussion about relations between the sexes, closed in a relatively relaxed climate.

The same climate prevailed in the nineteenth group session, during most of which two members, Helka and Aphrodite, tried to take positive advantage of the negative resonance they felt regarding Katerina's "male" position. This was in the sense that they focused on the difficulties created in their conjugal lives by the fact that Helka unconsciously adopted a "male" position toward her husband ("ordering" him to do chores) while the latter (Aphrodite), on the contrary, felt that her own female position was being seized by her husband (who does all the women's work by himself).

Nevertheless, the clash between Angeliki and Katerina was simmering and found fertile ground in which to manifest itself in the group's twentieth session. In essence, this session was little more than a repetition of the eighteenth, in a stronger form and with the conditions reversed, in the sense that now Katerina assumed the representation of the id and Angeliki that of the archaic superego. Angeliki was the first to arrive at the group, after a long period away, and hastened to occupy the "conductor's" chair, while Katerina came twenty minutes late and sat on Angeliki's right. On the occasion of Katerina's lateness and until she arrived, Angeliki suggested to the group that she resented Katerina's presence and more or less because of her was experiencing the group as a "cold womb". When Katerina arrived, she attributed her lateness to a recent "involvement", which was, in essence, nothing but her acting out her strong incestuous tendencies and the concomitant feeling of guilt that she had been feeling for a long time in the group:

> By the time I got ready, I was already a little late . . . meantime I had got involved with this couple . . . and because of this I started thinking about some things . . . This is a couple of neighbours who have two little girls . . . I've been spending time with them recently . . . The woman does not accept her husband sexually on the one hand, but on the other she is jealous of him if he goes with other women . . . I don't understand this . . . Meanwhile, I saw the way she was washing one of her daughters, and there was something erotic in it . . . She is also depressed and frequently feels like throwing the children out the window. Her husband considers me the absolute sex object, I mean he sends me these messages saying "Come on over, my wife wants to see you," when I know that he wants to see me himself, just like my father, who used to say "Come on, your sister wants you" when he wanted me himself. I know that this is something like incest and my guilt is almost unbearable. Incest would be any erotic relationship in here, inside or outside the group. And even though I know this, and can see that it won't happen here, I feel as though I'm doing it with this other family.

These words, through which she was dealing with one of the harshest projective identifications in the group as a whole, resonated immediately in Angeliki who, in her effort not to be completely identified with Katerina's projection, reacted by saying that "all this is very boring, unpleasant and affected, not, of course, in the sense that it's a lie, but a fantasy that is being deliberately cultivated", a view with which Vassilis agreed immediately. At that point, the conductor intervened, saying that, irrespective of what is reality or fantasy, what is important is that all these things stir up feelings with great depth, feelings which, due to the relative similarity of Angeliki and Katerina's case histories, were mutual and that it would be good if they could be worked out and overcome mainly through analysis, and not only through projection and acting out. This intervention, although it temporarily relieved the group, did not appear to satisfy either of the two members, particularly Katerina, since, from what was shown by their non-verbal stance, each one of them expected the conductor to defend her exclusively (unconsciously: his attraction towards incest). During this and immediately afterwards, Katerina turned to Angeliki and asked directly, "What do mean to say about your feelings towards me?" She received an equally harsh reply: "If I told you what I feel . . . better not. I do feel dislike for what you say!" and, thus, she retorted immediately in an explosive manner, "Me too. I get the feeling that if we met somewhere else, we might even punch each other out!" At this point the conductor once again intervened, urging the members to express their feelings as openly as possible—especially jealousy and envy—among themselves, apart from Angeliki and Katerina, who denied that they had such feelings, but most of the other members expressed feelings of liking for the others but also feelings of jealousy/envy among themselves but mainly towards Katerina and Angeliki and, of course, towards the conductor. They also expressed a profound feeling of fear of Angeliki, since she is opposed to any prohibition and of Katerina because, while she presents herself as a champion of prohibitions, she also appears to circumvent them quickly. The session closed in a comparatively relaxed climate.

The third phase: unblocking genitality and dropping out

Despite all this, Katerina had already adopted the position of scapegoat, a fact that began to be more clearly visible and to take place during the group's third phase. This phase lasted for between four and six months (sessions twenty-one to forty-five) and corresponded to group's transition from the anal-expulsive to the anal-retentive phase (Agmon & Schneider, 1998), from the counterdependence:fight phase to the power:authority issue phase (Agazarian & Peters, 1981), from the paranoid–schizoid to the depressive position (Bion, 1992; Klein, 1946), and from the basic assumption dependence and fight–flight to the basic assumption pairing (Bion, 1961). During this phase, the group's unconscious pressure to "expel" Katerina began, especially on the part of Angeliki and Vassilis, at the same time as the equally unconscious instigation of this pressure by Katerina herself, a fact which, in conjunction with the subsequent entrance of a new member (birth of a new child) would lead to her dropping out. Thus, even though the phenomenon had been frequently interpreted from multiple aspects, the two members most involved were warned adequately about the unconscious motives on which they based their constant desire to occupy the "conductor's" place.

During the first three sessions that followed the clash between the two members (twenty-one and twenty-three), even though both Katerina and Angeliki usually came to the group more calmly, they were, at the same time, subject to the same unconscious motives—a fact that was clearly imprinted on the way in which they tried to find a place in the group: Katerina rushed to be the first to occupy the "conductor's" chair, while Angeliki struggled, if not to sit in the same place, at least not to be beside Katerina. Katerina continued to refer to the "familiar theme of the couple that has preoccupied me for some time", which she frequently associated with the issue that, in contrast to the birth of her first child, the birth of the second child distressed her significantly: "It was a very difficult period for me . . . I had many sexual urges."

From then on, however, obviously to avoid any malignant mirroring of the couple that upset her, either by the pairing of Angeliki and Vassilis or by the representation/union of the conductor and the group, Katerina began to be absent from the group without notification (sometimes she overslept at the time of the session, and sometimes she told us her legs would not carry her) and she would come once every three times; during these sessions and given that Angeliki would rush to occupy the "conductor's" chair, Katerina was careful to sit on the right of the conductor.

Nevertheless, gradually the game with the chairs and the seating arrangement began to ease off and become more flexible. This was a direct result of the fact that the group, as its analysis process advanced (with the participation of Angeliki and Katerina and with a comparative improvement in their relations), the confusion between the mother (group) and father (conductor) was clearing up, and passing to the level of relatively calm and mature grief. Katerina stopped referring so persistently to the "couple" and focused on the analysis of her mother's behaviour. Angeliki, even though she still regarded what Katerina reported as "exaggerations" and was certainly not comfortable in her presence, focused on distinguishing her mother from Katerina's. At the same time, she was trying to find an outlet in her "male" identity with Katerina by acting it out, and started a new affair with a German. Under these conditions, the desire was also stirred up within her to have two children, even though, as she used to say, objectively she was not yet in a position to do so. A similar desire—but for one child, even an adopted one—was expressed by Helka, even though, as she said, she was also afraid that with the arrival of the child she would "lose" her husband (i.e., she would cease to be his "child"), in precisely the same way as, upon her birth, she "lost" her father (her parents separated). Even Vassilis declared such a desire indirectly when he reported to the group that he was thinking of marrying the girl he was living with.

It was by now obvious that the group's impulsive drive toward genitality (the desire for a child), especially as it was being pressed by the opposite unconscious impulse of Katerina (and to some degree of the other members), was seeking a way out. Within the group dynamic this was translated into the desire for the arrival of a new member, which was expected to be helped by genitality even if the newborn (new member) under these conditions (as a product of the union of the group and the conductor, or of a substitute union–pairing) would be unable, at least at the beginning, to have any dimension other than that of Messiah (Bion, 1961). Thus, while the group's third phase seemed to be somehow arriving at completion, the conductor, through a series of interventions (analysis of the individual and group resistance to date, and emphasis on the particular value that the group's expansion, or growing up, would have on the intrapsychic evolution of the members), began to prepare the group for the entrance of a new member (twenty-ninth to thirty-fourth sessions).

The new member was a man named Stavros, twenty-seven years old, a private employee between the age of child and man, with a neurotic psychopathology, who could be expected in my opinion—as proved to be the case in the long term—to contribute to the transformation of the group's drive toward genitality and to making its urges that inevitably assumed a phobic and dependent nature (pairing, etc.) more erotic and oedipal. In the announcement of the new member's arrival (thirty-fifth session) the group in general reacted positively, projecting its desire (given that it did not know the gender of the new member) for a male member. Of the two members directly involved in the scapegoating, Angeliki put forward legitimate complaints, saying that while she wanted to have a new member, she would also have liked "us to be the way we are here, unchanged". Katerina reacted first by over-compensating for her profound fear of the arrival of a new member—which she experienced as the birth of her third child—and by projecting this fear to Angeliki (that was simultaneously an indirect attack): "When a child is to be born and you are still young, will parents ask you whether to have a child?" and then, in an open refusal, "As far as I'm concerned, I accept the new member, but I didn't give birth to him!"

At the next session, during which Stavros arrived, neither Angeliki nor Katerina came to the group, and neither had notified us. But they came to the session immediately after, during which Angeliki succeeded in achieving a first emotional bond with Stavros that would be extended later and would help her to escape gradually from the pairing with Vassilis, and generally to participate in the containment that the group provided him. On the contrary, Katerina maintained a formal polite attitude toward him and a remote stance toward the group. This session was, in fact, the last one in which Katerina participated. She then missed three sessions in a row, without notification, at which time, and after consultation with the group, I decided to telephone her, expressing both my desire and that of the group to help her in every possible way to reconnect with us. Katerina announced to me that under no circumstances did she wish to participate "in a group which brings forth new members, who have been born of the union, if not of the conductor with the group, certainly of Angeliki with Vassilis", and that this whole story had disturbed her greatly and she even blamed it indirectly for the miscarriage of a "two-week old embryo" that she had just had, and—despite my efforts to convince her that this is not the way things are done—said that she would come by my office with an envelope containing the fees she owed for last two months (which she never did).

Final remarks

The fantasy of Stavros as the child produced by an incestuous intercourse (of a more or less anal nature), "killing" it by acting out an abortion, and throwing it on to the group in the form of a dead embryo were the three key dramatic moments taken on by Katerina's constant and almost permanent projective identification ("penetration") on the group. These moments appear to constitute versions of the three corresponding forms assumed by projective identification on subjects in whom the psychotic part of their personality predominates in a torrential way and especially in its schizophrenic version (massive but, at the same time, fragile transference, rapid transformation of life instincts into death instincts, etc.). This is projective identification in the form of an illusory encapsulation in the objects, to which we have already referred, to the self-destructive projective identification in reverse, and to the final projective identification and action through which aggression and destructiveness are turned towards the objects (Bion, 1967).

In these terms, the comparison of Katerina's "penetration" into the group with one similar to that of *Spaltpilz* was the most lenient that could have been made and certainly did not have the anticipated results, given that she identified herself fully with the fungus and, in fact, turned its destructiveness towards herself, rather than towards the group, as a mother ought to do by absorbing the strong projections and sadistic attacks of the newborn (Winnicott, 1971), but which, nevertheless, "survived". Certainly, by "deadening" that part of her own genitality and "throwing" it on to the group (essentially on to her parents), Katerina gave a temporary outlet to the aggressiveness stemming from her strong incestuous/homosexual anxiety as linked with a very morbid inverted oedipal situation and her annihilation anxiety of psychotic origin. But this was done at the cost of injuring her femininity/maternity caused by exiling herself from the group—just like the dead embryo.

On the other hand, of course, the same injury was suffered by the group. Apart from anything else, the group found itself facing two states of mourning, the processing of which, apart from being somewhat early, was quite thorny and risky, to the degree that it entailed two confronting axes of serious psychopathology: the depressive, which came from the conflict brought about by the combination of the sudden loss/drop out with the strong aggressiveness that accompanied it and the manic—and largely schizophrenic—axis that arose from the coincidence/identification of the new life (new member) with death (dead embryo) with which the new member was in danger of being charged. In such cases, some members might be led to an exhibition of manic-depressive reactions and behaviours, following Klein's

(1935, 1940) views. In any event, the members of the group, given their many conflicts regarding genitality that remained largely unresolved during this period, were not able to sustain or contain one of the strongest and most intrusive projective identifications that Katerina repeatedly threw on them, by openly mirroring the members' difficulties on the genital level in her own very morbid conflicts, and also returned this mirroring to her, usually in an openly aggressive way, and, thus, pushed her to become a scapegoat and led her to drop out.

Nevertheless, step by step and through the appropriate process (protection of the new member and gradual admission of new members, anti-identification with the instincts of death, demonstration of the value of the life instincts, and representation of loss as a form of "parting", etc.), the group was able ultimately to process the mourning and events more generally, healing its trauma and transforming it in a positive direction. Thus, it is not strange that from that time to the present, in whatever affected it as a whole and its members separately, the group experienced a rapid increase in its genitality while at the same time—given that the group and the conductor alike (particularly regarding the selection of members)—became much more careful and had no further drop-outs.

Up to the present, the group has gradually taken into its ranks another four members (two women and two men) one of whom is a forty-year-old American woman named Hilary, married with two children, and with a stable neurotic personality organisation, who, in conjunction with Helka, has extended its transcultural nature. Regarding the members separately, Helka has already adopted a two-year-old boy and is systematically processing her intrapsychic conflicts (particularly with her father), and is preparing to leave. Vassilis married the girl he had been living with and is expecting the birth of his daughter, a fact that helped him to accept better the identification with his father. Angeliki, for two years now, appears to have a stable relationship with a man and is thinking seriously about marriage. Katy, thirty years old, a newly married teacher who entered the group right after Stavros, is pregnant, and expecting the birth of a little boy. Stavros, now thirty-one, was able, with the help of the group, to shake off the burden that had so prematurely fallen upon him through the scapegoating and drop out of Katerina, and has processed and significantly overcome his oedipal fixation on his mother, which was imprinted on a relationship that he recently formed with a girl who facially resembles Angeliki.

Regarding Katerina, my indirect information is that she continues her life at its usual pace. From time to time, her image certainly appears in the associations of the group—particularly when it is going through periods of great anxiety—associated mainly with the penetrating/invading behaviour of a *Spaltpilz*. Nevertheless, the members—especially the older ones—now know that Katerina, or the fungus, is only a representation, although to a lesser degree, of a corresponding part of their own personality, and that scapegoats of this type are consequently "international" and cannot change or improve the way they operate, other than in a group which has the features of a good enough mother figure and a conductor who demonstrates—through a *crescendo* move—the power of this figure and overcomes—through a *decrescendo* move—its archaic dimension as absolute (invasive) superego/leader (Foulkes, 1964).

However, despite these precautions, early ending of groupanalytic therapy is not always due to "wild" group phenomena such as scapegoating or, as we have verified in the previous chapter, envy, and neither can the group prevent it, even though it functions as a good enough mother with a surrogate good enough father/conductor. As will be seen in the following chapters, early or normal termination of group-analytic psychotherapy is interrelated with, and somewhat pre-determined by, the degree to which the patient's psychopathology suits the group's dynamic situation, or can at least cope adequately with it.

CHAPTER SIX

Early ending in group analysis and borderline conditions

Introduction

Psychoanalytic and psychotherapeutic clinical experience is generally agreed to have shown that the ending of such therapy, whatever form it may take, is inherent in its beginning (Schlesinger, 2014). This ending consists primarily of patients learning to separate themselves from the individual therapist or therapy group, after having developed attachment bonds with them usually lasting many years, and signifies that they are prepared to re-experience their separation, especially from the maternal object (and subsequently from the father figure) as represented by the therapist, the group, and the therapy milieu in general (Farber et al., 1995; Holmes, 1997). This is a separation that the patients are called upon to renegotiate during therapy in a healthier, more effective way than that which they learnt or did not learn in the course of their psychosocial development by achieving therapeutic goals as ideally reached through the patient's growth and inner independence, leading to freedom from anxiety, greed, envy, or jealousy and, thus, to self-realisation and development of the ability to love in a mature way (Fromm-Reichman, 1950).

Despite the above considerations, however, endings in psychoanalysis and psychotherapy are far more complicated than one would expect, mainly due to two parameters which are difficult, if not impossible, to manage effectively. The first parameter relies on Freud's (1937c) view that analysis usually risks becoming interminable because analysands cannot achieve a sufficient and effective combination of their male and female identifications, thus achieving resolution of the oedipal complex, which is the ultimate target of the psychoanalytic cure. The second parameter is based on Klein's (1950) views, according to which successful termination of analysis necessarily presupposes that object relations and the Oedipus complex have both been sufficiently released as persecutory anxiety in the paranoid–schizoid position (pre-oedipal situation) and depressive anxiety in the depressive position (oedipal situation). They must also have been considerably reduced through the resolution of envy of the maternal object, a successful mourning and an internalisation (instead of incorporation/introjection) of it, leading to identification with both parents as a combined union. This process is a very difficult to achieve because, on a level deeper than Freud has considered, it is running and terminates during the first year of the infant's life. In this sense, termination of a therapy, especially in cases of forced termination (Mikkelsen & Gutheil, 1979) or termination of the therapy of vulnerable patients such as patients with borderline personality disorder (Agraval et al., 2004; Schlesinger, 2014), is undoubtedly associated with re-experiencing feelings of death on a very archaic (oral–sadistic) level of regression (Wardi, 1989). This is the reason why ending one's therapy is undoubtedly the "Achilles heel" of psychoanalysis, which so far has not provided a paradigm for termination (Bergmann, 1997). In this chapter, we outline the phenomenology and attempt to suggest some causes and an initial explanation of early ending in group-analytic therapy by patients with a borderline and/or narcissistic personality disorder as first analysed systematically by Kernberg (1975) and Kohut (1971).

Early ending as masked drop-out and borderline pathology in group-analytic therapy

It is known that the treatment of patients with borderline personality disorder, whether in individual or group therapy, or in an inpatient or outpatient setting, presents serious difficulties that are mainly due to the patients' deep dependency needs, narcissistic injury, intolerance of frustration, somaticising, and usually negative feelings towards the therapist and the therapeutic milieu, together with a strong resistance to change (Horwitz, 1987; Kretsch et al., 1987; Schreter, 1980–1981; Skodol et al., 1983; Springer & Silk, 1996). In Bion's (1967, 1992) terms, the above difficulties are strongly associated with the patients' permanent and ever-changing oscillation between the psychotic and the neurotic part of their personality or between the paranoid–schizoid and the depressive position, together with the inability to transform beta-elements into alpha-elements due to severe disturbances in their relationship with the primary mothering person.

Despite the above difficulties, group-analytic psychotherapy has been proved a very advantageous therapeutic milieu in which to treat borderline personality disorders. A mere summary of Foulkes's (1964, 1990) views could convince one that this type of therapy is known to provide whatever is necessary to ensure both a systematic beginning and preparation for the ending in a direct and lively way. Its main advantage results from the fact that, as we have already seen, the group-analytic group is presented as a good enough familial environment favouring the renegotiation of the patients' inner conflicts and behaviours. However, the majority of patients in the same group-analytic environment discontinue their therapy prematurely. This might be due partially to the double-edged paradox presented by the group therapy of borderline patients and described by Horwitz (1987): the same qualities of the group that indicate a group treatment for these patients might simultaneously be counter-indicated. This does not mean that this discontinuance always takes the form of drop-out. It should be pointed out that, at least in these cases, the term "early ending" does not necessarily mean dropping out (even though it, too, can be entailed in an early ending). What is meant here is that ending which, even though it might include many of those features that characterise dropping out, is usually seen as early ending by the members involved as an intermediate stage in their therapy, and, in fact, an effort is made to have it declared and imposed as such on the group as a whole. These are intermediary states that are undoubtedly group phenomena and give the impression that they constitute the counterpart of what, on a personal level, we would call a borderline personality disorder. In fact, this disorder is usually characteristic of members who resort to this type of early ending, but it does not appear to constitute, in itself, an explanatory factor. It is also undoubtedly a disguised dropping out and for this reason we examine these two phenomena together later.

What, then, are the most fundamental causes of the phenomenon that can explain it to some degree, if we exclude reasons of erroneous technique, such as inadequate preparation of the patients for entering the group, an unstable therapeutic environment or failure to establish suitable treatment goals (Bernard & Drob, 1989; Fromm-Reichman, 1950), and, above all, countertransference reactions and behaviours (Dalenberg, 2000; Gabbard & Wilkinson, 1994; Racker, 1968; Schlesinger, 2014)? Let us keep in mind that, in the case we are dealing with here, there are no clear-cut causes that lead to an equally clear-cut early ending; at the same time, the boundaries between early ending and dropping out overlap. In the case of an overt dropping out, on the contrary, the reasons are much more easily discernible and some of them inevitably play a part in instances of early ending. Yalom (1970) and other authors have identified a number of factors that most therapists have had to confront during the daily practice of their profession. In my view, these factors do not explain the phenomenon adequately, at least from a psychoanalytic and group-analytic viewpoint. In any event, since the issue requires further systematic investigation, and for methodological reasons, early termination and dropping out is considered here as largely constituting the same thing.

From my own clinical experience, I have found that the most fundamental reason why people drop out, leading, by extension, to an early ending, around which all the other factors revolve, lies in a profound deficiency in the subject's symbiotic relationship with the pre-oedipal mother. This deficiency, at least as it appears within the framework of group dynamics, takes on the form of a syndrome known as the "symbiotic syndrome" (Mahler, 1968; Mahler et al., 1975). Of course, much more research must be conducted to identify patterns of this syndrome as expressed in group-analytic psychotherapy, especially with patients suffering from borderline personality disorder. In this chapter, I attempt solely to shed some light on aspects of the phenomenology of the "symbiotic syndrome" as it generally makes its appearance in the group-analytic group.

Early termination as a failed good-enough symbiosis

The absence of a good enough symbiosis is known to take the form of an excessive (malicious) or totally deficient symbiosis, and characterises subjects who are in either a psychotic state (open or latent) or have a severe form of borderline and/or narcissistic personality disorder (Kernberg, 1975; Kohut, 1971). In either case, the patients have not experienced successfully the phases and sub-phases of the separation–individuation and rapprochement process (Mahler, 1968; Mahler et al., 1975). Since they are constantly fixated on a deep pre-oedipal level, these patients mainly seek, although initially in a pathological way, either to re-experience the primary mothering bond or simply to construct such a bond from the beginning, rather than to resolve the conflicts resulting from a normal experience of the oedipal complex, which is usually only partially and fragmentarily experienced by them. In fact, as has already been pointed out, under these conditions group analysis is strongly indicated for borderline patients, although in some cases is counter-indicated (Robbins, 1982).

However, caution must be taken to ensure that the entrance of the patient into the group is not premature. The primary duty of the therapist is to establish an initial form of good enough symbiosis with the patient, first and foremost through individual psychotherapy sessions and, if this proves successful, to continue it later through the group (in which he can and should gradually emerge as the father figure) (Urlić, 1999). The individual therapeutic context, due to its inherent and explicit dyadic structure, can easily set limits to the patient's preponderant tendency for fusion, thus favouring reconstruction of the patient's not good enough symbiosis and transforming it into a good enough one to a greater degree and with greater safety than the group. The group also represents a maternal object, which, because of the multiplicity of its dimensions and behaviours as re-enacted by different people, might risk intensifying the patients' fusion needs, as would be the case with patients suffering from psychosis during their group psychotherapy (Hummelen, 1994). Also, since at least during its primordial phases the group is imagined as a devouring mouth (Anzieu, 1984), it could incite borderline patients' fear of being devoured. Furthermore, the group is subject to multiple triangular relations on the oedipal level (Martean, 2014). In either case, these factors would advise against the borderline patient beginning therapy as it could risk leading to the latter's strong fear of dependency on the group and, thus, perhaps to premature termination. This is why combined individual and group psychotherapy is usually indicated for persons with borderline personality deficiencies or disorders (De Zulueta & Mark, 2000; Lofton et al., 1983). If individual psychotherapy has succeeded in functioning primarily as the "good" side of the maternal imago by providing a benign symbiosis (normal oral–sadistic stage), it can then offer the patient a chance to stabilise this aspect further by acquiring the corresponding aspect of the group and to withstand the "bad" aspect (malicious symbiosis) of the same imago, which is likewise represented by the group on the level of the paranoid–schizoid position according to Klein's (1946) views.

Given that fixation in the either the oral–sadistic stage or the paranoid–schizoid position is the fundamental cause of schizophrenia and paranoia respectively (Klein, 1946), the patients who are suffering from one of these two psychopathologies react directly to the malicious mirroring created when they join the group and resort to dropping out soon after. Neither can the possibility be ruled out that they might remain in the group for a long time, or that there will be an extended delay of the dropping out, as happens in cases of borderline patients that we will examine below. By dropping out, the patients who suffer from psychosis seem to be using a form of acting out to speed up an "ending" with the "bad" maternal object. Interestingly, the patients who, without having psychosis, have a psychotic part to their personality that is fairly vulnerable in terms of a borderline personality disorder act out the "ending" with the "bad" object in a similar way. However, either at the beginning of their therapy or at some more advanced stage of it, the patients who suffer from psychosis usually disappear without notification, acting out and thereby avoiding the loss (of themselves), which they believe would have been the result of their remaining in the group and completing their therapy (Sandison, 1991, 1994). On the contrary, the borderline patients drop out with a fuss, by means of which they are seeking to leave their mark on the group, because even though they are afraid that the effort to transform the psychotic part of themselves into a neurosis will lead to the release of a psychosis, they behave as though they could have succeeded in achieving the transformation of this part to a neurotic one. Thus, they will either distance themselves completely from the group, after some formal notification or the regulation of their financial obligations, even though until then they had shown themselves, by overcompensation, to attend the group regularly, or they will request a leave-taking from the group, which they hope will be recorded as completed.

The signs of an imminent drop-out can be said to pre-exist and, indeed, are fairly visible. Patients with a borderline personality disorder do not feel at all comfortable in the group. The two main points of the group process—that is, contact with the "skin" of the mother/group, to paraphrase Anzieu's (1984, 1989) well-known metaphor of the "skin–ego", as it is symbolised by the circular seating arrangement of the members, and the relationship with the therapist in regard to the father figure that he represents (Foulkes, 1964)—are not possible for them. This is why they either glance at their watches fairly frequently or turn around in their chairs in an effort to "push" time or to familiarise themselves with something that does not suit them. Also, they resort persistently to a set of behaviours and reactions of particular social interest (discussion of social problems, etc.). These are fusion reactions through which the borderline patients try to curtail the emergence of the group's critical (unconscious) material and to create a fusion situation within which no one can be different from anyone else. Even the therapist should not be allowed to escape from this fusion, and the patients provoke him alternately with the group, with the aim of exhausting the last remnants of his patience and making him angry; in this way, it is very easy for the image of the therapist/father to fuse with the image of the mother/group, and an undifferentiated total is created that the borderline patients will be able to reject within themselves as a "bad" object and abandon in a much less painful way. All of this ultimately conceals the patients' inability to deal with frustration and the effort to cast the blame for this on the group.

Despite this, the therapist and the group should continue constantly to function as containers (alpha-elements) for the patients' projections and projective identifications (beta-elements), providing them with a dose of "good" object. This stance serves as a kind of catalytic group testing by means of which we can foresee the degree to which some "receptors" of good enough maternity and symbiosis operate in the patients' inner worlds in such a way that, according to this degree, the patients will finally either remain in the group or be led to drop out which, eventually, proves to be unavoidable.

Clinical vignettes

Using two clinical vignettes I describe briefly the way in which two people with borderline personality disorder, Jane, a thirty-two-year-old woman, and Stylianos, a forty-nine-year-old man, who were members of two different heterogeneous group-analytic groups of mine in private practice, terminated their therapeutic treatment early. Both groups were held at a different period of time between 2000 and 2008, respectively, and met once a week, in the hope that their frequency would permit the patients to introject the "good" maternal object in a mild and gradual way, as necessary for the successful outcome of their therapy.

Vignette one

Jane was a teacher at a private school. She entered therapy after a period of intense stress, which she attributed to her chronic involvement in a series of sexual relations with much older men. The roots of her problem went back to her troubled relationship with both her parents from early childhood until her current adult life. Both her father and mother were unfailingly critical, violent, and rejecting towards her, while, on the contrary, they were accepting and quite caring towards her younger sister and only other sibling, who usually drew admiration and esteem, especially after marrying and having a family.

Jane came to the group after about six months of individual psychotherapy sessions. During this time, and despite the existence of some elements that lent a negative colour to the transference, she seemed to have an honest desire to establish a relationship of trust and symbiosis with the therapist as maternal object (and, by extension, as paternal figure). She showed the same desire to the group for eight months or so after joining it, and specifically until the day when a new member entered the group, a thirty-five-year-old woman educator with a neurotic psychopathology. On that day, Jane's behaviour changed in a dramatic way. Even though her presence in the group was uninterrupted, Jane, in a psychotic-like manner, began to attack any linking in the group by creating constant and repeated interruptions in the normal coherent flow of the group process, thus hindering it from delving increasingly deeper. She also began to act out her profound self-degradation outside the group, frequently in a dangerous way, such as losing a lot of money playing cards, or driving at high speeds. When some members tried to stop her talking, Jane began to cry without stopping, like a helpless child, thus risking the deepening of her regression.

It was in this context that she had entered into a process of comparison with the new member, who represented her younger sister. Jane gradually perceived that, in contrast to her family, the group/mother and the conductor/father did not discriminate between its children/members. Instead, they functioned in their union as a good enough container for Jane's projective identifications in the sense that they provided support and guidance during her attacks (beta-elements), as well as an explanation and an interpretation of her behaviour (alpha-elements). However, Jane's maternity "receptors" and bridges of access to the oedipal state (relationship with the therapist) proved too fragile to permit her to contain the capacity of the group/mother, in other words, to reacquire the maternity of which she had been deprived for so many years. As she herself said in one session, her jealously of the new member had reached the level of wishing to murder the latter. After that, she decided to end her therapy. Four months had passed since the new member joined, and about a year since Jane had entered the group. The group made a final effort to keep her, but this proved impossible. It granted Jane the right to decide for herself what form she would give to her leave-taking, based on the period of time she had been in the group. She proposed to leave after a period of just four sessions, which the group accepted. But finally, Jane could not stand that. In the session immediately after the one in which the form of her leave-taking was discussed, she came to the group with pastries and gifts for the members and wanted to leave "on the spot". The group accepted it. During Jane's last session, an effort was made by the therapist to keep the group mood and climate relaxed and somewhat superficial in a mixture of grief and pleasure. Jane, who had strong difficulties mourning on the level of the depressive position, as linked with a farewell process, was satisfied. Thus, Jane's therapy came to an early end.

Vignette two

Stylianos was a high-level executive in a multi-national corporation. He was legally divorced and the father of two children, a daughter of sixteen and a son of fourteen years old. The most important reason for his coming to therapy consisted of the "unexplainable excitement and confusion" that he began to feel immediately after the death of his mother, which had occurred about one year before Stylianos entered therapy. As gradually became clear during the course of about twenty individual therapy sessions that took place before Stylianos joined the group, the confusion and excitement in question were derived from the fact that he was unable to take leave of his mother after her death; even worse, he was unable to grieve for his mother except through the hatred he felt for her and which, within the framework of an already latent melancholy, turned inwards on himself, with the result that sometimes he felt like injuring himself or even committing suicide. Stylianos's hatred stemmed from the fact that he had mainly introjected his mother, an indifferent, closed narcissistic personality, as "bad" object. As we know, it is impossible for one to take leave of such an object unless it is transformed, on many points, into a "good" object through therapy (Klein, 1936, 1940, 1946, 1957). Stylianos's relationship with his father was also very disturbed. His father, now retired, was a high-ranking military officer and was described as a "very frightened and profoundly compromised man".

The patient's attitude and behaviour in his individual sessions was characterised by his ambivalence towards the therapist, primarily as maternal object, and, by extension, as father figure. Every time Stylianos seemed to be seeking to establish a deeper relationship with the therapist conceived as a "good" object, he was also cultivating a profound distancing from him fantasied as a "bad" object that was manifested chiefly in two ways: (a) he avoided sitting directly opposite the therapist (face to face) in such a way as to signify that he was near to entering into a symbiotic relationship with him; instead, he used to move his chair to the left or right, so that he would be addressing someone else but not some specific person, and (b) despite the fact that his socialisation and wealth of associations contributed to "filling" the sessions, he often appeared to be experiencing the time of "symbiosis" in therapy as stifling; this became obvious in the way he kept looking at his watch.

Under these conditions, he agreed to continue his analysis in an analytic group. It was hoped that this could help him to discriminate better between the "good" and the "bad" representations of the maternal object. Initially, and for the space of about one month (four sessions), the entire effort seemed to be crowned with success. Stylianos came regularly to the group with which the first and most difficult contact appeared to have been made. But then, during the next two months (as long as his presence in the group lasted) he began to show that he felt suffocated by the fact that the group process in itself, through its relaxed, free associations, called upon him to form a deeper relationship with the group/maternal object, even though there were no events or reports in the group at this period that could easily be seen as factors referring to representations of a "bad" object.

Progressively, Stylianos began to feel uncomfortable in his seat, in which now, perhaps putting pressure on himself, he did not move out of the therapeutic circle, and kept track of time in the group with suppressed but manifest anxiety. In fact, during this time, in his effort to maintain some distance from the group/maternal object, with the hope that in so doing he would be able to split away from a representation of the "bad" object, as he had certainly begun to represent it, he arranged to be absent twice on the occasion of two business trips that he had to make outside Athens. Despite this, the hypothesis was, given that in his absence the maternal object is introjected even more, that the distance appeared to have intensified the representation of the group as "bad" object in his mind.

So, one day he telephoned the therapist saying that he was not going to return (because "I can't stand the group, any more than my mother finally") and that at least he had the hope that perhaps later, having sorted out his relationship with his former wife, he would be able to make a new start at therapy.

Conclusions

The meaning of terminating psychoanalysis, psychotherapy, and group analysis has not been defined as yet in a clear-cut way and the term remains ambiguous. However, a good enough ending can be defined as strictly linked with the patients' ability to close the therapy process with a farewell, after they have elaborated their main deficiencies and conflicts on the pre-oedipal (oral–sadistic stage and paranoid–schizoid position) and oedipal (depressive position) level, as defined by Klein (1946, 1957) and released their symptoms after a considerable number of years. In the case of patients with a borderline personality disorder, an early, rather than a mature, ending usually takes place. Analysis of the relevant material from two borderline patients who followed group-analytic psychotherapy and had a premature termination indicates that the main reason why these patients ended their therapy earlier is related to the fact that the group, despite its maternal qualities, is not by nature able to correspond to the patients' symbiotic needs, which, albeit not thoroughly psychotic, are linked with a very deficient or absent symbiotic maternal bond (Mahler, 1968; Mahler et al., 1975) which causes them to experience the group as a "bad", rather than as a "good", object (Klein, 1946, 1957). Borderline patients, thus, leave the group in either an open or a masked drop-out (meaning they present it as a form of mature ending). The group, however, whenever possible, by offering its maternal qualities to the maximum, can contain the patients' manipulations by proposing a good, albeit early, farewell.

CHAPTER SEVEN

Ending in group analysis and neurosis: from pathological narcissism to social consciousness*

Introduction

We have seen in the previous chapter that psychoanalytic therapies, including group analysis, are an adventure, because, on the one hand, the meaning of the therapy termination remains ambiguous and inconclusive in the psychoanalytic literature and, on the other, many patients who suffer mainly from borderline personality disorder likewise interrupt their therapy early by dropping out, openly or not. However, clinical experience indicates that, as well as borderline patients who terminate earlier, there are also patients with a neurotic personality and symptoms who, if they do not stop earlier, risk continuing their therapy without being able to end it.

There are, indeed, a number of factors that can contribute to causing an individual or group analysis to remain without termination. Unresolved countertransference on the part of the therapist and the secondary benefit derived from regressions and fixations on the part

---

* A small part of this chapter was presented at the Third Regional Mediterranean Conference IAGP-SEPTG, Barcelona, Spain, 28 February–2 March 2008.

of the patient have been regarded as two of the main factors that might keep the neurotic or borderline patient for many years in an analysis that could eventually turn out to be hallucinatory (Dalenberg, 2000; Fromm-Reichman, 1950; Gabbard & Wilkinson, 1994; Racker, 1968; Schlesinger, 2014; Wolberg, 1954). Above all, the danger of an unterminated analysis, oddly enough, can be unconsciously increased by the therapists themselves. Many therapists identify so strongly with the analytic process that they cannot conceive of their lives without it. In this way, the psychoanalytic sessions take the form of a symbiosis that often has the features of a strong pairing (Bion, 1961). Analysis is, in truth, the art of entering and leaving the unconscious as though having never entered, which does not prevent one from bearing that special sign that marks every adequate contact with the unconscious, that is, the sign of a good enough frustration (weaning from the breast/mother as real object), which is the mother's task, and of a good enough symbolic castration (weaning from the breast/ mother as imaginary object), which is the father's task (Lacan, 1994, 1998b). These are two functions that are known to make the patient capable of achieving the symbolic death of his or her parents and to enter the mourning process (Klein, 1940). This is why successful analysis must have an ending, its supreme moment, in frustration and, above all, in symbolic castration. Otherwise, the analysis is in danger of becoming an interminable process that merely prolongs the patient's non-castration *ad infinitum*. Symbolic castration is known to be indicated and more readily achieved in patients with a strong neurotic personality organisation. In the case of patients with a borderline personality organisation, we must do a great deal of work either by frustrating them (if they have never been frustrated or have been inadequately frustrated) or by making them capable of accepting frustration after a period of gratification (in the event that they are totally frustrated), before reaching the point of symbolic castration.

How can group analysis lead the neurotic patient to a good enough ending? The literature, despite its limitations, has been able to clarify some aspects of this issue, especially the link between the termination processes and the patient's re-experiencing of the separation–individuation phase, as described by Mahler (Kauff, 1977) and/or the conductor's stance (countertransference, etc.) (Maar, 1989; Peternel, 1991). Termination in group analysis has also been linked with the patient's disengagement from the womb, strongly symbolised by the group, and provider of absolute maternal safety (Wardi, 1989). This chapter attempts to approach the matter on a different level. In particular, it will link the successful termination of group analytic therapy with the achievement of a good enough frustration and symbolic castration, which, in turn, is associated with the patient's sublimation of his or her homosexual fixations. The ending of group analysis will be compared with the ending that takes place in psychoanalysis, as described first by Foulkes (1964). The difference between these two forms of ending will prove to be a difference in the way each one approaches symbolic castration, which is ultimately associated with a different approach to the concept of the symbolic father.

Theoretical and clinical considerations

Foulkes (1964, 1990) suggested that the ideal ending of group analysis is, in principle, the same as that of psychoanalysis: patients must go through and re-experience the three stages (oral–sadistic, anal–sadistic, and phallic) with greater success than they had previously achieved in their lives; they must redetermine their relations with their personal parental imagoes, as they appear, now corrected, in the imagoes of the group/mother and conductor/father, respectively, and, thus, achieve a good enough entry into the oedipal state and a successful resolution of the Oedipus complex, which presupposes the patient's identification with the conductor as paternal ego ideal. In Klein's and Bion's terms, the successful ending of analysis, on either an individual or group level, presupposes that the patient goes through the oral–sadistic stage and the paranoid–schizoid position repeatedly and successfully, so that he or she can become optimally established in the depressive position, and achieve a better negotiation between the paranoid–schizoid and depressive position (Bion, 1962, 1992; Klein, 1937, 1950, 1957), or, as Klein (1950) notes in reference to the transference level, to transform negative into positive transference, that is, to transform the "bad" object into a "good" object, wherever possible.

However, in Foulkes' view, that which differentiates ending in the analytic group from the ending to which the couch leads is ultimately the way in which the person's identification with the paternal ideal, in the Freudian sense of the ego ideal or superego, is achieved by overcoming the oedipal situation. When psychoanalysis ends, at least as

Freud (1924d), seems to define it, the analysand is identified with an ego ideal/superego. This is conceived as an evolved adult form of the ideal ego, a purely narcissistic formation of maternal origin during childhood, and strictly linked with the child's refusal to give up satisfaction (a libidinal correlate). The development of the ego ideal marks the transition of the child and, later, the adult to real sociality as opposed to the pseudo-sociality and narcissism expressed by the maternal qualities of the ideal ego (Freud, 1914c). However, this ego ideal tends to reconnect internalisation with the primal identification, that is, with the incorporation of the primal father/leader who has kept the primal group (horde) as well as the archaic mother figure under his absolute dominance (Freud, 1912–1913). On the other hand, the primal father is nothing but another version of the primal mother. This explains why, on the contrary, the ending of group-analytic therapy for Foulkes should lead the group member to identify with an ego ideal with the qualities and components of a mature and good enough maternal perspective (ideal ego), as the latter alone can express genuine sociality and group values as opposed to a sociality of narcissistic origin. This is a group ego ideal through which the fantasy of the primal father/leader is further repressed and its place is taken symbolically by the idea of a father/leader whose emergence is accomplished through the respect and recognition of the group (Foulkes, 1964, 1990).

Needless to say, repression of the primal father is, at the same time, according to both Foulkes (1964) and Klein (1946, 1957), repression of the primal mother as a dual "good" and "bad" imago and a much more realistic and symbolic re-engagement of her as a mature representative of the reality principle. In this sense, full leave-taking in group analysis pushes the patient to evade the psychotic part of his personality in which the fantasy of the primal father or primal mother, largely conceived as two imaginary figures fostering pathological narcissism and false consciousness, would tend to fixate him, and reinforces the neurotic part of his personality which favours genuine sociality and social consciousness. In contrast, psychoanalysis appears to foster the patient's fixation in the psychotic/narcissistic part of his personality and, as a result, makes the possibility of a fully successful ending of psychoanalytic therapy doubtful (Foulkes, 1964).

This is not the moment to delve into the extremely complex and difficult joust between psychoanalysis and group analysis over which of the two has the most effective therapeutic results, especially with regard to the fully completed ending of therapy. I would simply like to point out here that Foulkes' argument that psychoanalysis is in danger of leading the subject to a psychotic condition is overstated. A patient who is suitable for psychoanalysis, that is, whose personality has a well-organised neurotic component, is in no such danger. I would also like to note Foulkes' excessive optimism and oversimplified approach to the issue as compared to the reticence and critical stance adopted by Freud when even he, under certain conditions, casts doubt on the idea of a complete psychoanalytic ending. Freud (1937c) is known, in the end, to have linked the danger of unterminated analysis less to the analysand's unsuccessful identification with the ego ideal—and even less so to the very ambiguous idea of the primal father—and more to a failed repression of the subject's primordial identification with the opposite sex. What is repressed is none other than the female/passive side of the male and the male/active side of the female (Freud, 1937c). If the repression fails, a return of the repressed takes place, which is always associated with unresolved envy of the opposite sex, and undermines the subject's access to an integrated ego ideal or, as Klein (1937) suggests, access to reparation of the object through the transformation of envy and hatred of the object into love of it. Under these conditions, the patient's analysis might remain unterminated. Undoubtedly, Foulkes (1990) puts forward an ego ideal that favours a successful renegotiation of an inverted oedipal through the socialisation and communication that result from utilising the matrix and network of interpersonal and transpersonal relationships in the group. However, as Bion (1992) has shown, every sociocentric tendency is always accompanied by the corresponding narcissistic tendency. Beyond this, the fate of what Freud believed to constitute the core of the repressed, that is, the female tendency of the man and the male tendency of the woman, remains obscure and is only minimally susceptible to intrapsychic processing, in as much as this core is interwoven with groupishness as representing the maternal element in which it seeks to be sublimated in the therapy group. Groupishness can easily become strongly phallic (phallic mother), always indicating the degree to which it has regressed to pathogenic primary or secondary narcissism.

Yet, clearly, according to Foulkes (1964, 1990), the group does not function alone; it is guided by the therapist who, in a manner that shows him to have accepted and assimilated well the female part of himself, does not instruct it as a leader, but co-ordinates it as a conductor. The group, in turn, assimilates any phallic/male disposition it may have, works through and eventually achieves the symbolic death of the therapist as archaic father/leader (ego ideal/superego) and his emergence as the ego ideal that has become moderate and symbolic through its positive admixture with the group (as ideal ego). The conductor should act in such a way as to aim at his own symbolic death or, as Foulkes (1964, p. 62) puts it, to "dig his own grave": that is, by always putting the group first. Yet, there might perhaps be no more narcissistic and castrating stance than for the father to endeavour to put himself to death symbolically. This is why the group therapist, at some point, cannot fail to reconsider his position as a conductor, returning to the position of the archaic leader (Koukis, 2004). The same thing happened to the leader whom Bion, in his early therapy efforts, sought to eliminate altogether through the idea and application of leaderless groups (Bion, 1946). Bion (1992) himself recognised later that this idea has proved to be precarious. On the contrary, the idea of the therapist as intellectual leader that Bion (1992) was to adopt later (in his mature period) seems fairly consistent and could perhaps be the best we have, for the time being, in the context being discussed here. The intellectual leader does not try to dig his own grave by putting the group first. The group *per se* is an abstraction. Moreover, it is fundamentally structured on "bad" or beta-elements, that is, thoughts without thinking or thoughts in search of a thinker (Bion, 1970). The leader of the group, who is characterised initially by beta-elements, the leader of the basic group, becomes an intellectual leader only to the degree that the group, as it becomes a work group (Bion, 1961), acquires the ability (deep social consciousness) to transform its beta-elements into alpha-elements, or, in Freud's terms, to assimilate its male components as a female figure. For the leader of the work group, this is the model on the basis of which he can assimilate his female components as a male figure. In this way, psychoanalytic thinking could ideally be merged with group-analytic thinking, as expressed by Foulkes.

This does not imply that Foulkes' view about the conductor being the potentially "dead father" is not theoretically and clinically valid. It is, however, presented in a very general way. It would be more consistent to argue that the conductor should be flexible enough to be sometimes "dead" and sometimes "alive", according to the patient's psychopathology and the therapeutic course of the patient or the group. In this regard, the need might arise for the conductor to be "dead" and the group "alive", or *vice versa*. The only certainty is that Bion's view of the conductor as intellectual leader, owing to the fact that the intellectual state is linked to both "dead" and "alive" elements, covers the sense of leadership in both these aspects.

It is clear from the above that what is at stake in group-analytic psychotherapy, as in every kind of analytic psychotherapy, is none other than the fertile and creative re-creation and sublimation of the patient's deeper homosexual psychic components. This is precisely what analytic therapy demands and what determines whether its nature is interminable or not, in the sense described by Freud. The degree of the patient's homosexual components, created by distorted identifications with the parental figures, constitutes in some way a diagnostic tool for the therapist, indicating the extent to which the group member will be able to sublimate these components in order to arrive at a relatively complete ending to therapy. Within the group, the primary identification of both sexes with the breast/mother/ father/penis, an identification which, from the outset, leads to an inverted oedipal (Klein, 1955), is revived by the very entrance of the individual into the group/mother. The patients will have to fight very hard to disengage themselves from the inverted oedipal and pass to the oedipal and its resolution, which is the ultimate goal of therapy: internalisation of the conductor/father (identification for the boy and love object for the girl), in such a way that the fertile assimilation of the same-sex parameters that legitimately emerge takes place in one or the other direction (Freud, 1923b). The group members come into direct confrontation with a series of malignant mirrorings based on homosexual stimuli; these mirrorings must gradually be transformed into benign mirrorings, so that the members can arrive at a sublimation of their homosexual fixations. It is the successful sublimation of same-sex elements in males and females alike that will eventually constitute the fundamental bridge supporting the symbolic castration and radiance of the patients who have successfully entered on a new course towards the goal of personal integration, leading to the higher self-consciousness and social consciousness which is manifested in a successful ending. In contrast, the lack of a good enough sublimation of these elements leads in most cases to an early ending.

Clinical vignettes

These views can be corroborated by a brief presentation of some clinical vignettes. Reference is made here to three patients who are members of different group-analytic groups that met twice weekly between 2004 and 2012 and included an average of eight members each, four men and four women. All three of these patients completed their therapy successfully after approximately eight to ten years, each according to the measure of his or her own psychopathology. All three groups were conducted by the same therapist, me, who followed the views of Foulkes and Bion, and conducted these groups as intellectual leader, as described above.

Maria, a thirty-year-old woman, entered analysis owing to her profound fear of earthquakes. Her phobia was, in fact, fear of her own female nature, which had been strongly repressed and its place taken by many male traits. She had developed strong male identifications based on a distorted idea of the father. For Maria the ideal father (ego ideal) consisted more or less of the archaic fantasy of "a real omnipotent man". Under these premises, she devoted most of her time to her professional advancement, precluding any female attitudes and any idea of marriage or having children. This attitude was due to the fact that Maria, after her father's death when she was about six years old, had been obliged as she grew older to take her father's place, protecting both her mother and her older sister. Replacing her father was the least threatening position she could occupy, despite the fact that this development was linked directly to the inverted oedipal situation. For a long time, Maria wanted unconsciously to assume the role of conductor conceived as a strong and archaic leader in the group, that is a "living" father, in an effort to compensate for the "dead" father she had obviously introjected prematurely. She was always careful to speak and behave rationally, to preserve the balance, and to impose limits on the group that she felt the conductor should have done and, in her opinion, failed to do. Thus, she came into conflict with him. She also felt she had to protect the other group members, especially the women. She openly stated that she preferred to communicate with women rather than with men. This was a narcissistic attitude, and created a split between the conductor and the group. From the fifth year on, however, she became aware of her underlying problem and began to adopt a more female stance. She also began to be more sensitive about social issues, which indicated a rudimentary development of social consciousness. The confrontation with the therapist diminished. The conductor, due to the balance he maintained as intellectual leader between his attitude as either an "alive" or "dead" father, gradually became for her an object that she could accept and identify with. Deep down, however, for her this was not a full identification. Despite this, the identification was sufficient to enable Maria to think about marriage. In fact, she soon got married, and began thinking of having a child. Two years later, and as the symptom that had brought her into analysis was significantly reduced, Maria decided to leave the group and achieved a successful ending to her therapy.

Konstantin, a thirty-five-year-old man, entered analysis because he suffered from a long list of symptoms of a compulsive–neurotic personality disorder, including collecting and counting large numbers of small objects, counting the slabs of concrete on pavements and refusing to walk on them if the number was not right, etc. He was absorbed in his thoughts and symptoms in a narcissistic way as linked with a deep fixation on the maternal object from which he could not be separated. This fixation was reproduced as fixation on the group/mother. Konstantin was never absent, paid regularly, and was in general a "good guy" with a passive attitude towards the group. He had been in his group for about six years, and despite his progress, continued to hold a passive attitude towards the group and especially towards the conductor. In this way, Konstantin reproduced within the group the passive stance he had learnt to adopt towards his father, whom he hated because his father was always "an omnipotent, vigorous and active figure", although sometimes violent towards his wife, whom Konstantin adored, and on whom he was strongly fixated. This had led to an extremely difficult inverted oedipal situation, which was manifested in various ways in the group. Under these conditions, it never occurred to Konstantin to leave the group. The group and the conductor were, for him, a state that would be eternally unchanged. It is obvious that in this case, in contrast with the previous one, the conductor had to direct the group more as "dead" and less as "live" father, which he did for a long period of time, particularly with regard to his stance towards Konstantin. From the eighth year on, many things began to change within the subject. He appeared to have shed his passive attitude, and to have adopted a more active stance, which showed in his desire to become the group leader. He seemed to have entered a normal oedipal situation for the transcendence of which he would have fought fiercely. So, he was ready to accept frustration and symbolic castration. When the therapist told him he could not conduct the group, but that he would be capable of conducting other groups after he completed his therapy, Konstantin came into creative confrontation with the group and especially with the conductor, leading him to a good enough identification with the conductor, and made it possible for him, a year later, to effect a complete leave-taking from the group. This urged him to develop a strong social consciousness, with the result that some years later he became head of the political section of a dominant party of the left.

Kosmas, a twenty-eight-year-old man, came into therapy with an almost psychotic fixation on the maternal object. This fixation was created after the premature death of his father when Kosmas was eight years old. It led to a borderline and/or narcissistic personality disorder, but was kept on a fragile neurotic level owing to his symptom, which was to tear out his hair, as an expression of the profound grief he felt at the prospect of being separated from the maternal object and his inability to grieve for his father. His mother, in her efforts to compensate for the loss of her husband, gratified her son's every whim, thus reinforcing his fixation on her and his homosexual tendencies (as an adolescent, Kosmas had had a homosexual relationship for a year). His fixation was reproduced as fixation on the group, which continued for about six years. The group represented for him an object of identification in the sense of incorporation. In one sense, the group could not acquire a symbolic dimension for Kosmas. The conductor was, for Kosmas, sometimes a "dead" element, like his father; at others he was in fusion with the group/mother, so that he was barely differentiated from a mothering figure. In this case, the only thing the conductor should not have done was to "dig his own grave"; he had to remain "alive", but in such a way that gradually he would be distinguished from the group. Despite these efforts, the group could not achieve a symbolic dimension in Kosmas's mind; on the contrary, strange as it may sound, the paternal ideal had, in fact, been somewhat symbolised within him owing to the symbolism inherent in death. Nevertheless, his symptom diminished significantly. At a moment when things appeared to be stagnant, around the seventh year of his therapy, and in a last effort to shed his female fixation and to symbolise the group, Kosmas distanced himself from the group through extended absences. Meanwhile, he had not paid his fees for about ten months, fearing that the strong symbolism of payment would cause him to be violently and prematurely separated from the group. After some negotiation with the therapist and the group, who encouraged him to make the decision to leave the group after paying his debts, and after a very strong effort on the part of the therapist to frustrate him, Kosmas, for the first time, could see the group's conductor as a father figure, distinct from the figure of the group. He became very angry with the conductor and came into confrontation with him. Later, he thanked the therapist for permitting the confrontation as father to son. Also, in an outburst, he revealed that he was "profoundly jealous of the conductor" and of his father (whom he saw as "handsome" in photographs) and wished deep down to be conductor of the group. For the first time, Kosmas was ready to enter a complete oedipal situation in the context of which he was prepared to accept symbolic castration. Thus, after a few months, having understood that he could not become the conductor of the group, and after paying his debts, he decided to leave the group, which he did successfully, showing that he had assimilated the female elements of the group and had achieved a strong identification with the conductor. He had also developed a strong social consciousness, and later was involved in politics conceived by him as the best way to help the poor.

Conclusions and final remarks

A good enough ending in the group-analytic psychotherapy of patients with neurosis strongly depends on the patients' ability to accept frustration and symbolic castration. Group analysis, like psychoanalysis, is theoretically an unlimited process that, from one point on, can only be recycled. This is due to the fact that the patients' distorted identifications with the parental figures, mainly with the father, primarily conceived as either an archaic "living" or "dead" father/leader, are subject to continuous correction through a process of counter-identifications and new identifications with the conductor and/or the group. Furthermore, ending in group analysis presents special difficulties because it is founded on the precarious ground of a "spiral notion", as proposed by Foulkes (1990, p. 174): "at various times we arrive at a favourable moment of concluding treatment; if these points are missed, we have to count on a longer period until such a point is reached again". In this chapter, the view was supported that this privileged point is reached and leads to a successful farewell when the patient's inverted oedipal, which is preponderantly based on pathological narcissism, has been sufficiently transcended and the positive oedipal has been adequately re-experienced as linked with the development of higher self-awaraness and social consciousness. The conductor's attitude towards his own same-sex fixations takes on special significance, as it will determine whether he will try to restore the members' identifications by assuming the position of a leader in the group or conductor, or that of leader of the group, as described by Foulkes (1964). The leader of the group, as an archaic superego of narcissistic origin, seeks to subjugate the group because he has identified excessively with it as female figure and ideal ego; the conductor, on the other hand, does not aspire to dominate the group, because he has assimilated the female elements of the group (ideal ego) in a way that strengthens his male identity in terms of an ego ideal and/or mature superego, according to Foulkes (1990), or intellectual leader, following Bion's (1992) views, and, thus, fosters a better negotiation between narcissism and sociality, leading to self-consciousness and social consciousness alike.

PART III

GROUP-ANALYTIC PSYCHOTHERAPY AS A TREATMENT OF MAJOR DISORDERS

CHAPTER EIGHT

Group analysis and eating disorders: a study of the therapeutic impact of group-analytic psychotherapy on women suffering from anorexia and bulimia nervosa*

Introduction

Although their diagnostic criteria and status as autonomous clinical entities have been well defined from a psychiatric perspective (American Psychiatric Association, 1994), neither anorexia nervosa nor bulimia nervosa presents a clear-cut clinical picture. Both diseases usually co-exist with obsessive–compulsive disorder, borderline personality disorder, and especially depression, which interfere with their diagnostic evaluation, therapeutic approach, and outcome (Casper, 1998; Meyer et al., 2001; Thornton & Russell, 1997). The reasons why anorexia nervosa and bulimia nervosa afflict both sexes, but women much more frequently than men (Fombonne, 1995), remain likewise complex and controversial, as they range from childhood abuse (Rorty, 1994; Waller, 1992) to socio-cultural factors (Garner & Garfinkel, 1980; Simpson, 2002). The aetiology of both anorexia nervosa and bulimia nervosa, considered from a psychodynamic viewpoint, is also extremely complicated and inconsistent.

---

* Previously published in 2013, in *Group-Analytic Contexts*, 62: 49–64. Also published under the title "Group therapy and eating disorders", in *BPS Psychotherapy Section Review*, 55 (Autumn 2015): 69–79.

Klein (1952) considered anorexic and bulimic tendencies as symptoms of an infantile neurosis when a regression/fixation of the subject to the paranoid–schizoid position takes place in an effort to get rid of the mothering object that was introjected mainly as "bad" object during the oral–sadistic stage. Lacan (1994) regards anorexia as a psychotic-like symptom, rather than a disease, precipitated by the overwhelming prevalence of an omnipotent imaginary mother over the symbolic father (the Name-of-the-Father). Mahler and colleagues (1975) conceived of eating disorders as adaptive responses to disruptions of the late symbiotic or early differentiation sub-phase of the separation–individuation process, leading to an impairment of self-object differentiation. Kohut (1971) considered eating disorders, which are strictly linked with the development of an archaic body self, to be behaviour that acts as a substitute for a mothering object conceived as a bodily rather than idealised "self-object". All theories would agree that, in order to be effective, any kind of psychotherapy of eating disorders should first reconstitute the above deficiencies on the pre-oedipal level—mainly by transforming the internalised "bad" object into a "good" one in terms of a sufficient negotiation between the paranoid–schizoid position and the depressive position (Klein, 1937, 1946; Palazzoli, 1978) or into a "good enough" one (Winnicott, 1976) or a "container" (Bion, 1963), leading to the patients' identification with the mother as an idealised "self-object" (Kohut, 1971)—and later address deficiencies linked to identification with the symbolic father/Name-of-the-Father on the oedipal level.

However, given the complexity of these diseases, both psychoanalysis and even the modified psychoanalytic psychotherapy of anorexia nervosa and bulimia nervosa are counter-indicated as ineffective (Bruch, 1970; Palazzoli, 1978). Anorexic and bulimic patients in individual analytic therapy, when they do not negate or interrupt it, mainly develop an archaic self-object transference which can only be transformed assiduously into (and elaborated therapeutically as) an idealised self-object transference, through their fear of devouring the therapist(s) or being devoured by them, often counterbalanced by their splitting tendency and/or their psychic emptiness projected on the therapist(s) (Geist, 1989). This, in turn, incites strong countertransference feelings, which could undermine continuation of therapy and/or its outcome (Bruch, 1978; Farrell, 1995; Zerbe, 1992). Yet, some positive results in terms of the transformation of the patients' archaic self-object into an integrated/idealised self-object during analytic psychotherapy have been reported (Dellaverson, 1997). By contrast, individual and/or group cognitive–behavioural therapies, although they present high drop-out rates (Steel et al., 2000; Waller, 1997), have proved to be the most effective therapeutic approach especially to bulimia nervosa (Fairburn et al., 1986; Thompson-Brenner et al., 2003). Psychoanalytic/psychodynamic groups with eating disorders present insignificant outcomes (Harper-Giuffre & MacKenzie, 1992), while individual/interpersonal psychodynamic psychotherapy has been proved effective (Gabbard, 2004; Shedler, 2010).

The group-analytic psychotherapy of eating disorders has been only partially explored. Hudson and colleagues (1999) refer to the progress made by bulimic women, in terms of a better integration of their dissociated body image into the self, mainly on the projective level of the group (Foulkes, 1964), through the mutual mirroring developed between them in an inpatient short-term homogeneous group, the latter conceived as the therapeutic method of choice. Segercrantz (2006) also highlights mirroring due to homogeneity in outpatient short-term groups with bulimics as the most effective factor in recreating their self. Willis (1999) and Gold (1999) verified that the "bad" object as internalised by anorexia nervosa and bulimia nervosa patients can be transformed into a "good" one by using short-term heterogeneous, rather than homogeneous, inpatient groups. Heterogeneous groups deter the fusion of the members with the group that, mainly on what Foulkes (1964) describes as the group's archaic or oral level, is experienced by these patients as a "bad" object. According to Gold (1999), heterogeneous groups also permit members of different sexes to interact with each other and with the group therapist conceived as the Name-of-the-Father, and, thus, to better negotiate oedipal issues. Valbak (2001) refers to the complete therapy of nine out of ten severely bulimic patients with a serious borderline personality disorder that took place in an inpatient slow-open homogeneous group-analytic group following an eclectic group-analytic method. Valbak (2003) suggests that the outpatient heterogeneous group-analytic group could also be a promising specialised treatment for bulimic women.

However, the group-analytic models and research proposed above, in their modified form as either long-term or short-term, inpatient or outpatient, homogeneous or heterogeneous groups, inevitably undermine the "naturalistic" setting of the original group-analytic group, with the result that it is impossible to differentiate the group-analytic factors and processes that favour or hinder the therapeutic benefit. Furthermore, the research focuses on the generalisability of the therapeutic outcomes, thus missing the step-by-step analysis of individual cases and their therapeutic progress in relation to the therapeutic evolution of the group. Thus, many questions that are critical to the effectiveness of group analysis, as defined by Foulkes (1964), in the treatment of eating disorders remain unanswered. They include questions such as: in what sense does the group matrix—which, particularly on the group's archaic/oral level, is experienced by bulimic/ anorexic patients as an empty matrix governed by a "bad" Dragon Mother (Weston, 1999)—have an impact on the treatment of anorexia nervosa and bulimia nervosa? How can the matrix be re-activated to foster the patients' emotional connectedness with the group and negotiate their passage from the archaic–oral to the projective or bodily images level of the group strictly linked with Klein's paranoid–schizoid position? What mirror reactions and multiple transferences are produced on the projective level; how do they differ from relevant phenomena engendered during individual psychotherapy, and what is their impact on the therapeutic outcome? To what extent can anorexic and bulimic patients achieve a good enough passage to the mature reality level of the group or to Klein's depressive position?

In order to provide some answers to these questions, we decided to investigate the impact that group analysis could have on the treatment of eating disorders by analysing the therapeutic progress of two cases, a woman with anorexia nervosa and a woman with bulimia nervosa, which took place in a heterogeneous slow-open outpatient group-analytic group conducted following a modified version of Foulkes's group-analytic principles and method.

Method

Therapy group

The group was an outpatient slow-open group-analytic group that met once a week for an hour and a half at my private practice in Athens from 2002 to the present. The treatment of the patients with anorexia nervosa and bulimia nervosa took place between 2002 and 2007. The group was scheduled to include members suffering from neuroses, borderline personality disorder, and psychoses, excluding acute cases as defined by Foulkes (1975). The once-a-week group was estimated as a good enough therapeutic dose in order to avoid a massive incorporation of the group as "bad" mother, especially by the bulimic, anorexic, and psychotic patients. Treating neurotic and psychotic patients together in long-term psychotherapeutic groups has been reported as leading to favourable outcomes (Smith, 1999), and a similar one was expected to be achieved by treating anorexic/bulimic patients in a group-analytic group with neurotic and psychotic patients.

The group was initially made up of five founding members: Peter, a teacher, thirty-two years old, suffered from melancholic depression. Fotini, a bookkeeper, thirty years old, suffered from borderline personality disorder and depression leading to panic attacks and agoraphobia. Gabriella, a fifty-five-year-old housewife, suffered from mild depression. Socrates, an electrician, twenty-four years old, suffered from trichotillomania, a consequence of severe borderline personality disorder, depression, and obsessive–compulsive disorder. Antonis, a teacher of physics, twenty-eight years old, suffered from paranoid psychosis. He had been hospitalised twice and was under constant medication. A year later Anna, a twenty-five-year-old fashion model suffering from anorexia nervosa, entered the group, and a year after that, Dimitra, a twenty-eight-year-old speech therapist suffering from bulimia nervosa, joined the group. Eight months later, Alexander, twenty-seven years old and unemployed, suffering from schizophrenia, entered the group. Alexander had been hospitalised twice and was under medication. All members had finished once-a-week individual psychotherapy provided by me for between approximately six months and three years. Antonis, Alexander, Anna, and Socrates continued their individual therapy parallel to the group therapy for one to two years.

The main target for the bulimic/anorexic patients was for them to progressively introject the group as a sufficiently "good" object and later to effectively cope with separation from it by preparing some farewell. This is also regarded as the main target in the group psychotherapy of patients suffering from psychosis (Caparrós, 1999; Skolnick, 1998, 1999). Patients can experience all three group stages sufficiently, given that the latter, as mutually permeable phenomena with flexible duration, are repeated in cycles at both the individual and group level, each time on a more advanced level (Foulkes, 1975). This is on condition that a patient drop-out, defined as quitting before six months, can be avoided through the conductor's continuous efforts to translate and resolve any malignant mirroring or negative transferences developed in the group (Zinkin, 1983). The group was conducted following Foulkes' group-analytic technique, which is likewise indicated for the group psychotherapy of psychoses (Urlić, 1999), with the therapist being a leader following a directive and/or interpretative stance during the first stages of the group and on its archaic and projective level, thus diminishing the group's influence, and a conductor at the later stages of the group and on its mature level by leaving it to take the place of the therapist through the members' mutual support. Cognitive and behavioural elements, as well as directions regarding the members' medications, were also included in conducting the group.

Subjects

Both patients with eating disorders were referred to me by their psychiatrists. They went through an in-depth psychiatric and psychodynamic evaluation and were given a diagnosis of severe anorexia nervosa and the purging subtype of bulimia nervosa, respectively, as defined in the fourth edition of the *Diagnostic and Statistical Manual of Mental Disorders (DSM-IV)* (American Psychiatric Association, 1994). The average body mass index (BMI) of Anna and Dimitra was 19.6 and 26, respectively. Both patients were diagnosed on *DSM-III-R* axes I, II, IV and V following the global assessment of functioning (GAF) scale. Both had a diagnosis in axis I and II, indicating depression and borderline personality disorder, respectively, which was more severe in Anna than in Dimitra. Anna was prescribed anti-depressant medication which she continued taking throughout the period of her individual and group therapy. The GAF score (60–51) suggested that both were candidates for outpatient care.

Design and measures

The design was a single-subject study in a group-analytic context with assessment measures before and during treatment. The patients completed the eating attitudes test (EAT; Garner & Garfinkel, 1979) and the bulimia test-revised (BULIT-R; Thelen et al., 1991) and were interviewed following the eating disorder examination (EDE; Fairburn

& Cooper, 1993). They were also administered the eating disorder inventory-2 (EDI-2; Garner, 1991), the EDI symptom checklist (EDI-SC; Garner, 1991), the body shape questionnaire (BSQ; Cooper et al., 1987) and the multi-factorial assessment of eating disorder symptoms (MAEDS; Anderson et al., 1999). The measures indicated a more severe depression and a greater level of restrictive behaviour (drive for thinness, body dissatisfaction) for Anna than for Dimitra. A disturbance in body image (believing herself to be fat while weighing forty-nine kilogrammes) was present only in Anna.

The patients' motivation for therapy and level of introspection were evaluated and accepted as inclusion criteria. However, their individual therapies (Dimitra's for one year and Anna's for two), despite the higher levels of attendance and therapeutic alliance, were extremely difficult. Dimitra developed a superficially idealised self-object transference linked to her fear of devouring the object/therapist or being devoured by it. Anna's transference was established as an overwhelming tendency to represent the therapist as an omnipotent mother or bodily self-object. Any mirroring that favoured a relationship with him as separate/idealised self-object was tenaciously hindered by Anna's emptiness of feeling and/or frigid stance, which she permanently projected on the therapist. At the very end, both therapies presented mediocre success since, just before entering the group, Anna had gained only half a kilogramme. Her menstruation cycle was reconstituted, but she continued to consider herself fat and to complain about depression. Dimitra had just reduced her binge-eating and vomiting from three to two incidents weekly. In order to achieve a better outcome, it was decided that both should continue their therapy in the group.

Group treatment

Archaic level

Both patients experienced the group on the archaic/oral level, which lasted approximately six months, in an effective way. The group had already entered the projective stage (paranoid–schizoid position). The active but calm leadership model, the smooth development of verbal intercommunications and interactions, and the heterogeneity of the group as hindering massive regression or fusion phenomena helped them to experience the group matrix as a container and holding environment rather than as a devouring Dragon Mother (Weston, 1999) or an engulfing hall of mirrors (Foulkes & Anthony, 1957).

Anna, who was usually silent, developed a good enough emotional link, especially with Gabriella, Alexander, and Antonis, who represented calm mothering objects or siblings for her, and with the group as a whole, mainly through her non-verbal communication. She attended the group uninterruptedly and achieved the introjection of it as a bodily self-object, which was less threatening as sustained by the therapist/leader. "Unlike my mother, the group does not control me, and it is supported by a therapist who is a God", she said in one session. At the same period, Anna began to gain some weight, although her disturbed body image persisted.

Dimitra had serious difficulties in developing a bond with the group and persistently avoided it through pleasant yet superficial talking. However, she also attended the group regularly and progressively made a good enough attachment, especially with the neurotic members, with whom she felt safer, and with Anna, in whom she saw an alliance. In order not to "vomit" the group as an introjected bodily self-object like food, she took care to maintain an attitude that meant a gradual adult connection with it. Towards the end of this stage, she had lost weight and stopped vomiting.

Projective level

By the end of the archaic level, Anna's attitude to the group had changed greatly. "I feel as though the group is chasing me", she said in a subsequent session. The experience of the group on the projective level/paranoid–schizoid position, which lasted about one year, had begun and the group had become persecuting by being conceived as "bad" rather than "good" object. Although Anna's persecutory anxiety was mediocre, she could not quite respond to the benign mirroring provided by the neurotic or borderline group members (interestingly, malignant mirror phenomena were absent during this period of the group). When, in one session, Gabriella, Fotini, Socrates, and Peter insisted that she was beautiful, Anna resisted by replying, "I feel very fat, I weighed forty-nine kilos and now I weigh fifty." However, she accepted with pleasure the same remarks when expressed by the psychotic members, Antonis and Alexander. Later, Anna arrived at a deeper realisation. She said that she did not feel "a nothing" for the group, as she felt for her mother (who never looked at her), which indicated that she had assimilated new images of herself provided by the benign mirroring of the group as a whole.

Dimitra experienced a much deeper paranoid anxiety because of which she had great difficulties at the mirroring level. When the members told her that she was beautifully dressed, Dimitra replied that they were "making fun" of her, like her mother: "My mother used to say that I'd be really lovely if I weren't the size of a horse." The only mirroring that seemed acceptable to Dimitra was that which developed with Anna. Owing to this, they arrived at deeper levels of insight. In one session, Anna said and Dimitra agreed, "We both want to get rid of the bodily presence of our mother inside us, so you try to vomit it. I even refuse to eat because I'm afraid I'll expel it and then I'd be lost". This helped both Dimitra and Anna to accept the group as a "good", rather than "bad", object and to introject it as an idealised, rather than bodily, self-object.

Mature group reality level

After about three and two years of group analysis, respectively, both patients, following the group's evolution, entered the mature/reality level linked with the depressive position. Both women were constantly without symptoms. Dimitra had stopped binge-eating and purging behaviours. Anna had gained one more kilo and no longer considered herself fat. New assessments were administered, showing that depression had considerably diminished in both patients. With the agreement of the psychiatrist, Anna had also discontinued her medication. She had also completed her individual therapy. All members had exhibited impressive improvement, including the psychotic members, who had had no relapse.

In this period, major events took place in the group at the oedipal level. Gabriella stated that the conductor was a model father like her father. Peter and Socrates openly expressed their envy of the fact that Gabriella felt this way about the conductor. Surprisingly, Antonis said the same thing. Whereas Fotini complained to Antonis that she was jealous because whenever he spoke, he addressed either Gabriella or the conductor. Both Anna and Dimitra resisted the group's tendency to address oedipal issues. Anna declared that she saw the conductor exclusively as a mother. Dimitra said that she simply considered the conductor a friend. The conductor tried to counterbalance the oedipal dynamics just expressed with the pre-oedipal qualities of the father/therapist and the group. He feared that an immediate exposure of the anorexic/bulimic patients to the idea of the oedipal father would lead them to regressive states, with the danger of relapse and/or drop out. He maintained, in the form of a group intervention, that the father figure is as good enough as the mother figure and can prove to be a strong figure as long as he follows the deeper mindedness of the mother, without directing her or being passively subjected to her, as the conductor follows the group. The intervention pleased Anna especially, and the conductor's unconscious fear that some of the anorexia nervosa and bulimia nervosa patients would drop out was momentarily reassured.

Later, the group dynamics became interwoven with mourning processes related to separation/differentiation from parents. Anna began to be absent systematically. In one session, she stated that she wanted to withdraw from the group, and wanted only to live close to her mother "until she dies". All members unanimously replied that she needed to stay in the group a little longer, and linked Anna's wish to leave the group with the deep fear that she, too, might lose her mother. The conductor linked Anna's wish to leave the group with the difficulties that the group as a whole had to cope with in mourning the immature infantile part of self. This occasion was provided by the evolution of the group at this level of its development and is a critical and difficult moment. However, the members were able to deal with this experience by sharing it. Furthermore, the conductor, using a cognitive–behavioural approach (Heesacker & Neimeyer, 1990; Leung et al., 2000), said that Anna had mistakenly linked every separation process with her mother's loss, which was a maladaptive parental bonding schema. Anna asked for an individual session and the conductor agreed. However, she did not come to the individual session and gave no notice. But she was present at the next group session and kept coming to group after this. She did not feel depressed and said that she had no need to return to medication.

Dimitra tried to experience the depressive feelings aroused during the mature phase of the group. However, in one session, she announced that she had decided to accept a job she had been offered in another town. She said that this was a real reason and it was not due to the difficulties in her therapy, which she really tried to cope with. All members, and the therapist, asked Dimitra whether other alternative solutions were possible and expressed their willingness to help. However, Dimitra had definitely decided. Before she left for her new job, she wanted to have just one farewell session with us (normally the termination of group therapy lasts for two months, meaning that two months beforehand, the member who is completing therapy pre-announces their last farewell session). Dimitra's farewell took place in a deep emotional climate with interactions between the members. All members were present, including Anna, who said goodbye to Dimitra very warmly. Interestingly, this kind of farewell resembles the farewell performed by some patients with psychosis when their therapy is relatively complete (exceptionally, Antonis and Socrates, when they left the group four years later, were to take one month to prepare their farewell).

In the session after Dimitra's farewell, Anna was absent. After the session, she called me saying that she would prefer not to have a farewell, and that she was going to discontinue therapy. For some months after her farewell, Dimitra continued her contact with the group by writing about life in her new home and sending cards. Anna did not re-appear until three years later, when she telephoned me to say that she was fine. Today, she is married and has two children. Dimitra lives alone, has no symptoms, and works in a Children's Hospital Centre in her new town.

Discussion

This study analyses the therapeutic evolution of two women patients suffering from anorexia nervosa and bulimia nervosa, which took place in a once-a-week heterogeneous group-analytic group in an outpatient setting. The group consisted of patients with neuroses, borderline personality disorder, and psychoses and was conducted by me, following Foulkes' (1964, 1975) group-analytic method combined with cognitive–behavioural elements (Birchwood et al., 2000), psychoanalysis, and object relations theories. A continuous reassessment of anorexic and bulimic patients during group treatment was combined with individual psychotherapy and medication control. Patients were assessed before individual treatment by the psychiatrist who referred them and the individual/group therapist for precise diagnosis, motivation, and anticipated treatment outcome.

Avoiding dropping out, defined as quitting therapy before six months have elapsed, and achieving a good enough long-term attendance in the group, leading to reduced symptoms, was the first target in the group-analytic psychotherapy of both patients. Given that the minimum duration of group therapy for any individual is one year (Foulkes, 1975), the fact that group therapy lasted three and two years for the anorexia nervosa and bulimia nervosa patient, respectively, and that the patients' symptoms had fully receded by the end of their presence in the group, indicates that their therapeutic progress was undoubtedly successful. This result is consistent with Gold's (1999), Willis's (1999), and Valbak's (2003) view that modified group analysis can be effectively used with eating disorder patients not only in homogeneous, but also in heterogeneous, inpatient or outpatient group-analytic groups.

The second major target was that these two patients with anorexia nervosa and bulimia nervosa would transform the mothering object which they had introjected as "bad" into a "good" one (Klein, 1937, 1946) by first introjecting the group as a good enough mother and holding environment (Winnicott, 1976) or as container (Bion, 1963) sustaining, in terms of an idealised self-object (Kohut, 1971), the differentiation of the infant's self from the mother's self through mutual mirroring and recognition. This was largely achieved: (a) during the group's archaic–oral stage by the patients experiencing the group matrix of intercommunications as a reassuring, rather than a Dragon Mother (Weston, 1999), and (b) during the group's projective level (paranoid–schizoid position), which, through the multiple mirroring phenomena that developed—unlike their individual therapy—provided the patients with valuable self-images that were progressively assimilated, leading to a better integration of their body image into their self structure. Both aims were further supported by the fact that the heterogeneity of the group deterred fusion states, according to Gold (1999) and Willis (1999), that the patients' persecutory anxiety incited during paranoid–schizoid position was mediocre, and that the therapist, during these two group pre-oedipal stages, functioned as leader rather than as conductor, as provided during the third mature (depressive position) group's oedipal level.

The last, less ambitious, target was that the patients would experience adequately the group's reality-based stage/level (depressive position), which is linked to identification with the mothering object and the group conceived as preponderantly "good" (Klein, 1937, 1946), thus leading to separation from it or to the last phase of the separation–individuation process according to Mahler and colleagues (1975), and also marks the patients' passage to the oedipal situation (Foulkes, 1964). This aim was minimally achieved by the bulimia nervosa patient, who prepared a one-session farewell before leaving the group, and was completely avoided by the anorexia nervosa patient, who preferred to interrupt her therapy rather than prepare a farewell. Both patients, especially the patient with anorexia nervosa, avoided following the mourning processes developed in the group, and neither did these two members consistently develop a transference on the oedipal level with either the therapist as conductor or symbolic father (Name-of-the-Father) or the men of the group that could be elaborated, thereby refuting Willis's (1999) and Gold's (1999) relevant views.

The above results have considerable implications for the further investigation of the group-analytic approach to eating disorders. By revealing both the strong (oral–archaic and projective paranoid–schizoid position level) and weak (mature depressive position level) points of this approach, according to Klein's (1946) and Foulkes's (1964) views, they suggest that both anorexia nervosa and bulimia nervosa can be effectively treated by systematically elaborating the psychotic part of the patients' self (Bion, 1967) on the group's pre-oedipal level of oral gratification. They also show the need for mirroring and intercommunication provided by the mothering qualities of the group matrix and the supportive role of the group therapist, rather than the non-psychotic part of the self on the oedipal level linked with separation–individuation processes and identification with the group therapist as symbolic father. Foulkes (1975), although he generally considered group analysis as a suitable means of treating psychosomatic illnesses, has left these factors completely unexplored, as well as a number of other factors, specific and unspecific (Foulkes, 1964; Foulkes & Anthony, 1957), that this study has not investigated. These factors should be systematically explored. Group analysis, as this study has indicated, could also be used to obtain a minute, step-by-step diagnosis of eating disorders, especially with regard to their psychotic parameters.

However, the applicability of the above results has certain limitations. First, they are based on a very small sample of individual cases, which precludes any possibility of generalisation. Second, the results cannot be compared with other relative findings or considered to replicate them, since there is no other study investigating the therapeutic progress of eating disorder patients in a slow-open heterogeneous group-analytic group in the literature and it is not the dominant paradigm. Third, a follow-up study is also missing, since the patients, although remarkably improved, abruptly prepared a farewell or avoided it and interrupted their therapy. Finally, the present study was not able to adequately investigate the degree to which the group was effective in reducing the patients' borderline personality disorder and depression, thus improving their eating disorder symptoms indirectly, or whether the reverse is true. Similarly, the study was unable to investigate whether, as shown in the different quality of the patients' termination phases, group-analytic psychotherapy would be more effective in the treatment of bulimia than of anorexia, or whether group effectiveness depends on the different level of severity of the patients' eating disorder symptoms, on their different restrictive characteristics, or the level of their borderline personality disorder and depression. Studies on group cognitive–behavioural therapy with bulimic women have verified that the higher drop-out rates are not due to the severity of the patients' bulimic behaviours, but to higher rates of their secondary psychopathology, such as depression (Steel et al., 2000) restrictive tendencies (McKisack & Waller, 1996) or borderline personality disorder (Coker et al., 1993). The present study seems to support the same conclusion, but with regard to anorexic, rather than bulimic, patients. It would be extremely valuable for this issue to be further investigated, together with the other themes opened up in this discussion.

CHAPTER NINE

Depression in schizophrenia and the therapeutic impact of the group-analytic group*

Theoretical and clinical remarks

The psychoanalytic approach

Even though a secondary depression syndrome is not unusual in schizophrenia, no evidence has been found since the time of Kraepelin and Bleuler to indicate a direct aetiological link between them; in fact, the question of whether schizophrenia and affective disorders are biologically and psychologically distinct or a continuum is still unanswered and might remain so for some time (Kendell & Brockington, 1980; Lake, 2008; Siris, 1991; Taylor, 1992).

In any event, our experience permits us to claim that depression, although it often accompanies schizophrenia, does not seem to constitute a structural element of the latter disorder; on the contrary, access to depression appears to be a constant and necessary requirement for a partial way out of schizophrenia. Whatever its form, depression presupposes a rudimentary internalisation of the maternal object, which is achieved when the infant ceases to see the mother primarily

---

* First published in 2009 in *Psychosis*, 1(2): 167–177.

as a "good" (gratification) or "bad" (frustration) breast (Klein's oral–sadistic stage), or as a breast or partial object that is more "bad" and persecuting than "good" (Klein's paranoid–schizoid position), and sees it well enough as an integrated whole person with its "good" and "bad" aspects (Klein's depressive position) (Klein, 1935, 1940, 1946, 1960). It should be noted here that the paranoid–schizoid position and the depressive position or, as Bion says, the "Positions", "are not to be regarded simply . . . as something that is achieved once for all during infancy, but as a continuously active process" (Bion, 1992, pp. 199–200). One position interacts with the other in a continuous to-and-fro, operating smoothly and changing rapidly. As a result, the subject should acquire the ability to enter the depressive position, go back to the paranoid–schizoid position, and then return to the depressive position continually in a flexible way. This leads subjects to withstand the paranoid–schizoid position, to become stabilised in the depressive position, and to better manage the anxiety stemming from the latter that the object might die. When this anxiety goes beyond a certain point and under certain conditions, it is known to lead to depression as a disorder (Klein, 1935, 1940, 1960). The patient with schizophrenia lives in an archaic state without object (Freud, 1915e), that is, a state that seems to precede even the oral–sadistic stage, where the object has already become "dead" and is, therefore, equated to a thing that is completely hallucinated and persecuting (Bion, 1967, 1992). This means that patients suffering from schizophrenia lack the flexibility to negotiate between the paranoid–schizoid and depressive positions. They enter the depressive position under the impetus of either the treatment or their own mental development, while remaining strongly fixated in the paranoid–schizoid position, and, above all, in the oral stage. As a result, they split off the depressive anxiety and guilt—the latter of which applies to destroying the internalised object or what seems to be such—and project it to objects or, as Bion (1967, 1992) claims, to their own thought, which is, thus, fragmented and eventually destroyed. Under these circumstances, some depressive components of the patient's self are not elements of an authentic depressive anxiety, but elements of an archaic mental situation, largely a mixture of anger, envy, and revenge, and are simply encapsulated in various depression-like forms (Searles, 1965).

However, the presence of these depression-like elements is preferable to their absence. They indicate that a considerable part of the internal object remains "alive" and demands to be reconstructed in order to lead to healthy behaviour. The only problem is that this demand, in order not to be harmful, cannot and must not be totally realised through therapy. A good enough therapy for the patient who suffers from schizophrenia does not consist of transforming the depression-like syndrome into a real depression, which can later be treated, that is, in achieving access to the depressive position. This is not possible, and when it is presented as possible or forced (e.g., through medication), it can only lead to access to the depressive position, but probably in a destructive way. As Bion (1992) has shown, any effort to lead the patient with schizophrenia to an immediate encounter with the whole object would be destructive. Such patients perceive a fully internalised object as a "dead" object and, by extension, as a murderous superego. They might then turn their murderous feelings against themselves, leading to suicide.

Under these conditions, we can understand why patients suffering from schizophrenia, since they are under the pressure created by the negotiation between the paranoid–schizoid and the depressive position, tend to regress permanently to the oral–sadistic stage in a tragic way: on the one hand, they want to fulfil their insatiable need for a "good" breast, and, on the other, they hate this breast and resist it (Searles, 1965). This is why a good enough therapy of patients with schizophrenia should go hand in hand with their tendency to regress to the oral–sadistic stage, aiming at a good enough recreation of the latter. This gradually permits the release of a reasonable amount of depressive feelings and their de-encapsulation in such a way that patients can assimilate them as part of their psychic reality.

The contribution of group-analytic psychotherapy

In this chapter, I support the view that, parallel to medication and after any other form of therapy patients might receive (individual psychotherapy, family therapy etc.), group-analytic therapy can constitute a very effective therapeutic milieu for patients suffering from schizophrenia, especially if the latter is accompanied by a depression-like syndrome. I am not referring here to a homogeneous group, which is a group exclusively composed of patients with schizophrenia or other psychoses. This type of group (which is conducted by two or more therapists) is today highly developed with well-known and very good results (Schermer & Pines, 1999). I am referring to the heterogeneous group-analytic group as conceived and initiated by Foulkes (1948, 1964) and Foulkes and Anthony (1957). This should be an inpatient or outpatient slow-open analytic group that meets once or preferably twice a week, at a constant place and time (an hour and a half) with eight being the ideal number of members. This group is conducted preferably by one therapist, whereas its members can consist of patients of all psychopathologies except for "pronouncedly paranoid people", "acutely psychotic patients", "acutely depressed or suicidal persons" and "anti-social psychopathic individuals" (Foulkes, 1975, p. 66).

Foulkes was minimally preoccupied with the issue of whether psychotic patients could be treated within the framework of any group-analytic group. Moreover, since Foulkes's time, this issue has remained largely unexplored. The only literature based on the Foulkesian perspective today consists of a few articles about either the group treatment of patients suffering from psychosis alone (Urlić, 1999) or the group treatment of people with psychosis (schizophrenia and bipolar psychosis) together with borderline personalities (Chazan, 1999).

Nevertheless, after many years of personal experience in group analysis with neurotic and borderline personality patients, and in conjunction with the group psychotherapy of psychoses, I decided to attempt a treatment of patients with schizophrenia in a group-analytic group of mixed psychopathology. I was very hesitant at the beginning. But as time passed, and as I became increasingly aware of the group's impact on the socialisation of the patients, including patients with schizophrenia or other psychoses, without the threat of serious complications, I decided to try it, employing the following basic principles:

- The group in question would be a once-weekly group, since in contrast to the twice-weekly group, it permits the gradual "digestion" of the therapeutic elements by the patient with schizophrenia.
- The group should be an outpatient group conducted by one group analyst and consisting of six or seven members of mixed psychopathology, preferably members whose personality is characterised by a borderline or psychotic structure rather than a

neurotic one as well as members with severe psychosomatics such as eating disorders. Patients with a borderline personality are known to constitute a group with difficulty similar to that of a group of patients with schizophrenia (Chazan, 1999; Milders, 1994; Ryle & Golynkina, 2000).

- Before entering the group, all members, especially those suffering from schizophrenia or other psychoses, must have spent considerable time in individual psychotherapy with the same therapist, who would later be their group therapist. It is through individual psychotherapy (from approximately six months to two years or more) that a primary link is constructed from the beginning with the therapist, conceived mainly as a partial object/breast and less so as a whole object, which is known to be represented by the group (Urlić, 1999). Yet, although the link formed in the individual therapy of such patients remains always the barometer of their therapeutic evolution, the group is what allows the patient to become readily familiarised with the object conceived initially as a continuation of the breast/partial object on the social level, and then gradually with the object as a whole (this familiarisation could also be achieved in a good enough individual psychotherapy).

The group-analytic factors that could contribute to a good enough treatment for the patient with schizophrenia can be classified as follows:

1. As a mature representative of internal or external reality, the group reduces the danger of a malignant symbiosis between therapist and patient. In order for the group to be effective in this, the analyst must work with the group mainly on its current or projective level (the level of bodily and mental images) avoiding emphasis on the primordial or archaic level, which, by its nature, is highly regressive (Foulkes, 1964). Otherwise, the member with schizophrenia will feel the group as a devouring mother (Foguel, 1994).
2. Sharing emotions, feelings, ideas, etc. among the members through intercommunication is the privilege of the group-analytic group (Foulkes, 19664; Foulkes & Anthony, 1957). This permits the therapist to work effectively in the oral–sadistic stage,

which, in this case, is our goal. Intercommunication in the group forms a common shared ground, so that the two major and difficult axes of the oral–sadistic stage, that is "suckling" the group conceived as breast on the one hand, and frustration and weaning from it on the other, take place in a commonly acceptable way that does not permit either of them to exceed moderation, thus facilitating their good enough function.

3. By emphasising the dialogic and social nature of the mind (Ryle & Golynkina, 2000), the group takes on a psycho-educational role, thus helping patients with schizophrenia to rehabilitate their neurocognitive dysfunctions, if such exist, and promoting social cognition. The group-analytic group, like the cognitive analytic-based therapy model, helps patients with schizophrenia, especially those with schizophrenia accompanied by depression (Birchwood et al., 2000), to cope with their voices in the sense that, based on the members' interventions, patients tend gradually to attribute the voices to the self rather than to external sources (Bentall et al., 1994).

4. Multiple mirroring is also a common shared ground of the group (Foulkes, 1964; Foulkes & Anthony, 1957; Pines, 1984; Weinberg & Toder, 2004). As a result, members suffering from schizophrenia can gradually receive and absorb a reasonable number of images of themselves, thus better reconstructing the good enough self-image that they lack and that is normally formed in early infancy through the mother's eye as primary mirror (Winnicott, 1971). Of course, such patients' exposure to mirroring must be gradual and gentle. All kinds of malignant mirroring in the group must be confronted and resolved as soon as possible (Zinkin, 1983; Weinberg & Toder, 2004). Otherwise, the patient's narcissism could easily regress to an archaic state without object.

5. The group is always characterised by a large number of interpersonal and transpersonal relationships (two persons and three and more persons, respectively) (Foulkes, 1964; Foulkes & Anthony, 1957). As a result, a set of oedipal (triangular) situations is formed, especially the oedipal situation represented by the group analyst (father's position), the group (mother's position) and the members (children's position). This does not of course permit members suffering from schizophrenia to enter the oedipal situation, which is not possible, but at least they will feel less

fear of it and become gradually familiar with it. This is helped by the fact that the therapist's style of directing the group, without lacking a leadership profile when required, goes hand in hand with respect for the group as a mother figure, and its promotion as a major therapeutic figure. This is why the group analyst is called a conductor (Foulkes, 1948, 1964, 1990). Under such conditions, the patient gradually forms an image of the combined parents, that is, the union of the conductor and the group, which is the core of the transition from the paranoid–schizoid position to the depressive position (Ancona & Mangiarotti, 1999; Bion, 1992; Klein, 1957). This image is not destructive, but offers sufficient harmony for the patient suffering from schizophrenia.

A typical vignette will now be presented of the good enough therapy of Nikos, a patient of mine who suffers from schizophrenia with strong depressive components, in a group-analytic group in the sense described above.

A clinical vignette

Nikos was the only child of a very disorganised family. His father was completely withdrawn. For as long as Nikos could remember, his mother was exclusively engaged with her dogs and cats, of which she always had large numbers, and never with Nikos, whom she treated like one of her pets. Undoubtedly, Nikos had dangerously regressed to a pre-narcissistic state without object in the context of which he had also introjected his mother as a "dead" object. Nevertheless, Nikos succeeded in getting through high school and then entering higher education. He began to study electronics in which he was very talented. Unfortunately, when he was twenty-two years old and just before writing his last exams to receive his degree, Nikos presented his first schizophrenic crisis. No pre-psychotic depressive symptoms or serious cognitive deficits (which usually precede psychosis) were present. One day, feeling himself suddenly oppressed by an uncontrollable sense of unprovoked anger and vengefulness, together with, as he described it, "a lot of little people" who crowded into his mind and annoyed him, sometimes making him laugh and other times making him feel crazy, he began to quarrel with one of his friends so intensely that Nikos beat his friend badly and then, with feelings of despair and guilt, tried to cut his own wrists. The quarrel was over a girl. Nikos thought (more in his imagination than in reality) that the girl was in love with him, but the girl had already formed a relationship with his friend. After that, Nikos began to quarrel with his parents and, by extension, with anyone he met on the street whom he saw as an incarnation of the "little people" he had inside him. Then, the "little people" began to mock him in a stronger and more violent way, by telling him he was totally useless and that his life had no value or meaning.

His family had him admitted to a psychiatric hospital where he began pharmaceutical treatment that continues to the present time, now on a maintenance dosage. With the help of medication, the symptoms declined perceptibly. Despite this, on many occasions, Nikos would present symptoms of depression that were clearly not due to the negative-symptom syndrome of schizophrenia; on the contrary, it seemed to be much closer to a post-psychotic depression-like syndrome. It was a mixture of anger, guilt, and revenge behind which lay profound schizophrenic material that Nikos expressed through a strongly depressed mood with suicidal tendencies and acts of vindictiveness and self-mutilation.

After he left the hospital, Nikos was sent to a psychiatrist–psychotherapist in private practice. The therapist treated Nikos for about a year and a half in once-weekly individual supportive psychotherapy. When required, he prescribed and modified the medication. Despite this, one day Nikos presented a second crisis, which was more serious this time, and was again admitted to hospital (a private one). After Nikos was released from hospital his therapist expressed his disappointment to me on the phone and decided to refer his patient to me for individual analysis and eventually for group therapy.

Nikos entered once-weekly individual psychotherapy with me for about two years. From the very beginning it was obvious that a good enough symbiotic relationship would gradually be established with me. Nikos felt that, in a deeper and secret part of myself, I was always with his psychosis. We were unequal and at the same time equal. During one of our first sessions, Nikos very vividly and characteristically showed me how his depressive emotions had been encapsulated in his mind, leading him to schizophrenic behaviour:

Many times, I feel very angry deep inside. This is my insanity; it is, I believe, my only psychological problem. Every two weeks, I get upset and I shout, but I shout inside me. It's like I have no voice and I make a lot of gestures to send my anger away. And I also feel vengefulness. I feel unbearably vindictive towards some people, not all people, just those who distress me. But the main problem is anger. Anger drives me crazy, like when I had that episode. I was so mad I could hardly see. That's why I want to be cured. I don't want many things, just to be able to hold down a job and find a girl who will love me without trying to control me. I'm afraid that this anger will make me so sad one day that it will eventually lead me to depression. But I want to try. I want to change, to make myself better, because, after these crises of anger, I want to die.

After we had established strong enough bonds in two years of individual therapy, we decided to end this type of therapy and continue in a group. When the time was right, Nikos joined a group-analytic group in the sense described above. The symbiotic bond he had established with me continued without any problem and gradually consolidated as a bond with the group. A contributing factor in this regard was the very close friendship he quickly developed with George, a twenty-five-year-old mathematician, who suffered from paranoid psychosis. George imagined he was God. His first psychotic crisis came when he thought he would be able to fly from his third-floor balcony to the one next door and jumped, injuring himself very seriously. He went through many crises and treatments in hospital, and spent two years in once-weekly individual psychotherapy with me, both inpatient and outpatient. He was a member of this group from its outset (2000), about a year and a half before Nikos entered it. The other founding members of the group, who had also had individual once-weekly psychotherapy with me (from between six months and three years) were: Helena, a twenty-six-year-old teacher with anorexia followed by depression, Mary, a twenty-seven-year-old nurse with bulimia, and John, a thirty-two-year-old economist suffering from a very serious compulsive neurosis based on a fragile pre-psychotic structure. John had a strong fear of leaving his house; every time he went out, he felt so dizzy he thought he was going to fall down and die. The group gradually made it possible for him to go out more easily. There was also Georgia, a fifty-six-year-old housewife, who was very badly and continuously abused by her husband, a senior officer in the army, whose behaviour was highly archaic and destructive.

The successful linking of Nikos with the group was not without obstacles and a year or so was required for it to be established well enough. Nikos had found a mother/breast/group that, unlike his personal mother, was "alive" and ready to "suckle" him (the group's oral–sadistic stage), but, since this was a unique experience for him, he wanted to accept it at his own pace. As a result, from time to time Nikos would forget to come to the group, quarrel with his parents or friends, or mutilate himself (without entering a crisis). Nevertheless, these difficulties were soon overcome. Nikos began to attend the group regularly and was rarely absent.

Nikos' group therapy lasted eight years (2001–2009). During this period, new members with auditory verbal hallucinations entered the group; they had either a neurotic personality or psychosis. Interestingly, in the meantime, unlike Nikos and George, all the other members of the group terminated their therapy early, after no more than two years in the group. For reasons that are probably associated with the psychotic fear of regression to the oral–sadistic stage caused by the enormous devouring needs of the anorexic or bulimic woman (Segercrantz, 2006; Weston, 1999), there was for a long time a subtle malignant mirroring between Nikos and Mary and Nikos and Helena. Yet this mirroring was very soon counter-balanced by a good enough benign mirroring existing between George, Mary, and Helena. In addition, a very strong benign mirroring had taken place from the beginning, as has already been pointed out, between Nikos and George. In this way, just after he entered the group, Nikos gradually introduced George, who had until then avoided all contact with technology as it aroused in him strong notions of persecution, to computer games. Nikos and George would meet at one or the other's house for computer lessons, which they talked about extensively in the group. George, in turn, despite his own deep fear of girls, but because he was more familiar with them owing to his good relations with his sister, tried to "teach" Nikos how to behave with females. They talked a lot about this, too, in the group. All these relationships have greatly helped Nikos to rebuild to some extent his lost narcissism.

Communication in the form it takes in the group gradually permitted Nikos to talk about his symptoms, especially about the "voices", of which he was initially so ashamed. The group members carefully avoided treating the voices he heard as a hallucination and accepted them as an internal reality for him, which they told him openly. Later, they pointed out that these voices were probably no different from the conversations heard among themselves in the group; it was just that, in some way, they seemed to have been transferred to Nikos' mind and to have gained some autonomy. This helped Nikos to focus more on talking to the members and largely to forget the voices he heard in his mind. Gradually, the voices diminished appreciably.

Then, about one year later, the difficult times began, now on an advanced level indicating the passage of the members and the group as a whole from the oral–sadistic stage to the paranoid–schizoid position (Bion, 1992; Klein, 1946, 1957). Under the influence of the announcement of some leave-takings and the entrance of new members into the group (which was linked with a somewhat premature experience of the depressive position), Nikos, through the evolution of the group and his own personal development, followed the difficult path of accepting a number of deprivations and frustrations. Without ceasing to be accepted, he was no longer the centre of attention. Once again, he seemed to be entering a phase of depression that led him to a permanent silence, which was sometimes interspersed with pointless laughter in the group, and to tendencies to self-mutilation outside the group (after quarrelling with his parents, he tried twice to cut his wrists). All these forms of acting out obviously represented Nikos' difficulties and resistance to achieving a flexible negotiation between the paranoid–schizoid and the depressive position (Bion, 1992) and to confronting well enough what Mahler (1968) considers the separation–individuation process.

Below is a typical dialogue between Nikos and the group members at the first session following his two absences, during which the acting out described above occurred. At this session, Nikos returned to the group very pensive and moody, which was unusual for him. He avoided looking people in the eye and gazed at the floor, sitting quietly in his chair after saying a cordial "Hello" to the members. It was clear that there was something wrong. George, opening the dialogue, asked him, with the directness characteristic of their friendship,

What's the matter, Nikos?

Nikos: Nothing.

George: Is anything the matter at home?

Nikos: (*speaking rapidly*) No. Nothing. I went up to the bachelor apartment over our apartment, but two days later, I wasn't feeling well and I started to go up and down the stairs. I told my Mum and she told me to come back down. Now she has assigned me to look after the dogs and to take them out for a walk two or three times a day. The dogs shit on the newspaper that's on the floor which I then have to pick up. I find all this tiring.

Mary: You must be very angry or sad about this.

Nikos: I don't know. I don't want to know. I don't like that sort of thing. I love my parents. I feel closer to my Dad but I am bonded with my Mum.

George: The fact is you don't look very well. Don't tell me you did anything to your wrists again . . .

Nikos: No. I just took a little more medication, and passed out. Fortunately my mother found me. Then when I came to, I quarrelled with my Mum and left the house, slamming the door. I don't know where I went, I wandered around all day and finally my father found me in a park.

Helena: Why didn't you come to the group? Did we do something wrong?

Nikos: I wanted to come; I love my group. But I couldn't. I was ashamed. But I wanted to see how I'd be without the group.

Analyst: And how were you?

Nikos: I don't know. At that moment, you all didn't exist for me.

Analyst: Do we exist now?

Nikos: Yes. Here, things are better. My parents are the absolute good and absolute bad at the same time.

George: Don't worry. The same thing's true in my case, too.

Helena: Anyway, Nikos, I want you to promise me personally that you won't try and hurt yourself again.

Nikos: (*sadly and with some emotion*) I promise.

With the help of the group, Nikos soon returned to his previous state. After about six years of therapy, he was able to express his anger, the targets of which seemed interchangeable: sometimes he appeared to be protecting the group and to be angry with the conductor, at others he seemed to be protecting the conductor, while turning his anger against the group. It was obvious that Nikos was trying to challenge the union of the therapeutic parental couple (conductor and group) before accepting it, by splitting off, although, in a mild way, the depressive position, following Klein's (1946, 1957) views. Later, in 2009, after eight years in the group, he was able one day to say in front of its members "In fact, I empathise with all of you".

Nikos was now feeling stronger and capable of continuing his life outside the group. Influenced by George, who had said goodbye a year previously, Nikos also asked to leave. It is significant to note here that the leave-takings of patients who suffer from psychosis are never complete; they are intermediate in the sense that, in a once-weekly group-analytic group, they usually last for one month instead of two, which is four group sessions instead of eight. The group accepted Nikos' request, and he said farewell to the degree that all people with psychosis do. The major emotional and symbolic events of the farewell by a neurotic member do not take place (the expression of deeper feelings of grief, the exchange of gifts, etc., are missing). But, without being superficial, these farewells have their own emotional and symbolic value for the psychotic patient as well as for the neurotic. The patient with psychosis leaves the group, but never leaves his/her psychotic self. This self is imprinted on the mind of the group, teaching its members that life is much better without the burden of neurotic conflicts.

A year after completing his therapy, Nikos told me that he was able to cope with his mother's death from cancer without suffering an episode. A year after that, he asked to have an individual session with me once a month. During this period, which lasted for about a year, we discussed different topics concerning his follow-up each month. Influenced by the fact that George, thanks to the passage of a law that provided for temporary jobs in public agencies for persons who have recovered from psychosis, began working in a tax office, Nikos began considering a job in electronics. He also started having occasional relationships with the girls he met through the Internet. Even though he frequently entered into these relationships, when they broke up, he would fall once again into depression (without having a crisis). It was obvious that Nikos was now continuing the dialectic of "suckling" the mother/group and accepting frustration and weaning from it that he had learnt during his group therapy.

Now that our sessions have finished, Nikos works in a business he set up in collaboration with one of his friends. He continues to look for girls on the Internet but now, as he tells me when he calls me once a month or so, he is more careful. George also phones me (although less frequently than Nikos). He works in the tax office to which I belong, and so has access to my tax returns. Which is why, in some of his phone calls, he laughingly reminds me that if he catches me in some illegality, he will see that I am punished!

Conclusions

Patients with schizophrenia, particularly those who also develop symptoms of depression, despite their regression to a pre-narcissistic state without object (Freud, 1915e), can be treated effectively in a group-analytic group composed of members of mixed psychopathology (preferably patients with borderline personality disorder, patients with other forms of psychosis, and people with psychosomatic illness). The group, as representing a primordial good enough mother (Winnicott, 1971, 1976), is well equipped with many qualities that are mainly focused on communication, multiple mirroring phenomena, interpersonal and transpersonal relations (Foulkes, 1964), and the idea of a mature parental couple as represented by the union of the conductor with the group, following Klein's (1946, 1957) views. The careful utilisation of these qualities permits the group to reconstruct the narcissism of patients with schizophrenia adequately, that is, to rebuild from the very beginning their relationship with an internal mother figure, which, in these cases, is absent or "dead", according to Bion (1992), thus helping them to re-experience sufficiently the transition from the paranoid–schizoid to the depressive position. Members with schizophrenia that is also accompanied by a depressive syndrome tend to cope with their transition to the depressive position in a auto-destructive way, and so can profit greatly from the qualities of the group-analytic group with good therapeutic prospects. The ability of the group to create a common shared ground within which everything has its meaning and value could eventually constitute the optimal method of treating severe mental disturbances, including schizophrenia.

CHAPTER TEN

Dreaming and psychosis: coping with hearing voices in group analysis*

Auditory verbal hallucinations: research overview and clinical implications

Auditory verbal hallucinations or "hearing voices" are major psychiatric symptoms that afflict sixty to seventy-five per cent of people suffering from schizophrenia or schizo-affective disorder (Wing et al., 1974). Auditory verbal hallucinations may start during childhood or late adolescence and are heard (either inside or outside the head) as spoken by a source outside the voice-hearer (Leudar et al., 1997; Romme & Escher, 1989). Theories founded on experiments using the efficient generation mechanism (EGM) argue that auditory verbal hallucinations constitute an abnormal expression of subvocal, inner speech production in the frontal lobe (Gould, 1949; Green & Kinsbourne, 1990). Other theories assert that auditory verbal hallucinations emanate from either the impaired monitoring of intended speech (Hoffman, 1986) or the defective monitoring of verbal thoughts as they are generated, leading to their misidentification as

---

* Part of this chapter was presented at the Sixth World Hearing Voices Congress, Thessaloniki, Greece, 10–12 October 2014.

alien voices (Frith, 1987). However, there is no more than limited psychological and neuropsychological evidence to support these theories (Johns & McGuire, 1999). Other theories suggest that the voices are construed as either benevolent or malevolent depending on the autobiographical cognitive schemata characteristic of the patient's past symbiosis with significant others (Chadwick & Birchwood, 1994). In any case, a set of patterns of therapeutic intervention or coping strategies has been proposed on the basis of the above theories, aiming at either preventing auditory verbal hallucinations by blocking or transforming subvocal activity through behavioural treatment (Green & Kinsbourne, 1990), or modifying the morbid cognitive schemata that lead to hearing voices in individual or group cognitive–behavioural therapy (Chadwick & Birchwood, 1994). Yet, although individual and, above all, group cognitive–behavioural therapy was usually found to reduce auditory verbal hallucinations, their positive effects were not replicated in other studies (Lawrence et al., 2006).

Psychoanalysis is known to have made a decisive contribution to our understanding of psychosis. Freud maintained that in psychosis, unlike neurosis, the unconscious representations of thing (mothering object) have been de-invested while the preconscious representations of word have been super-invested (Freud, 1915d). This is because the patient with schizophrenia regresses to an archaic narcissism without object, in which any mirroring with the mothering person is absent (Freud, 1915d,e). For this reason, an alienation of the word from the thing is produced (Freud, 1917d), which results in hearing voices (Freud, 1911c). Freud also considered hearing voices as defence mechanisms. Derogatory voices could emanate from a harsh superego that fights the drives of the id, and advisory voices from a superego that has been somewhat soothed by the ego (Freud, 1924e).

Following and extending Freud's views, Bion argued that the mothering person (in Freud's terms, the "thing") inside people with psychosis, especially schizophrenia, is "dead" in the sense that, mainly during the infant's oral–sadistic stage, it cannot return the sadistic attacks or bad objects that have been projected to the mother by the infant's excessive projective identification in the form of good ("live") objects, but only as "dead" objects (Bion, 1962, 1967, 1992). Thus, infants and, later, patients are forced to use a destructive projective identification against themselves during the paranoid–schizoid position by fragmenting all internal processes of sensory impressions, perceptions, thought, and language as developed during entry into the depressive position. They place the fragmented parts of self (even words) to be encapsulated in external objects, and then reabsorb the encapsulated things or words (as things) by using projective identification in reverse. The senses are, thus, overwhelmed, resulting in visual and auditory hallucinations (Bion, 1963, 1967, 1992).

The psychodynamic-orientated group-psychotherapy approach to psychosis, on the other hand, has proved to be very effective. Yalom's (1970) supportive model is based mainly on inpatient groups of patients with schizophrenia and strongly emphasises crucial therapeutic factors, especially group cohesiveness and the instillation of hope. Smith's model (1999) suggests a mixed group of people with both schizophrenia and neurosis as being more effective. Of great relevance are psychodynamic models based on the ideas of Bion (Skolnick, 1999) and, finally, the group-analytic model as inspired by the theories of Foulkes. None of these models, however, including the group-analytic one as well as psychoanalytic approaches, has been used to treat patients who hear voices, and neither have they considered dreaming as an important means of achieving the therapeutic reconstitution of these patients. This might be due to the psychoanalytic conviction that people with psychosis are unable to dream, as stated mainly by Bion (1992). Contrary to Bion's view, in this chapter we will demonstrate that patients with psychosis, although they initially present themselves as unable to dream, progressively rediscover their ability to produce proper dreams, as long as their therapy evolves in the context of a heterogeneous group-analytic group.

Group analysis as a healing dreaming matrix: psychotic dreaming and hearing voices

In fact, Freud never questioned the ability of patients suffering from psychosis to dream normally. Psychotic dreaming, even in schizophrenia, despite its hallucinatory character, continues to be authentic because of the great similarities between dreaming as a neurotic activity and both the psychotic background of the primary process and psychosis itself (Freud, 1900a, 1911c, 1917d). In contrast, Bion (1967, 1992) believed that people suffering from psychosis tend to present as dreams their invisible–visual hallucinations. Patients with psychosis have suckled a "dead" breast (thus leading to a continuous hallucinated desire for it as real); this is why they can only produce dreams in the sense of morbid hallucinations, which are, in essence, minutely fragmented images of the mothering person that have been distorted by the patient through excessive projective identification and that persecute the patient in the paranoid–schizoid position. These images essentially lack "pictorial imagery" and "pictorial symbol" (Bion, 1992, pp. 46, 53). Through them, the production of an entire image, as happens in normal dreaming, is avoided because it would signify that the patient accepts experiencing the depressive position in the context of which the mothering person emerges as a murderous superego, a fact that would lead to severe depression.

Foulkes (1964), on the other hand, believed that dreams, whether produced by a patient suffering from psychosis or neurosis, are recounted in the group in order for the dreamer in the transference context (which is a morbid, psychotic-like state) to achieve a more personal symbiotic psychotic relationship with the group therapist or conductor of the group, who is represented imaginatively as an omnipotent archaic father/leader or God. It is hoped that any dream recounted, just like any other mode of group communication, will be progressively absorbed by the matrix of the group (Foulkes, 1964). The group process itself represents a dreaming process which evolves on a much more mature level than that of the individual dream, as analysed by Freud (1900a). This also favours the production of group dreams rather than individual dreams. The group dreaming matrix, like the individual dream, has two dimensions, the manifest content of communication and its latent meaning. However, the manifest content of group communication largely coincides with its latent meaning (one being more conscious than the other) and both are expressions of the group as a mature mothering person, which, together with the group therapist conceived as a father figure in the sense of conductor rather than of leader, represent adult social life (Foulkes, 1964). In any case, dreams are expressed following the evolution of the group from the primordial archaic to the current level. The ideal for the group is to achieve a fairly stable evolution on the current level. This level coincides with the awareness that the real strength relies on the empowerment of the group. The manifest content of the group matrix as dreaming matrix is much richer than the manifest content of the individual dream, since it contains and expresses the latter's major features on the level of group and human sociality. These features are group-specific factors, and include mirror phenomena and mirror reactions, or transposition phenomena, resonance, location, and others (Foulkes, 1964). It is in this sense that the group encourages its members to recount their dreams as a means of communication (Foulkes, 1964).

Under these premises, Foulkes was not expected to enlarge upon the contribution of the group to restoring the ability of patients with psychosis to dream. Nevertheless, group analytic principles, especially mirroring and communication (Gonzalez de Chavez, 2009) have all proved to be of great therapeutic relevance in either the supportive or the group-analytic Foulkesian group psychotherapy of schizophrenia in inpatient and outpatient settings alike. Despite this, there is no analytic reference in the literature to people hearing voices in a group, or how they dream, or how they regain the ability to dream. This absence motivated me to undertake in this chapter an initial analysis of the dreams of the patients who hear voices and participate in a heterogeneous group-analytic group. The effectiveness of group therapy for outpatients with psychosis, especially schizophrenia, was clearly verified in literature reviews (Kanas, 1986). Similarly, the treatment of people with schizophrenia in groups together with psychoneurotic patients has also proved effective (Hulse, 1958; Smith, 1999). An impressive feature was the rapidity with which patients with auditory verbal hallucinations in our group reconstituted their ability to produce a proper dream and, consequently, ceased hearing voices after some sessions. The main reason for this seems to have been the fact that a good enough mirroring existed between the free-floating discussions in the group conceived as a dreaming matrix (Lawrence & Biran, 2002) that functioned in the group as though on stage, and the significant dreaming and theatrical nature of the very act of hearing voices. This fact, once the patients decided to share their experiences with the group, soon led to the decompression of the patients' super-invested preconscious, the reinvestment of their unconscious with a "live" rather than "dead" new mothering object, according to the views of Freud (1915e) and Bion (1992), and, by extension, to the reconstitution of their ability to dream. Another factor that contributed strongly to this was that the group-analytic group was conducted in an analytic culture, without censorship, reflecting Foulkes' views (1948, 1964), which, given that the voices heard by the patients are usually derogatory, as though emanating from the severe superego of a primal carer, significantly favoured the patients' free associations and dream-telling in the group. However, the progress in rediscovering their ability to dream properly was better in patients of both sexes with schizophrenia than those with schizo-affective disorder; it was also better for men than women, which could be attributed to the fact that the women who heard voices in the group had been victims of incest in childhood, which is a particularly damaging trauma, strictly linked with the development of hallucinations, especially auditory ones, rather than delusions (Einsink, 1994; Read & Argyle, 1999).

Clinical example

Setting, membership, and therapeutic factors

The group to which we are referring here is already known from the previous chapter. It is a heterogeneous outpatient one that has been running continuously from 2000 to the present and has been structured in such a way as always to function as a mixed group of people with neuroses, psychoses, and psychosomatic illnesses. The group takes place in my private office in Athens once a week, since this helps patients with psychosis to assimilate the group progressively as a good enough mothering figure. In accordance with a modified group-analytic theory that comprises supportive and cognitive–behavioural elements more than an analytical interpretative stance, the group is conducted by one therapist, me, with the patients having entered it after some months or years of individual psychotherapy with me.

All members with psychosis and auditory verbal hallucinations—except George—entered the group gradually as new members. Kostas, who has completed his therapy successfully, has stopped hearing voices and continues to take a minimum of medication. Sofia has terminated her medication somewhat prematurely but, despite the severity of her illness, has stopped hearing voices; she completed her therapy in 2010. Kate and Nikos are the other two members who hear voices. Both stopped hearing voices some months after entering the group. George is the other (founding) member with paranoid schizophrenia and does not hear voices. Despite the severity of his illness, the prognosis has improved. He completed his therapy successfully in 2008. All the members with psychosis take the medication prescribed by their psychiatrist, who referred them to me. Some of them have been hospitalised. They all live alone or with their primary family. Kate has been diagnosed with schizo-affective disorder, Sofia and Kostas with schizophrenia, and Nikos with schizophrenia together with severe depression, all based on *DSM-4* (American Psychiatric Association, 1994) and "comprehensive assessment of symptoms and history" (CASH) diagnostic criteria (Andreasen et al., 1992). For all members, the severity of hearing voices was further confirmed by their completing the "psychotic symptoms rating scales" (PSYRATS) and the "beliefs about voices questionnaire-1" (BAVQ-1) (Chadwick et al., 2000; Haddock et al., 1999). The members have also completed the "childhood trauma questionnaire" (CTQ) developed by Bernstein and Fink (1998). It verified that Kate was sexually abused by her father, while Sofia was probably seduced by her brother during their early childhood.

Sofia, a twenty-six-year-old social worker, after entering university, kept hearing voices of either men or women inside her head. The voices openly accused her of being "dirty", while others very confusingly reported something like "a brother annoyed his sister from behind".

Kate, forty-two years old, an economist, heard voices continuously from outside her head. They were "various groans" or something like "voices and breathing".

Kostas, a thirty-three-year-old electronics engineer, starting in late adolescence, when he had his first psychotic episode, kept hearing voices either inside or outside his head inciting him to murder his father through the hissed message: "Kill him".

Nikos, an electronics technician, twenty-seven years old, suffers from hearing the voices of "little people" inside his head. The "little people" also mock him from outside his head, by telling him he is totally useless. Nikos was hospitalised twice and has been taking medication ever since.

George, twenty-six years old and a mathematician, had developed severe paranoid schizophrenia from his early adolescence, which was mainly a delirium of omnipotence that continuously led him to believe he was God. He was hospitalised twice after his attempts to commit suicide and was constantly and systematically in medication throughout his therapy.

The other four members of the group were all present during the phases of group therapy described below (between 2002 and 2008), together with the patients suffering from psychosis. Three of them continue their therapy and one, Michael, has bid a successful farewell to the group. All these members suffered from neurotic disturbances. Michael, a thirty-nine-year-old merchant, married and the father of a young child, suffered from depression, obsessive compulsive disorder, and panic attacks. Anita, fifty-eight years old, a retired teacher, was married and had a son, thirty-two years old, a physician who suffered from paranoid psychosis. She suffered from depression. Lila, a thirty-six-year-old nurse, married and the mother of a young child, suffered from agoraphobia as a borderline personality disorder. Panos, thirty-one years old and an unmarried mathematician, suffered from obsessive–compulsive disorder and psychosomatic symptoms.

Over the six years or so in which the above members were together in the group, a high level of group dynamics and intercommunication developed between themselves and between them and the conductor, based mainly on trust, sharing, and familiarity as a consequence of mutual benign mirroring and resonance. The analysis of these phenomena is not within the scope of this chapter, and neither can we further discuss the therapeutic interventions and stance of either the conductor or of the group as a whole, the main emphasis here being on the development of the group's dreaming matrix and the healing power it contains in itself. Of great relevance was also the mutual understanding that developed among all members, irrespective of whether they suffered from neurosis or psychosis. It is worth noting that this climate greatly helped patients hearing voices as it enabled them to express their experience in front of the group and then to stop hearing voices when the group responded by telling them that the voices were, in fact, the patients' own inner thoughts, an inner dialogue like the dialogues within the group, and that the patients should accept them as an experience of this kind. Then there was the dreaming matrix that developed progressively in the group as the neurotic members began to recount their dreams, the majority of which consisted of group dreams, which further helped the patients with psychosis who were hearing voices to strongly resonate with the latter with the result that they stopped hesitating and progressively began to recount their first dreams. These dreams were psychotic in nature, but, as the group evolved from the primordial (oral) to the projective and transference or current level, or from the paranoid–schizoid position to the depressive position (Bion, 1992; Klein, 1946), they gradually acquired the features of neurotic dreaming based on rich symbolism and refined imagery as described by Freud (1900a). Below, I shall refer selectively to some instances of the evolution of the group's dreaming matrix, indicating the progress of patients who heard voices in reconstructing their ability to dream.

First phase

As long as the members and the group re-experienced the oral–sadistic stage, which lasted about one year or so, the dreams recounted by even the healthiest neurotic patients expressed their oral needs of dependence on the conductor or on the group, as Foulkes (1964) argued. In contrast, the dreams recounted by the patients with psychosis expressed their hallucinations directly or indirectly or, in the case of patients with auditory verbal hallucinations, their experience of hearing voices, as Bion (1992) noted. Thus, during one of the sessions in the group's second year, a significant dreaming matrix was developed through the dynamics of fear on the part of most members toward the group and the conductor. Michael said that he had dreamed about "dogs who were the same colour as the shirt worn by our conductor". This dream clearly revealed Michael's fear of being castrated by the group or the conductor on the pre-oedipal or oedipal level, respectively. Lila said she dreamed that "I was digging deep into a tunnel, and I found a sword and a lot of jewellery". It was a dream that the group and the conductor translated as Lila's effort to rediscover her repressed female identity. George said that he, too, had a dream: "I dreamt I was God", a dream that openly expressed the patient's constant hallucination. After George, Kostas talked about his dream. "It was probably like I was killing some relative." This dream represented the basic message passed on by the voices he heard. Kate told the group that she dreamed "a lot of voices and groans", like the voices she kept hearing that probably represented the voice and groans of her father, by whom she had been sexually abused. Sofia said she dreamed "that my mother was naked with a penis in front". Her dream seemed rather like a hallucination in waking hours through which the terrible masculinity that had led to her sexual seduction by her brother was transposed to her mother. Nikos, in contrast, instead of a dream, preferred to refer, in a minute and expressive way, to the process of hearing voices, which was very similar to the process of neurotic dreaming (paradoxical though it sounds, Nikos was well aware of how the normal dreaming process works by contrasting it to his own experience of hearing voices!):

> Different voices can be heard, as though some people were speaking, one behind me, the other beside me and making fun of me. "You're a piece of garbage" they keep telling me, "you're worth nothing." I insult them, too. There is somebody else who's laughing so hard that he makes me laugh, too. It's like a dream, but not exactly, because in a dream you can see the faces, but here you can't see them, you can only hear their voices. You might be able to distinguish something out of the corner of your eye, but you can't see clearly. Basically, it's the voices. You can hear them and see that their lips aren't moving at all, as in the dream, Here too, like the dream, you can see that their mouth isn't moving but you can hear the words.

Shortly after this description, Nikos remembered that he also had had a dream that night: "I dreamed that I was shouting at my father and quarrelling with my mother." It was evident that while the experience of hearing voices, as described above, was similar to the manifest content of a dream, what was expressed later as a dream was, in fact, something like the latent content of the unconscious thoughts and desires of daily life. Nikos' desire to have a confrontation with his father and mother and to differentiate himself from them was strongly censored by a severe parental superego that led to his hearing voices in the sense that it was not Nikos shouting at his parents, but the voices of his parents, who despised him.

Second phase

During the second projective phase of the group-analytic process, which coincides with the anal–sadistic stage or paranoid–schizoid position and lasts for between one and two years, interspersed with tendencies of backsliding to the oral–sadistic stage or going forward to the phallic stage or to the depressive position (Bion, 1992; Klein, 1946), the dreams recounted by the non-psychotic members became more group dreams than personal ones, while, at the same time, the dreams of patients with psychosis who hear voices lost much of their hallucinatory nature and began to acquire an initial representational character, like neurotic dreams on the paranoid–schizoid position level.

In one group session during this period, in which most members experienced a lot of paranoid anxiety, with the group as a somewhat persecutory figure, Lila said, "I dreamed about the group. It was something like a bum or anus." It was a dream that expressed the group's anal phase. Panos recounted the following dream: "I was sitting in our group. I take out a knife and throw it at the conductor." The attack on the conductor with the knife as symbol expressed persecution anxiety (paranoid–schizoid position) leading to the preliminary transition to the depressive position. Sofia said she dreamed "that I am sleeping on my stomach and a knife comes from above and pierces me". This dream expressed in a significant symbolic form her fear of being sexually abused from behind, which was also the content of her hearing voices. George also remembered a dream: "I dreamed I went to see some fish or a ship that I was travelling on." The tone of his voice indicated that he had begun to feel safer in the group conceived as a ship and the members represented as fish.

Third phase

When the group has achieved a somewhat stable transition to the depressive position, which is the third phallic phase and continues to develop in parallel with the paranoid–schizoid position after some years of therapy, it is a significant and simultaneously critical period for all members, especially patients with psychosis. As this phase is strongly correlated with the major issue of separation–individuation (Mahler, 1968), with castration anxieties and fears on the oedipal level, and with conflicts linked to oedipal antagonism in general (Foulkes, 1964), emotional states of great tension, grief, and bereavement prevail in the group. Things become more complicated by the fact that some members think of ending their therapy and preparing a farewell. At the same time, new members had entered the group. Meanwhile, Sofia, George, and Michael discussed the possibility of bidding farewell to the group in the future. So, it was logical that, during this phase, the content of dreams, usually group dreams (in which the group is represented as itself or as a carriage, church, or theatre) as recounted mainly by patients with neurosis, included their father's or mother's death as a means of separation–individuation from their parents and identification with the parent of the same sex, and in combination with marriage (meaning identification with one's own sex) or of castration anxiety as a result of the desire of men for the women in the group and the conductor's anger thus engendered. In many dreams of this period, both separation–individuation and castration anxiety appears through the symbolism of teeth that are falling out, which is a customary related symbolism, according to Freud (1900a).

In one of the sessions during this period, Lila said, "I dreamed I saw a dead man, probably my father. I think it was in something like a carriage and many of you were there." Anita also said, "I dreamed about a dead man like my father." Michael said, "I dreamed that my mother had died." Anita said, "I dreamed about my teeth falling out." Panos said, "I dreamed I was in something like a church, together with the women in the group. I was going to molest them, but our conductor cut me off. And then I had another dream, that I was marrying my mother." Kate and Kostas had no dreams for a long time during this period. George said that he had a dream. It was a hallucination, but this time in a more evolved form of a group dream, in which the group was a church, the conductor was Christ, and George was God:

> I went into a church and was on the right (his usual place in the group). Christ appeared beside me. He asked me to give him the coat I was wearing. I didn't. "I'm God too', I told him."

Sofia also had a dream. It signified the symbolic death–killing of parents in the group represented as theatre:

> I was in a theatre. I was sitting with some other people. It was dark and on the stage there were two posts on which were the heads of two unknown people. And then the heads died.

But among the dreams of patients with psychosis and/or hearing voices, the dreams showing the most progress were those recounted by Nikos. They all referred to two major symbols indicating a considerable degree of acceptance of castration on the oedipal level, such as hair-cutting and/or losing teeth (Freud, 1900a), with exemplary neurotic imagery. "I dreamed that I was bald but my father had grown hair." At the end he added, "I dreamed that my teeth were becoming loose".

Conclusions

Group-analytic psychotherapy, as conducted in a mixed group comprising patients with neurosis, psychosis, and psychosomatic symptoms, provides decisive help to patients hearing voices as they gradually reconstruct their ability to produce proper neurotic dreams with exemplary symbolism and imagery on the phenomenological level. The patients' auditory verbal hallucinations might perhaps be linked with a thoroughly "bad" object as described by Klein (1946) or a "dead" object inside them according to Bion (1992), or a super-invested preconscious rather than an invested unconscious, according to Freud (1915d,e), due either to their malign symbiosis with a mothering person and devaluation of the father figure, or to their maltreatment by indifferent or strict and derogatory significant others, or, in the case of women patients, to their sexual abuse by the latter. Although the prognosis was better for patients with schizophrenia than for those with schizo-affective disorder, and better for men than women (indicating that sexual abuse leads almost inevitably to serious trauma), reconstituting the ability to dream in patients who hear voices was significantly enhanced by the deep dream-like similarity between the act of hearing voices and the matrix of the group, which, by its very nature, evolves in the form of a dreaming matrix.

CHAPTER ELEVEN

The ontology and phenomenology of dreaming in psychosis: a group-analytic approach with a neuropsychological perspective[*]

Introduction

In this chapter, I elaborate further the idea previously discussed, which was first presented systematically in my book (Koukis, 2004), that group analysis can help patients suffering from psychosis to reconstruct their ability to dream, thereby easing their symptoms. In addition, by utilising the questions arising from the analysis as a whole, I briefly indicate the directions in which the deficit in the phenomenology of dreaming in psychosis, especially the attempt to reconstitute it through group analysis, could be further investigated by neuroscientific research.

In his mature work, Freud (1917d) believed that people with schizophrenia totally lack the ability to dream because their unconscious has been de-invested of representations of thing, the cornerstone of dreaming. This is not the case in paranoia, in which the ontology of dreaming, which is depiction of the fantasy of the primal scene, and is regarded as the umbilical cord of dreaming in both

---

[*] First published in 2015 in *Psychology Research*, 5(3): 153–160.

neurotic and psychotic patients (Freud, 1918b), together with its phenomenology, which is mainly based on the transformation of the ontology into relevant imagery, remain essentially intact even though they are presented in a hallucinated way (Freud, 1911c). For Freud, dreaming was a psychotic-like process, which in the case of neuroses was transcended by the fact that its ontology was effectively repressed by depicting it with refined imagery on the phenomenological level. In his later work, however, leaving aside the role of the primal scene fantasy, Freud analysed dreaming solely as a phenomenological product whose sole remote ontological substratum was the neurotic subject's repressed oedipal desires, as initially studied in his *Interpretation of Dreams* (Freud, 1900a).

Klein (1935, 1940) restated the value of reproducing the fantasy of the primal scene in dreams. For her, dreams normally have a psychotic nucleus, since they clearly depict the dreamer's attack on the fantasy of the primal scene that has emerged during the oral–sadistic stage and tends to develop as the idea of a mature parental union in the paranoid–schizoid position and especially in the depressive position. The evolution of dreaming from representing parental intercourse in a persecuting way (paranoid–schizoid position) to representing it in a way that indicates acceptance of the parents' symbolic death (depressive position) marks the transition from psychotic dreams to dreaming proper.

Bion (1967, 1992) further explored Klein's views on dreaming. For him, contrary to Freud, the ontological nucleus of dreaming is not desire but the imagery of the primal scene, which is the phenomenology of dreaming. Dreams are the inner projections of visual images of the mothering person that resulted from a good enough suckling during early infancy, and from images of the fantasy of the primal scene in its highest form as it evolved from a simple sensual experience into an "ideogram" and algorithm of the parental union, and marks the transition from the oral stage to the paranoid–schizoid position and the depressive position as a mature oedipal situation (Bion, 1992, pp. 52, 64). He sees dreaming, or "dream-work-alpha" (for the sake of brevity "dream-work-α", or α) as the ability to digest mentally the primeval psychic material (the need for the breast as real) day and night and consists of re-suckling at the breast on a symbolic level and of interacting with it through the projective identifications developed with the primordial mother as a means of communication and as a prototype of linking by projecting visual images (alpha-elements) on the dream screen, or as suckling by recounting dreams in a psychoanalytic session. Patients with psychosis are unable to dream (they lack the "dream-work-α"), because they can depict the primal scene solely as a sensual and fragmentary experience on the ontological level (Bion, 1992, pp. 62–68, 179–187). This is a result of the hallucinated suckling they received from a mother conceived as a "dead" object inside them, as a result of which they continuously desire (and retain a strong memory of) the breast as real thing. This is why they can only visualise the mother in the form of fragmented images (beta-elements) that persecute them during the paranoid–schizoid position. People with psychosis fragment the images in their dreams by means of excessive projective identifications against themselves. An image thus articulated would be equivalent to a mothering superego formed during the depressive position that proved to be murderous (Bion, 1992). Thus, psychotic dreams are only "invisible–visual hallucinations" (Bion, 1967, p. 96) that are projected on the therapist or the group through their recounting. Bion (1967, 1992) does not rule out the possibility that psychotic patients in psychoanalysis could, to some extent, depict the fantasy of the primal scene in an ideogram form, but, like Klein and Freud, he does not present any supporting material.

Foulkes (1964), on the other hand, although he has approached this issue only partially and presented few examples, argues that dreams constitute narcissistic encapsulations and are, therefore, by nature a psychotic process in either their neurotic or psychotic form. Dreaming by patients suffering from neurosis or psychosis can become a healthy activity only on condition that it is produced in the form of group dreams in a group-analytic group by expressing the quality of the dynamics in its matrix based on a number of group phenomena and factors, such as communication, resonance, condenser phenomena, mirror reactions and phenomena, transposition, etc. The phenomenology of this group communication, as expressed on the intermediate level or phase of the group's bodily and mental images (Freud's anal–sadistic stage or Klein's paranoid–schizoid position) and principally on the mature third current level or phase (Freud's phallic stage or Klein's depressive position), constitutes—unlike the ontology of the group as manifested on its first archaic or primordial (oral–sadistic) level or phase—a dreaming process that the members' dreams depict as group dreams.

Foulkes' approach, however, presents the formation of group dreams dogmatically, primarily on the group's current/neurotic level, as the only authentic form of dreaming, which creates a split between the individual and the social. Dreams of patients with neurosis or psychosis which, through group dreams, express the group as a reproduction of the fantasy of the primal scene on the primordial level, or as an idea of the parental union represented by the union of the therapist and the group on a more mature level, are totally neglected. Contemporary psychological research has verified the view that the origins of human sociality, of which dreaming is a basic manifestation, go as far as developing primordial defence mechanisms such as projection, splitting, or projective identification, as described by Klein and Bion (Thomas, 1996). To this we could also add archaic fantasies, such as that of the primal scene, as constituting the primeval nucleus of human linking. In this study, the role of the group in the production of dreams is reconsidered as a representation of the fantasy of the primal scene. The salient point of my argument is that it is this representation of the group that helps patients with psychosis in group analysis to reconstitute, to some degree, their ability to dream properly.

Dreaming as the evolution of the fantasy of the primal scene in the group

Introductory remarks

The quality of dreaming by patients with psychosis or neurosis is strongly correlated with the progressive evolution of the group from representing the imaginary union of therapist and group as a fantasy of the primal scene to representing the union of the conductor and the group as a highly symbolic idea of the parental couple. This evolution, which Bion (1992) regards as the oedipal fate of the primal scene, follows the evolution of the group from its oral stage to the paranoid–schizoid position and the depressive position, and of the therapist from a directive figure (leader of the group) to a conductor (leader in the group), trust in whom reveals the group's pre-eminent maturity, as described by Foulkes (1964).

This view does not imply that certain of the factors stressed by Foulkes are irrelevant. As noted in the previous chapter, the concept of the matrix, especially in its form as social dreaming matrix (Lawrence & Biran, 2002) has contributed greatly to familiarising psychotic patients with the group and inciting them to produce dreams. The dreaming matrix likewise functions, in Bion's terms (1962), as a container of the patients' projective identifications expressed by recounting dreams. It has also given the group a "capacity for reverie", a style that, according to Bion (1992, p. 53), characterises the good enough mother in particular but is lacking in the mother of patients with psychosis and, of course, in these patients themselves, while also helping the therapist, who needs to avoid any related interpretations. All these factors have contributed to the constitution of the group as a good enough mother in the oral–sadistic stage, which later favours a better negotiation between the paranoid–schizoid position and the depressive position and a better integration of the fantasy of the primal scene as the idea of the parental couple on the oedipal level.

Here, we shall briefly present the way in which two patients with psychosis, Sofia and George, were able to dream properly by depicting in their dreams the fantasy of the primal scene and its evolution towards the idea of combined parents, in accordance with the evolution of the members and the group as a whole from the oral–sadistic stage to the paranoid–schizoid and the depressive position. This process was assisted significantly by other patients recounting their dreams within the context of a dreaming matrix. The patients were members of a heterogeneous once-a-week group-analytic group (reported in the two previous chapters) running continuously from 2000 to the present. They entered the group after about three and four years, respectively, of once-a-week individual psychotherapy. Sofia is a social worker, twenty-six years old, who lives alone. Her symptoms included schizophrenic pathology such as hearing voices and believing that people kept talking about her on television. She entered the group as a new member and left it in 2010, after about six years of therapy, when her symptoms receded considerably and her ability to dream had been significantly reconstituted. George, a twenty-six-year-old mathematician, who also lives alone, was a founding member of the group. He suffered from acute paranoid psychosis. He usually imagined that he was God and was hospitalised twice. Through his individual and group therapy and medication, the symptoms progressively receded, there were no further hospitalisations, the ability to dream was sufficiently reconstructed, and George was able to bid a successful farewell to the group in 2008, after eight years or so of therapy.

First stage

During the first stage, which lasted from six months to one year or so, the patients' initial recounted dreams indicated that the fantasy of the primal scene, and of the group conceived as such, was either hidden in dreams that had all the features of delirium (George's dream), or was depicted in the form of another primary fantasy, such as that of the mother with the penis (Sofia's dream). Both dreams were somewhat similar to many dreams recounted by other members, who had entered the group recently and whose psychopathology ranged between severe neurosis and borderline states. In these dreams, the primal scene was presented as totally split, in the sense that the maternal body was depicted as a total of paternal penises (usually symbolised by snake images) and infants (symbolised by babies) that are "dead" (dreams of Jim and Christos). All dreams reveal that the primal scene cannot be represented because the patients' mirroring in the maternal object/group, and an initial benevolent split from it, is absent in this phase due to their fixation in the oral–sadistic stage and on the primordial level of the group. This is illustrated by one of Christos's dreams in which women and men, including the group therapist, are depicted without eyes. Through their recounting, dreams of this kind constitute destructive projective identifications that aim to stir up the corresponding primeval/psychotic experience which, at least in its initial phase, the group inevitably encompasses.

> *George*: It wasn't clear where and how, but I dreamed I was God.
>
> *Jim*: I dreamed that a snake was threatening me, or faces from the past that disappear quickly, and lots of babies and dead people.
>
> *Sofia*: I dreamed that my mother was naked with a penis in front.
>
> *Christos*: I saw men and women who have no eyes and that our therapist had no eyes.

Second stage

During the second stage, which lasted from about one to two years, the dreams of the patient who suffers from psychosis recounted in the group, in their form as either individual productions or, more often, as group dreams, evidently emerged from a first mirroring of the dreaming person with the group conceived as a good enough dreaming process. The dreams mainly express the paranoid anxiety that occurs in the paranoid–schizoid position, but the projective identification with the group, which is used to evacuate unwanted material, is now much milder. It can then be contained by the group and, in turn, supports the function of the group as container (Friedman, 2000).

The fantasy of the primal scene has begun to be represented specifically in a persecutory way, either in the form of the father's or mother's penis (symbolised by a knife) that tries to penetrate the patient from behind (Sofia's first dream), or as the fantasy of the mother with the penis in a milder, more effeminate form (Sofia's second dream). It can also take the form of the union of the conductor conceived as Christ and the group as church (i.e., as two good objects) within a state that continues to express delirium and in which the patient is still God (George's dream).

Importantly, these dreams do not differ essentially in content from the dreams reported by neurotic or borderline patients during the same period. A dream reported by Maria-Helena, a neurotic patient suffering from panic attacks, expressed the paranoid–schizoid position depicted as an attack against the patient by dogs (representing the conductor). The dreams of non-psychotic patients, however, differ from psychotic dreams in terms of the higher level of their representational quality and emotional tone, the finer selection of dream symbols, and the sophisticated use of language either in the process of dreaming itself or its narration.

> *Sofia*: I dreamed that I was sleeping on my stomach and, a knife comes from above and pierces me.
>
> *George*: I enter a church. I am wearing a long cloak. Suddenly Christ appears. He asks me to give him the cloak. I don't want to give it to him. "I am God, too", I say to him.
>
> *Sofia*: It was in a place sort of like where the group meets. Suddenly a naked woman appeared; she had a plastic vulva and inside this plastic thing was a penis, also plastic.
>
> *Maria-Helena*: I dreamed that a pack of dogs was coming toward me.

Third stage

During the third stage, in which the depressive position continues to develop uninterruptedly in the group in negotiation with the paranoid–schizoid position, the dreams reported by the patients suffering from psychosis seem to possess a number of neurotic features, thus indicating the patients' first sufficient, although unstable, entrance into the depressive position. Dreams are of a finer group character and are narrated through projective identification in the sense of a good enough communication, but lack any deeper emotional tone or associative process linked with the emotional experience. However, as the group (the maternal body) is now better represented, the patient is better mirrored in the group and is mirrored by it more effectively. The fantasy of the mother with the penis seems now to be sufficiently repressed, and this is helped by dreaming itself, by the mother allowing her penis to fall off (Sofia's first dream). After that, the primal scene, although it is still homosexual in nature as a union of two men (the father and the phallic mother), indicates the patient's first attempt to achieve the parents' symbolic death by using the depressive position, although in a wild archaic way (Sofia's second dream). In other cases, the primal scene is symbolised in dreams as the marriage of the person's parents (or the "marriage" of the conductor and the group), even though the couple either cannot be clearly discerned (George's first dream) or it is the friend's father, not the patient's father, who marries the patient's mother (George's second dream), or, later, as a marriage of his parents (or group and conductor) within the group as symbolised by a carriage in a way that indicates to some extent the parents' symbolic death (George's third dream).

Again, these dreams essentially lack the symbolic and imaginative plasticity that characterises the dreams of neurotic patients. For example, in Maria-Helena's dreams, the primal scene is symbolised by her own wedding linked with the symbolic death of her parents (or group and conductor).

> *Sofia*: I dreamt about a naked woman; in place of her pudenda was a very small penis that suddenly fell off.
>
> *George*: I dreamt I'd gone to a wedding, but couldn't figure out who the newlyweds were.
>
> *George*: I dreamt that the father of my friend married my mother.

George: I dreamt about a dead man, maybe my father. But then everything was like a wedding. It was inside something like a carriage and many of you were there.

Sofia: I was in a place like an ancient theatre. It was dark and on the stage there were two posts on which were the heads of two unknown men; the heads were alive. Then the heads died. And all the spectators including me applauded.

Maria-Helena: I dreamt that some people have died, maybe my parents. I'm preparing for the funeral and crying but suddenly I am to be married and getting ready to go and see about a wedding dress.

Conclusions and remarks about future neuroscientific research

Dreaming in psychosis, which is initially a hallucinatory or delusional activity, can evolve into dreaming with neurotic features in a heterogeneous group-analytic group, as first described by Foulkes (1964), thereby making a decisive contribution to the patient's therapy. Like dreaming in neurosis, it follows and expresses the group's evolution (conceived as the union of the therapist and the group as a whole) from the primordial level, on which it represents the fantasy of the primal scene as a sensual experience, to the final current level representing an ideal parental couple. These findings confirm the psychoanalytical view—which Freud (1918b) first expressed but then abandoned, and was later taken up by Klein (1935) and Bion (1992), but neglected by Foulkes—that the nucleus of dreaming, and by extension the basic means of transforming psychotic dreaming into a neurotic process, consists of representing the primal scene on an ever higher imaginative and symbolic level. However, the conclusion that for psychotic patients to visualise the primal scene in their dreams, according to the evolution of the group, entails a real reconstitution of their ability to dream should be accepted with some reservations. In fact, we are still a long way from the possibility of helping patients with psychosis to dream in the way patients with neurosis do. Although the latter's dreams also express the primal scene on the ontological level, the phenomenology of neurotic patients' dreams is much more sophisticated in the use of language, imagery, and symbolism than that of dreams by patients with psychosis.

What, then, is the factor missing in the primal emotional experience, as lived and spoken of by patients with psychosis, that hinders the transformation of the ontology of dreaming, that is, its archaic reality, into a phenomenology based on high quality sublimations of the ontological substratum in the form of refined imagery and vivid dream content? Neuroscientific research has already verified Freud's views of a core common to dreaming and psychosis (Gottesmann, 2006; Hobson, 2004; Scarone et al., 2008) and important neuroscientific studies have been conducted about dreaming processes in psychosis. Further extension of this research would, thus, be of great help in elucidating the above question. To what extent, for example, is the lack of any phenomenological articulation of psychotic dreaming related to an enduring memory of, and desire for, a real breast, as Bion argues, and in what respects are psychotic memory and desire the result of either the defective inhibition of dream memory due to pathological alterations linked with the action of vasotocin in the brain (Kelly, 1998) or the representation of a failure of the superior temporal and inferior parietal deactivation (Fletcher et al., 1998)? Or, should we elaborate on the hypothesis first formulated by Crick and Mitchison (1983) and Hopfield and colleagues (1983) that, in the case of psychotic patients, some potential memories have not been eliminated before being stored in the long-term memory, thus resulting in inefficient memory processing, which, in turn, seems to be linked with the hypothesis of reduced cerebral metabolism in frontal areas due to the reductions of synaptic density caused by excessive axonal pruning (Feinberg, 1982–1983; Hoffman & Dobscha, 1989)? Or should we link the lack of imagery in psychotic dreaming to the fact that people with psychosis develop hallucinatory activity during waking hours (which, according to Bion, is also a dream-like activity), instead of during rapid eye movement (REM) sleep, owing to serotonin depletion (Dement et al., 1969; Zarcone et al., 1975)? In addition, could any phenomenological deficiency in psychotic dreaming—since it inevitably involves the patient's inability to be mirrored by other people or to mirror them—be interpreted in terms of a deficiency in the mirror neurons system (Rizzolatti & Craighero, 2004)? And is the mirror neurons system sufficient to explain the production of group dreams conceived as encompassing a system of multi-mirroring processes among people (Schermer, 2013)? At the same time, could this system verify individual dreams as psychotic by-products, as

Foulkes (1964) maintained, or could it explain the fundamental role played by the fantasy of the primal scene—as primarily based on the mirroring between parents and child—in the formation of dreams in psychotic and neurotic patients alike? Last but not least, given the strong similarities between psychosis and normal dreaming, could the lack of phenomenological elaboration in psychotic dreaming be conceived as a disturbance which is simply greater than that occurring in neurotic dreaming but qualitatively on the same continuum with it, which was Freud's hypothesis, or should it be considered as a quantitatively different disturbance which is much more serious than the disturbance provided by neurotic dreaming, as Bion has maintained?

These are some of the basic questions arising from the above analysis, which future psychoanalytic and group-analytic research should investigate through the appropriate use of neuropsychology, neuropsychoanalysis, and psycholinguistics, to ascertain whether or not the findings reported here can be further validated and open new perspectives in understanding psychosis and, by extension, in approaching it more effectively through psychotherapy.

PART IV

GROUP ANALYSIS AND ITS RELATIONSHIP WITH THE SOCIAL UNCONSCIOUS AND ART

CHAPTER TWELVE

Desire and despair in postmodern times: aspects of the social unconscious in a declining world and the significance of group analysis for future prosperity

Desire as an ideal psychosocial construct and its modern decline

Despite centuries of evolution, human thought was never sufficiently concerned with desire to formulate a definition of it, until the development of psychoanalysis. It was Freud (1900a) who first initiated a systematic study of desire as disguised and expressed mainly through dreams. Inspired by Plato's ideal of Eros, Freud associated desire with libido, mainly conceived as "desexualised Eros" (Freud, 1923b, p. 44). He linked the roots of desire primarily to the infant's desire for the parent of the opposite sex, as manifested in the oedipal state, and concluded that, although it initially constitutes an inter-individual and family state, desire gradually acquires a mature social form when the child resolves his or her Oedipus complex and can then progress to the mature selection of a non-parental love object (Freud, 1905d, 1923e, 1924d).

However, since the social dimension of Freud's concept of desire is associated with resolution of the Oedipus complex (1924d), desire in its initial form is limited to the individual level, causing it to lack many of its characteristic social aspects, and independently of its psychobiological roots. This is why Freud's idea of libido, despite its Platonic idealistic parameters, is fundamentally based on the force of impulses or instincts, the concept of a frontier between the mental and the physical that, although represented by thoughts and ideas in the unconscious, never loses its biological substratum. Thus, the meaning of the libido/Eros/sexuality remained necessarily bound to the idea that desire is simply to want something, especially in the biological sense (Freud, 1915c,e).

From the mid-twentieth century on, Freud's thought was extended by Lacan, who investigated desire in depth, giving it a social dimension that went beyond the strict limits of individuality as determined by psychobiological premises. Like Freud, Lacan accepted the oedipal dimension of desire. He, too, recognised that the roots of desire go back to the infant's bond with its mother as primary object, and tried to define desire as resulting from the resolution of the Oedipus complex (post-oedipal state) by differentiating it from the two mental states that precede it: the need for the mother as feeding person (pre-oedipal level, oral–sadistic stage) and the demand for her love as loving person (pre-oedipal and oedipal level) (Lacan, 1988, 1994, 1998b, 2006b). According to him, the human infant is initially in a state of need for the mother as breast. Lacan calls this the state of "real" ("réel") in the sense that the mother/object is exclusively linked with bodily reality, which is not invested with the imaginary aspects that will be developed later through the infant's mirroring with her and lead, following the relevant views of Freud (1924e), as expressed in a different perspective, in their union with her symbolic aspects, to the constitution of the reality principle. Later, on a higher level, that is, the mirror stage (Lacan, 2006a), the infant arrives at a state of demand for love as provided not only through suckling, but also through the "good" or "bad" image of self that the mother reflects to the child. This level, which was also explored by Klein in terms of the infant's relation with the "good" or "bad" breast (Klein, 1937, 1946), is based on the fact that the two parts of the primal dyad exchange images of themselves according to what they imagine the other to be. This is what Lacan calls an imaginary level (Lacan, 1994, 1998b, 2006a, 2006c). As we have already seen, in Freud's terms, both states represent the undifferentiated mother-as-thing, as a real body by which one can be nourished physically and emotionally. According to Lacan, it is at the imaginary level that desire begins to be constructed in the sense that

DESIRE AND DESPAIR IN POSTMODERN TIMES   179

the infant desires to be its mother's desire. Yet, desire in its proper form presupposes transcendence of the state of the imaginary. This transcendence is based on the infant having been weaned from its mother's breast (real), and on the child's perception of its mother as an oedipal or imaginary mother (an object of desire in its imaginary form), at the limits of experiencing the oedipal state. The resolution of this state—through the symbolic castration that takes place mainly through the father—leads both sexes to recognition of and identification with the father or mother as symbolically "dead", that is, as representing not real or imaginary entities strictly linked to their bodily presence, but to the idea of fatherhood and motherhood disengaged from the parents' physical presence and linked to their symbolic absence (symbolic mother, symbolic father). This is what Lacan refers to as the symbolic level (Lacan, 1994, 1998b).

However, for Lacan, resolution of the Oedipus complex is not in itself sufficient to allow the human being to reach the state of desire, because, despite this resolution, the subject continues to be fixated on the mother-as-thing. For the subject to have access to desire, a symbolic castration is required that is broader than that of the oedipal level. It can only be achieved through the subject's profound awareness that the mother-as-thing is forever impossible to attain and that this castration is enforced by a law that, as noted previously in this book, is not only imposed by the subject's personal father, but also pre-exists in societies in the form of the general symbolic paternal order, which is the law of the signifier, the language that exists in the form of a paradigmatic axis on which the human infant lives from the moment of its birth. This order is the Name-of-the-Father, a set of names of the father expressed through social institutions (Juranville, 1984; Lacan, 1998b, 2004, 2006c).

More analytically, according to Lacan, a primordial signifier, the signifier of the Other, exists in the universe as well as in the unconscious (individual or personal) in the form of God, Mother, Being, or something else, and is represented by the Phallus (Φ), a symbolic power in its absolute symbolic as well as imaginary form. Individuals and societies at the very early stages of their development are completely identified with absolute Phallus. This is a state of absolute fusion and chaos in the sense that, since the phallus cannot be symbolised to engender meaning, it leads the subject and societies to the sole desire to be the desire of the Other/Phallus, that is, to be possessed by the Phallus, which they then try to impose on others at the level of total inadequacy and lawlessness. This would be potentially disastrous for societies, leading them to succumb to absolute socio-political powers and authorities that disorganise the symbolic order on which they must be founded. Yet, for the Phallus to function in a positive and constructive way, thus engendering symbolic meaning, the subject and the society must undergo castration in its absolute possession (symbolic castration) and represent the Phallus as a means of producing meaning in conventional everyday life, that is, as a partial signifier ($-\varphi$) which imposes the law directly. The law as partial signifier is none other than the signifier of the Other, who has accepted symbolic castration from the outset, that is knowing that he cannot possess the Phallus in its absolute form. And, because he recognises the absence of the absolute Phallus, he can represent it symbolically, thereby giving the Phallus its symbolic dimension and society its symbolic order. This Other, or signifier, is the idea of father or, rather, the Name-of-the-Father. This means that at the individual level, the infant arrives at the level of desire when it ceases to identify with the Phallus in its absolute (imaginary) form, or the Other in its non-castrating dimension, with whom the infant identifies initially, which is the mother as an object of its need and demand for love, and thus is able to identify later with the Name-of-the-Father (Juranville, 1984; Lacan, 1988, 1993, 1994, 1998b, 2006c). The Other, in the sense of an imaginary and absolute Phallus, could also be the father to the degree that he has not accepted symbolic castration. Rejection, or rather "foreclosure" ("forclusion") of the Name-of-the-Father in the subject's psychology leads to absolute fixation on the mother-as-thing and then to psychosis (Lacan, 1993).

It follows that desire is desire for the Other's desire, not in the sense of desire to be the phallus of the Other, but, rather, desire for the desire of the person who has accepted symbolic castration. This is why the law simultaneously prohibits and demands desire: it prohibits desire as a person's drive to possess the mother-as-thing absolutely, but also as the mother's drive to be the absolute phallus. Yet, the law also imposes desire, in the sense of the charm exerted by the mother-as-object on the imaginary level, so that when the imaginary is somewhat moderated by castration, the person gains access to the symbolic/paternal order (Lacan, 2006b). This implies that the imaginary element, in the form of either mother/object and her surrogates or things/commodities in which the mother/object is reflected and represented, is an essential prerequisite of the symbolic element. By desiring in this way, the person arrives at recognition of the symbolic element as expressed in different social forms, and recognises both himself and the Other as social beings with their own personal desire rather than as beings determined by need and demand. This means that desire in Lacan (1988, 2006b) is the person's desire for recognition in the social context, or to be recognised as a desiring subject by another desiring subject. Thus, desire, as the cornerstone of the unconscious social processes corresponding to what Hegel (1977), on the philosophical level, calls self-consciousness as the foundation of society, is the tendency of the mind—which is no more than an expression of the evolution of the Spirit governing history—to be recognised as free by another mind, and, thus, to become conscious of itself.

On the basis of Lacan's views, it can be said that the individual's desire is, to a considerable degree, socially constructed; its content is determined by the prevailing cultural and social values. Every society has its own mode of desiring, which is unconsciously imposed by the socio-political and economic structure and by the interpersonal relationships that develop within this structure. In this sense, Hopper, in his investigation of the social unconscious (Hopper, 1997, 2001), connects desire, in its lower form of insatiability and achievement, with social mobility, in which "mobility might be a source of interpersonal experiences that were likely to cause insatiability for economic status and political power" (Hopper, 1981, p. 5). In this chapter, I support the view that the dominant form of desire in contemporary postmodern societies has ominously lost the symbolic form that had largely been achieved during the modern era, since what is manifested and put forward as desire is no more than a disguised form of need (real) and demand (imaginary). This, in turn, means that, in postmodern societies, the subject, and, by extension, the society as a whole, has, to a large extent, lost the ability to repress need and demand. In other words, need and demand (unconscious level) have come to the conscious level, as in psychosis (Bion, 1992). This is one of the reasons why the Name-of-the-Father is in decline in modern societies (Koukis, 2009). In order for desire to function and be creative for the individual and society alike, and to avoid need and demand in the sense described above, it must always be repressed sufficiently, as outlined by Freud or Lacan (Freud, 1915d; Lacan, 2006b). In this case, it is not desire itself that is repressed, but, rather, desire in its absolute form, because of which desire could regress to the states of need or demand. After being repressed, desire in this sense can resurface in as pure a form as possible. Repression helps the subject not to grab the desired object (which is merely a substitute for the mother's body) immediately, as a needy or demanding person or social system might do, and, in this way, the subject learns to postpone gratification. The benefit resulting from delayed gratification on a personal and social level is incalculable. The need and/or demand for love, which is strictly related to insatiability, results in devouring and draining the object, whether commodities or human relations, or, in Klein's terms, the mother-as-breast, thus leading to profound despair due to profound guilt over the object that has been destroyed (Klein, 1937). Consequently, satisfaction of the need and demand for love causes desire to atrophy. The person regresses to a narcissistic state and is cut off from relations with others and from the community that is assumed to maintain the balance between the tendency to insatiability and the desire for relatedness.

On the basis of the above analysis, we can now explore more specifically both the ways in which desire has deviated from its genuine symbolic position in the transition from the industrial to the post-industrial society and how group analysis can make a significant contribution to restoring desire to its rightful position.

Desire and despair: from modernity to postmodernity

Since its earliest historical forms, society has made a decisive contribution—through laws, institutions, and ideologies that favoured frustration—to helping people repress the deeper search for mother-as-thing, that is, need and demand, finding in this way an access to desire. Since mother-as-thing can only be a "dead" object, an object of need that cannot be imagined or symbolised, it can be said that societies unconsciously understood that desire, as long as it transcended the search for mother-as-thing, always kept the object "alive", and, in this way, the object itself remained "alive", meaning that the object is imagined as something beyond need and demand, and, by extension, as something that could fulfil the requirements of the symbolic order. Under these conditions, the object, in the form of either commodity or personal social achievement or relatedness, was never fully acquired, so the subject was obliged to keep struggling to obtain it. Here, a balance is created between what Lacan (1988, 1993, 1994, 1998b, 2004, 2006c) called the real (mother-as-thing, as an object of pure need), the imaginary (mother as a primarily loved and admired person and as the exclusive instrument of producing meaning at the imaginary level through personal or social discourse), and the symbolic (language which, since it is detached from the continuous search for meaning in its imaginary sense, imposes castration on the imaginary and is expressed by the father) (Žižek, 1989).

It should be assumed that keeping this dialectic in balance was a fundamental condition for the generation of hope and the avoidance of profound psychotic despair on the part of individuals and societies alike. In Lacanian terms, psychotic despair could stem from an overwhelming predominance of one factor over the other, that of the real, which, in fact, is the domain of the unsymbolised and non-imaginary (common in all psychoses), that of the imaginary, when the powerful frustration that follows its contradiction by reality, in conjunction with lack of the symbolic, would plunge the subject again into despair and from there into the real (as in the case of paranoia), or that of the symbolic, which, having ossified the imaginary that is the moving force of the symbolic, would have taken the form of a "dead" symbolic similar in many ways to the real (as in the case of schizophrenia). On the contrary, the increased balance between the three retains the hope that the object, although forbidden, has not been lost, thus minimising frustration and leading to a moderate and bearable despair. Since this kind of despair is sometimes connected with the development of neurosis and with a neurotic state, it can be assumed that neurosis was the minimum price societies had to pay in their effort to set limits to need and demand and to bring their desire to fruition.

There is reason to believe that this balance between the real, the imaginary, and the symbolic culminated in the period of industrial capitalism. This society, in comparison with earlier ones, had the appropriate economic and political structure within which a relatively balanced dialectic was created between the real, the imaginary, and the symbolic. This did not preclude the possibility that the dialectic in question would become disorganised and lead to destruction, which would then be followed by a period of creation and reconstruction until destruction returned, as in a vicious circle. One might say that the dialectic between the real, imaginary, and symbolic was based on what Marx (1906) called "reification" ("Verdinglichung") as expressed in industrial capitalism (Žižek, 1989). According to Marx, owing to the new capitalist relationship developed between commodities and their exchange value, which coincided with the amount of labour and time spent on their production, plus the amount of ideational value or money that they cost (symbolic level), the commodities ceased to be objects with simple use value (real level) and appeared to be invested, in some supernatural and mystic way, with the social relationship developed by human beings as producers. These relationships were then reflected by the commodities, as social relationships belonging to them by nature as the phantasmagoric form of relationships between things.

In this sense, an equilibrium was created between the real, imaginary, and symbolic in the economic sense of an equilibrium between supply and demand (need, demand for love, which is the real and imaginary level) and the purchasing power achieved through money (desire, symbolic level), in such a way as to be favourable to the development of capitalism, while minimising crises as much as possible. It is testified by the fact that, as Max Weber (1930) showed, during this period, following the ideology imposed by the spirit of Protestantism, the earning of money was constantly considered as a result of virtue and avoidance of all spontaneous enjoyment of life. Yet, it was a risky and borderline dialectic that often led to an overspill of the imaginary (demand for love) as unbridled commercialisation (supply and demand), which, in turn, conduced to the absolute dominance of the real (need) and the destruction of both the imaginary and the symbolic (money). The causes of many of the wars waged in history, culminating in the two world wars that led people to the brink of despair, should be seen in this light, together, of course, with the other contributing factors. However, in industrial societies, a relatively stable balance between the three elements was maintained.

Through two unprecedented world wars, and from the mid-twentieth century on, the balance between the real, the imaginary, and the symbolic was reversed in such a way that it is now difficult to predict what paths it will take in the future. At the same time, the development of capitalism in its post-industrial form, especially after 1980–1990, led to the end of ideologies as sources by which the real is invested with the imaginary and symbolic, and to the serious dispute of liberal democracy as the system that stabilised this dialectic (Jameson, 1991; Mandel, 1978). The development of high-technology modes of production and the movement of capital in analogous forms have caused over-consumption to become a vital prerequisite for the survival of these societies. A kind of insatiability, linked with the fantasy that human resources are unlimited (a fantasy that is due to, and accompanied by, the regression of societies to a state of identification with the absolute Phallus), is thus created which, on the one hand, is a prerequisite for societal cohesion and, on the other, undermines society from within.

Over-consumption imposes the concept that desires must be gratified immediately, before they are even manifested. Although this could have led to a freer expression of desire (symbolic) through repression of the deeper need to devour (real level), it has, in fact, led to precisely the opposite, causing desire to be suppressed and, in some way, "deadened", and generating a great need to devour the commodity. It is as though the positions of desire and need have been reversed. Over-consumption has led subjects to a "symbiotic" relationship with the commodity, which covers both their need for food (real level) and their demand for love (imaginary level). In this sense, we can speak of the saturation of the imaginary through ceaseless consumption of the commodity. But this is a saturation of the imaginary that eventually turns in on and invalidates itself, with the result that the commodity, even though a great deal of imaginary power has been bestowed on it, is no more than a thing (real level). The object is no more than a breast that, after being used, is regarded merely as a thing, leaving the individual empty, without real satisfaction or gratification, and conducing to addiction and compulsive repetition. In Green's (1996) terms, the object resembles here the patched breast of a "dead" mother, a mother who is absorbed by her bereavement, thus leading the subject to a continuous search for her as a living person without whom life is meaningless (Kohon, 1999). By extension, human relations have become "reified", and this reality tends to be dangerously disengaged from imaginary and symbolic power (Žižek, 2006). All the symbolic means of expression, such as money, language, communication, etc., become merely signs used just to be used, in a manner that serves the investment process and leads to the domination of need (Jameson, 1991). Subjects are obliged to keep buying commodities ("shopping therapy"), without needing them, precisely because their desire is only the need to buy, meaning to devour the commodity. Marcuse (1964) had already predicted this when he stated that advanced industrial societies create false needs.

The above situation creates discontent in the subject, which is not the discontent of a neurotic subject, as described by Freud (1930a). Neurotic discontent stems from the conflict between the person's desire and the limitations favouring its repression that are imposed by civilisation; it could, thus, be considered a source from which hope is continuously generated for individuals and communities, and that is bound up with many options for future-making and self-fulfilment. On the contrary, the current discontent stems from a distortion of desire and hope, and gradually acquires the features of psychotic despair that could destroy our lives and the achievements of our civilisation.

This development has also reversed the existing balance between the real, the imaginary, and the symbolic that were invested in the notions of the individual and the group. Before entering the post-modern period, the subject, as Freud (1921c) has shown, was able to invest his or her desire in the group or in the leader, as representing, in Lacan's (1994, 1998b) terms, the mother and father, respectively, in a relatively harmonious co-ordination of their roles as real, imaginary, and symbolic parents. The subject was said to have become accustomed to seeing the leader (father) of the group (mother)—following Lacan's relevant dialectic as noted in Chapter Two—either as an imaginary father (deprives on the imaginary level the mother and, by extension, the child of the real possession of penis and of its symbolic dimension as phallus in order to help him later acquire it himself), or as an archaically real (castrates the child from being the mother's imaginary phallus/desire) and symbolic (real possessor of the phallus as signifying desire on the symbolic rather than the imaginary level) father. Freud's symbolic father is considered as a precursor of the symbolic father later conceived by Lacan as the Name-of-the-Father, a figure endowed with symbolic powers who would be capable of fostering all the elements in the group to promote its members' desire, which is also linked with promotion of the common good (Lacan, 1994, 1998b). Under the auspices of and with the protection provided by the father in the above three dimensions, the mother, or group as a representation of her, was also able to function as imaginary (sees the child as the phallic extension of herself, which is the main target of her desire), real (does not meet the child's demand for the breast, conceived as a demand for love, so as the breast becomes symbolic), and symbolic (frustrates the child from the breast as real on the level of need) mother. This helped the symbolic father/leader to achieve the symbolic castration of the child/citizen and, by extension, the mother/group as a somewhat morbid extension of the imaginary phallus, thus leading them to identify with the symbolic (desire) as the nodal point of the union of the real (need) and the imaginary (demand) as preponderantly representing the father. However, under postmodernism, the notion of globalisation might have dissolved the idea of the mother/group and the father/leader in their contemporary sense. The power of any group, local, social, or political, and that of its leader/father, is minimal in its genuine real, imaginary, and symbolic parameters. The group/mother is conceived only as an exuberant and hallucinatory globalised entity, or serves solely as a functional category expressing the crudely real, economic interests of the society, which must be considered primarily as a globalised entity subject to the financial parameters imposed by consumer capitalism. In this light, we may be able to explain the subordination of political parties and governments (the representatives of the symbolic) to the "rules" of the international financial markets in Europe and the USA. Yet, it is clear that there is no such thing as a global group (imaginary mother), and that there is no less valid a notion than that as soon as we desire something, we should be able to acquire it immediately in a "state of real" by plucking it off some Internet shelf. This is an enormous overflow of the real and the imaginary, which is humanity conceived as a real/imaginary mother, which, by excluding the role of the conventional imaginary mother (group) as well as by rejecting the Name-of-the-Father (leader as symbolic father), leads gradually and insidiously to the weakening, and even fragmentation, of people's self-image, while, at the same time, blunting the human ability to lend objects an imaginary and symbolic dimension that supplements and transcends their function as real, useful objects. In this sense, social arrangements can create pressure for a psychotic-type regression to the state of need on both the personal and social level.

Thus, desire is "deadened" and unconsciously reduced to the need and demand for love. A typical example of this is a twenty-four-year-old patient of mine with a borderline personality. He has been in group analysis for the past three years, because the obsessive–

compulsive neurosis from which he suffers has kept him away from university (he is afraid to approach the building) and his studies. A characteristic remark of his was: "It's not just me, but my entire generation who've had their 'fingers burned'. We do absolutely nothing, we don't want anything; we just live. And this is because we're helpless, but also because the society provides everything or gives the illusion that it provides everything." On the other hand, desire is pseudo-invested with an imaginary and symbolic element in the sense of an insatiable demand that the subject be accepted and an insatiable desire for imaginary recognition (mirroring) by all humanity. This is evident in the popularity of the glamour-orientated culture and the reality shows in which everyone is a star, just because of the routine activities he/she is seen doing worldwide. We are witnessing an increase of narcissism in contemporary society, although it should be noted that reference here is to a conventional subject broadly conceived as neurotic. Because desire in its higher symbolic (genital) stage has atrophied, the subject, according to Lacan (1994, 1998b), regresses to a very fragile primary narcissism, strictly linked with desire as desire for the mother or as need for the mother (oral–sadistic stage). Interestingly, this development does not appear to affect persons suffering from psychosis, perhaps because, in Freud's terms (1914c), the cause of their disease consists precisely of a strong fixation in the narcissistic stage or in a pre-narcissistic stage of libido (e.g., schizophrenia) to which the patients have become accustomed. This is not a paradox. This (pre)narcissistic stage is pathological in the sense that it consists of a morbid return to the ego, which either overcompensates for the absence of primary narcissism, such as that which comes into being under the regard of the Other (mother), or resists a primary narcissism based on the absolutely intrusive regard of the Other. In both cases, contact with the Internet as substitute for the physical presence of the Other can be a great comfort, and might even exert some therapeutic influence in at least a few cases of persons suffering from psychosis. In other words, the patient who suffers from psychosis can have contact with the Other without fearing that it will traumatise him again. Many such patients are in analysis with me, especially patients with schizophrenia or schizo-affective disorder. One of them said: "During the hours I spend on the Internet, my symptoms disappear." However, this is not the case with the average neurotic subject. In this subject, the idea of the group/mother remains intact but it tends to become de-structured through the imposition of the imaginary (globalised) dimension of the whole.

What can group analysis propose as an antidote to these conditions?

Group analysis: an alternative to the postmodern crisis

Group analysis and the transformation of the idea of the group

Group analysis developed during the crisis of the industrial culture before it made the transition to its post-industrial form. Analysis in this form should, therefore, be regarded as one of the most serious critical efforts to transcend this culture, on both the short-term and long-term level, in both its industrial and post-industrial form. The goal of group analysis was to revalorise the idea of the group in its proper form, which, up to then, had been considered as inferior to the individual, according to the ideology of modernity and individualism. The modern ideology had prevailed since the early modern period, even when the concept of the group and the collective spirit sometimes appeared to hold primacy. Apart from the period of its heyday in which, on the basis of Carlyle's (1841) ideas, it attributed primacy exclusively to the idea of the individual/hero, modernism gradually came to recognise the power of the group, on condition that it was under the constant control of the leader (Le Bon, 2002). But the notion of the group in this case was a formalised pattern (Mannheim, 1985), the primacy of which served to defuse the popular demands for social action that were being disseminated rapidly at that time. So, by the mid-twentieth century, at least in western societies, desire was not the mature result of the cultivation of relationships of mutual recognition between subjects in the context of the group/community as conducted by a leader/symbolic father; on the contrary, desire expressed personal needs on the imaginary level, that is, the demand for love which would be derived from the group as directed by a leader/imaginary father.

The Second World War, however, especially the phenomena of Nazism and Stalinism in which we encounter the concept of collectivity in its most psychotic form (Hobsbawm, 1994; Mosse, 1999), offered dramatic proof that from then on, the hypothesis of desire should be truly collective, that is, based on the most neurotic possible representation of the group. In short, the Second World War demonstrated that the representation of the group and, through it, the representation of desire that had prevailed until then, was totally hallucinatory. Subjects had set the group as their pre-eminent object of desire, in other words, as a mature entity conducted by a mature leader, or symbolic father, who promotes the development of group members in the direction of maturity and independence. Yet, what they desired, in essence, was that the group be strongly directed by a leader as imaginary father: a father who cultivates and incites the group members' infantilism and dependence. The group was just a reflection or mirroring of the imaginary father/leader, who could sweep societies to ruination. This fact was flagrantly expressed by the dictatorships that flourished during this period. Dictators initially were considered in a deceptive way as good/symbolic fathers, but soon showed their true face as entirely imaginary, deluded, and destructive fathers (Mosse, 1999).

More significantly, the modernist imago of the group was seen by the prevailing ideology as the sole true one (Le Bon, 2002), to such a degree that it was adopted by Freud (1921c), who certainly did not regard the group as a mass, as Le Bon did, but, rather, as an artificial entity. For Freud, a group tended to acquire unity only in so far as the members projected their ego ideal to the group leader as the group's pre-eminent personality or ego ideal, or as the primordial symbolic father, in order to put it later as one and the same object in the place of their ego ideal and, thus, achieve an identification with one another and with the leader/father in their ego. To a large extent, however, this father was an imaginary father.

Group analysis attempted to bring about a radical refutation of this imago. It was at Northfield Hospital in 1942 that Bion initially attempted to treat soldiers in large group settings directed by alternative leaders. However, Bion's radical effort failed because it sowed confusion in the hospital environment and brought him into conflict with the military leadership. His effort continued at the same hospital in 1943, under Foulkes, who conducted small groups under the direction of a leader/therapist (de Maré, 1983; Hinshelwood, 1999). Bion and Foulkes paved the way for redefining the idea of the leader as expressed through the therapist's leading position. Bion succeeded in doing this in the long term by eliminating the leader from the group. The group—which is initially a basic group dominated by psychotic defence mechanisms or a relevant basic assumption (dependence, fight–flight, pairing)—should be led alternatively by the appropriate leader on whom the group projects the corresponding basic assumption (basic-assumption- group leader). To the extent that the group can mature and develop neurotic defence mechanisms (work group) by exploiting its own most positive elements and by identifying the leader/therapist as a mature leader, it should be led by the latter as an intellectual leader (leader of the work group), so that it can be transformed ideally into a leaderless group (Bion, 1961, 1992). Foulkes achieved this by considering that the therapist will no longer direct the group as leader, but will conduct it, like the conductor of an orchestra, leaving it gradually to mature by utilising its own positive elements (Foulkes, 1964, 1990). This is why, subsequent to their efforts, the therapist in the symbolic position of father/leader no longer represented an ego ideal of which the group, conceived as representation of an archetypal "good" or/and "bad" mother, following Klein's (1946) views, was simply a reflection, as modern ideology dictated for persons with leadership qualities. Since then, the leader has had to work constantly to retain the position of ego ideal by expressing and formulating the deepest needs of the group, especially its need to make the transition from a fusion state to a state of representing reality (Bion, 1992), thus showing that he has learned to take advantage of, and to foster, the positive elements of the group (as good enough mother or ideal ego) from which he, too, was derived and promoted as its most mature member.

In Lacanian terms, the group/mother under these conditions ceased to be the primary imago of the subject's desire in the sense of being determined decisively by need or demand. The concept of the group became less associated with the subject's tendency to withhold the object absolutely and more closely linked with his or her awareness that, in order for desire to be disengaged from need and demand, the group as initial object must eventually be lost in the sense that the member who belonged to the group for some years can be separated from it.

Group analysis vs. globalisation: its main tools

The above objective can be achieved in small therapeutic groups with an analytic culture (Foulkes, 1964, 1975, 1990). The transition from the individual to the group level of therapy brought the group to the fore as a mature (maternal) figure of adult life, which, thus, became the signifier of the subject's mature expression of desire (Nitsun, 2006; Nitzgen, 1999). By directing the subject's personal complexes to the group milieu (Foulkes & Anthony, 1957), Foulkes made a significant contribution to preventing desire from being corrupted. Of great importance is the set of stable but dynamic principles that are embodied by the group and constitute "the operational basis" on which group dynamics can be demonstrated and analysed. Two of these principles, called "group-specific factors" (Foulkes, 1964, pp. 33–34, 76–77, 1990, p. 156), are paramount, in my view: the matrix and mirror reactions.

Foulkes uses the term matrix—a term deeply imbued with female parameters—to designate the "hypothetical web of communication and relationship in a given group" (Foulkes, 1964, p. 292). Group relationships and communications are interpersonal but chiefly transpersonal (Foulkes & Anthony, 1957). Undoubtedly, group dynamics determine the development of the matrix and *vice versa*, which is why Foulkes spoke of the matrix mainly as a dynamic matrix (Foulkes, 1964, 1990; Foulkes & Anthony, 1957). However, in order to be meaningful and effective, the dynamic matrix must be based on what Foulkes called the "foundation matrix", a matrix in the broad sense of "a firm pre-existing community or communion between the members, founded eventually on the fact that they are all human" and "have the same qualities as a species" (Foulkes, 1990, p. 212). Although linked with biological parameters, the foundation matrix is primarily based on the idea that human society, essentially founded on language, culture, and social classes, is constituted on the basis of a common shared communicational ground (Scholz, 2003). In Lacanian terms, we could say that the foundation matrix is always strongly symbolic in nature, expressing the universal values recorded in the corpus of tradition and formulated through language. In this sense, the dynamic matrix, unless it is linked with the foundation matrix, its initial nuclear core, is in danger of becoming an abstract notion in the form imposed today by the post-modern view of the world as a global village. In sociological terms, the small group is more a social system that exists and is influenced by the larger social system on which it depends, and less an autonomous self-sufficient structure that depends solely on the face-to-face interactions and intercommunications between its members (Hopper & Weyman, 1975). In this sense, the social unconscious would undoubtedly also be reflected in the small group processes.

The matrix, as conceived by Foulkes, is a key concept through whose gradual dissemination and extension group analysis might be able to correct the globalised view of the world. By explicitly imposing the idea of a globalised matrix, globalisation distorts the idea of the group by reducing it to an abstract concept but, worse still, makes the idea of the group a traumatic one. As conceived by the spirit of globalisation, the social matrix assumes an absolutely imaginary character that diminishes the symbolic power of the dynamic matrix and, above all, that of the foundation matrix, thus drawing the subject into psychotic states. What might be called the universal social network can easily be imagined as a global dragon mother who is always ready to devour the subject, leading him or her to an absolutely naked real that precedes even the level of need. Even worse is the idea of a patrix, conceived as what one might call the shared sense of paternal authority that might be expressed by the conductor or one who intervenes in different local large group settings (Skynner, 1974; Wilke, 2014) or, in Lacan's terms, the Name-of-the-Father, also risks being dangerously diminished and could eventually collapse.

Of great relevance also are mirror reactions as specific group phenomena. The group as a whole can be seen as a hall of mirrors (Pines, 1984) in which an individual is confronted with various aspects of his own social, psychological, or body image (Foulkes & Anthony, 1957; Weinberg & Toder, 2004). Mirror reactions help the members' transition to a better contact with reality (symbolic level) (Foulkes & Anthony, 1957; Pines, 1984). In Lacan's terms, the mirror reactions between individuals as social beings favour the expression of desire on its most mature level (Laxenaire, 1983). However, for the mirror to be effective, dual interpersonal relations must be transcended, and transpersonal relations, which are interpersonal relations mediated by a third person, must not be overextended. Any fixation on interpersonal relations (imaginary level) leads to distorted mirror reactions, or malignant mirrorings (Zinkin, 1983). Any overextension of transpersonal relations (symbolic level) in an indefinite social sense leads to the fragmentation of mirroring and of self-images, or fragmentation of the imaginary, which is also fragmentation of the symbolic. In both cases, a deep psychotic anxiety is activated, leading the subject to the realm of the unsymbolised real and from there to despair. Good enough mirror reactions are possible and effective only in the limited matrix that is the community matrix. Cultivating the spirit of community as conceived by group analysis could counteract the fragmentation of the self-image, which, at the same time, is the fragmentation of thought, to which the modern globalised society leads subjects.

Consequences on the clinical level

The fact is that group analysis has only a limited ability to intervene in the current post-industrial world on the social level in order to redefine the relation between desire (symbolic), need (real), and demand (imaginary) and, thus, to foster the mature cultivation of desire. The main obstacle here lies in the fact that the idea of the group, with its qualitatively rich symbolic components, mainly the foundation matrix, has atrophied in the social unconscious and, as noted above, has become traumatic. Owing to this fact, the maternal and, especially, the paternal function have diminished alarmingly in terms of their symbolic effectiveness. The two parental figures must serve essentially as mature representatives of the reality principle and, consequently, as regulators of the subject's desire, in the sense that they promote it as disengaged as much as possible from need and demand. In the present postmodern world, however, if parents—and, by extension, therapeutic contexts, either individual or group therapies, and, more broadly, parental surrogates such as social institutions, public services, etc.—do not function chiefly as feeders, that is, as real or imaginary mothers/fathers through whom subjects gratify their need for feeding and/or their demand for love, they are nothing. In some way, contemporary parents are, thus, transformed into things. This fact, to use Marx's term again, constitutes a deeply traumatic and disastrous aspect of reification.

This reification is often evident in group psychotherapy today, especially among young patients. Depending on the deficiencies in patients' mental and social development, patients frequently find themselves in a state of permanent need and vulnerability. It can be confirmed that, in the course of their analysis, patients tend to become extremely demanding and to exhibit minimal tolerance of frustration and symbolic castration. This is also revealed by the fact that it is very difficult for them to see the group—and the therapist, who is regarded as an extension of the group—as anything more than a process that should support or "suckle" them perpetually. Under these premises, adequate weaning leading to frustration cannot be achieved either. Even worse, patients are unable to perceive the group on a higher level as the union of a mature paternal figure (conductor) and a mature maternal re-enactment (group), a union that they should symbolise through regular payment of their therapy fees, thus dealing with the symbolic castration that takes place through the powerful symbolism of money, as we have analysed in a previous chapter. In this sense, the majority of patients constantly pay their therapy fees with a delay that makes the castration (as attained by the chronological proximity between therapy and payment) relatively inactive. Interestingly, the patients who present the most difficulties in payment are those with the highest incomes. The same people who treat payment of fees for therapy as "mental stinginess" indulge in flagrant over-consumption.

Under these conditions, in order to be effective, group analysis must take into account that the idea of the group as a mature process has become fragmented within postmodern subjects. In Bion's (1967) terms, postmodern subjects should be considered as functioning more with the psychotic or borderline part of their personality rather than with the neurotic one, and should be gradually familiarised with the idea of the matrix, otherwise they run the risk of experiencing it as a devouring mother (Foguel, 1994). Familiarisation of the contemporary postmodern subject with the matrix is no more than his or her familiarisation with desire itself, in the sense that as the matrix must always be restructured to take on more mature forms, so desire, as an expression of the subject's contact with the matrix, must constantly be redefined, differentiating itself from need and demand. But, for today's subject, every immediate and overextended contact with the matrix, or desire in its mature form, might turn out to be a highly traumatic event that could lead him/her to a deeper level of regression. In this regard, it is important for the group therapy patient to become familiar with the foundation matrix early and to assimilate many of its features long before coming in contact with the complex and conflictual field of the dynamic matrix. Cultivation of the foundation matrix is the safest way for the subject to avoid being trapped in the psychotic dimension of desire as need (real) or demand for love (imaginary). In particular, the foundation matrix can help the subject to invest objects (persons or things) at the outset with a broad symbolic meaning based on the concept of a common human destiny and of a shared communal spirit, and in this way to develop a symbiotic relationship with them that will help him or her later to deal with desire on the neurotic level in which the dynamic matrix unfolds.

Cultivation of the foundation matrix as a primary good is particularly urgent today, as it could constitute a powerful antidote to the disastrous psychic trauma engendered by the current financial crisis in western societies, especially in countries such as Greece, which have become much more accustomed to over-consumption than production. The resulting fiscal crisis has obliged consumer capitalism to place limits on this over-consumption by means of strict cuts in salaries, etc., representing an abrupt termination of "suckling", and reducing these countries to a state of economic, social, and political chaos. The financial crisis extending from 2008–2009 to the present—which is the reverse side of overabundance and over-consumption—might push the subject more deeply into psychosis, by reducing him or her to a subject of need, the need for an ordinary commercial object, considered and pursued exclusively as the means of survival. Thus, the economic crisis does not conduce to the subject's symbolic castration, as one might initially and erroneously believe. On the contrary, since the postmodern subject is addicted to considering the object mainly in terms of need (real level), it is expected that the economic crisis castrates subjects in a primary manner, depriving them of both the dynamic of the imaginary (fantasy of the object) and, even more so, of the symbolic (which lends meaning to the object). Familiarisation with the foundation matrix could raise a serious barrier to the drifting of both the subject and society into the psychotic state of absolute need.

Conclusions and further remarks

Contemporary postmodern society, influenced by the principles of the new globalised consumer capitalism, has imposed the concept that, in a milieu in which abundance and over-consumption are taken for granted as indisputable laws of socio-economic life, the subject's desires can and must be gratified immediately. This view is embodied on the level of the social unconscious in its postmodern, post-ideological trends and lends a completely illusory nature to desire, causing it to regress, in Lacan's (1994, 1998b, 2004, 2006c) terms, from its mature state, which is the state of independence and autonomy (symbolic level), to its previous states of dependence on the need for the mother as a feeding person (real level) and demand for her love as loving person (imaginary level). In the form of instant gratification (need), which, at the same time, is registered as acceptance and love (demand), desire is closed in a vicious circle that brings it into conflict with the reality principle, strips it of its symbolic dimension and eventually "deadens" it. Subjects and societies are led, not paradoxically, to the same stage of need and demand by the restriction of conspicuous consumption through the salary cuts and other financial austerity measures imposed in today's serious fiscal crisis, which is the reverse of consumer capitalism.

The highlight of the new imaginary, as well as the new real form that desire has acquired on the social level, is the view that all commodities and relational goods can be offered immediately and somehow magically by humanity conceived as the individual's globalised group/family, enjoyed by him or her without the intermediary of ordinary human relations based on a balanced combination of real, imaginary, and symbolic elements. This idea of a globalised group that supplies everything immediately—as introjected through the social unconscious by the average neurotic or borderline person, but not persons suffering from psychoses—is strictly linked to the representation of an archaic, imaginary, devouring mother to which the subject has regressed. Thus, it paves the way for a "psychoticisation" of the person and of societies strictly linked with reification processes according to Marx (1906) and fixation on narcissistic or even pre-narcissistic states, according to Freud (1914c). This situation is interrelated with a degeneration of desire as it functioned during the period of modern capitalism, expressing a good enough combination of the real, the imaginary, and the symbolic, mainly through the ideology of strong paternal leadership as ego ideal on the political level, while simultaneously constituting its continuation and disrupting the disengagement of the symbolic and the imaginary from the real and the latter's disastrous over-prevalence.

Thus, what is sanctioned today as an authentic group idea and sociality, based on the ability to communicate immediately with everyone internationally through Internet relations, despite its capacity to provide some "healing" of borderline or psychotic deficiencies by permitting contact with an imaginary non-intrusive other, is no more than a deeply narcissistic, psychotic attitude In fact, it seems that the mirror stage, as Lacan (2006a) described, has not been normally experienced on either the personal or social level, and the subject, since it cannot naturally be mirrored by an extended and chaotic global matrix, is constantly in danger of being devoured by it. It regresses then to states that permit mirroring only of its personal image/face (e.g., by taking selfies!). This status invalidates the concept of the group and gradually makes it traumatic; at the same time, it devalorises the Name-of-the-Father (Lacan, 1994, 1994, 1998b, 2004, 2006c) as substantiated in the authority and social meaning provided by social institutions, traditions, and laws, but especially by communication rules, symbols, and codes based on the symbolic use of language as a pre-established structure, which is the necessary presupposition for desire to retain its authentic mature state by transcending the state of need and the demand for love.

Group analysis—the development of which is an evolution of democratic liberalism towards new radical perspectives after the Second World War on the historical level, by restating the idea of the group and sociality on less authoritarian leader-dependent premises—is founded on the union of a mature parental couple as expressed by the conductor/symbolic father, as assimilating and respecting all the qualities of the maternal imago, and the group as imaginary and symbolic mother who follows the conductor's/father's authority, according to the views of Foulkes (1964, 1990), of Klein (1946, 1957), and Bion (1992). On this basis, it ensures the development of good enough mirroring and, thus, the subjects' good enough primary narcissism and their identification with the Name-of-the-Father as expressed in the context of group interactions in the here-and-now of a situation based mainly on the foundation matrix and the idea of community as based on a commonly shared, local, counter-international matrix and meaningful personal, interpersonal, and transpersonal communication. By fostering and expanding the idea of a group-analytic symbolically meaningful matrix, group analysis could constitute an antidote to the overwhelming power of a postmodern, globalised, devouring matrix of relationships and, thus, help analysands, as well as society more generally, to transcend this morass and perhaps to rediscover their lost desire.

CHAPTER THIRTEEN

Group analysis and music: similarities and differences between conducting a group-analytic group and conducting an orchestra*

Introduction

After studying the deeper social dimensions of group analysis, conceived as the group therapist's act of forming and conducting small groups, this book closes by exploring the interrelation of group analysis with art and, more specifically, with music. Does the act of conducting a group-analytic group, which is a scientific activity in a clinical setting, present substantial similarities with the act of conducting an orchestra, a highly artistic procedure in a performance context? As has already been noted many times in this book, this view was first expounded by Foulkes (1948, 1964, 1990), who frequently refers to the group–orchestra analogy and to the group analyst as conductor (a term he prefers to therapist), indicating that he conceived the similarity between conducting a group and conducting an orchestra as a matter of fact rather than just a metaphor. The issue has not yet been explored systematically, although there are a few studies that draw a general analogy between listening to music

---

* First published in 2015 in *Group-Analytic Contexts*, 69: 30–48. Also published in *BPS Psychotherapy Section Review*, 57 (Spring) 2016: 70–85.

and listening to a group, since both are based on an evolution of themes and processes (Powell, 1983; Strich, 1983), or further conceive the group matrix metaphorically as the true music of the group by considering the conductor as a significant note (the tonic or dominant one) among other notes (group members) and the group as a concerto which, due to its rhythmic temporal patterns of tension, is attuned to the release caused by the resonating intersubjective time of group interrelationships and the construction of joint meaning founded on innate human musicality (Thygesen, 2008; Wotton, 2013a,b). Others emphasise their similarities by tracing some strong analogies between conducting an orchestra and a group-analytic group (Pisani, 2014). In recent decades, research has demonstrated the great therapeutic effects of music, especially in terms of promoting brain plasticity (Koelsch, 2012), allowing the hypothesis that music also exercises a great therapeutic influence on the members of an orchestra and on its conductor (Sluming et al., 2002). It has also been shown that the improvisation of music, the cornerstone of both life and music-making (Barenboim, 2008), as used in the group-analytic group or in music therapy groups following group-analytic principles, further facilitates the patients' therapeutic evolution owing to the similarities between musical and verbal interactions (Davies & Richards, 2010). However, unless a systematic elaboration of the issue is conducted, it seems difficult to argue the reverse view, that the therapeutic process of group analysis itself encompasses behavioural and attitudinal elements which, on a deeper level, resemble musical units.

An attempt will be made in this chapter to corroborate Foulkes' view of the substantial similarity between conducting an orchestra and conducting a group-analytic group through a systematic study of the rationale and technique of both acts. Theory will be linked with related clinical material, and ways will be shown in which group analysis can be conceived as both a science and an artistic activity, further strengthening its therapeutic effect.

The orchestra as group and the group as orchestra

At first sight, an orchestra and a group-analytic group have nothing in common. The group-analytic group is an artificial entity functioning in a clinical setting (Foulkes, 1948, 1964). A small group of patients, ideally eight, meet together in a calm chamber under the guidance of the therapist/group analyst once or twice a week in a session that lasts for an hour and a half. The lifetime of the group is theoretically endless, although the average duration of each patient's therapy is from two to three years, during which new members enter the group and others leave it. The target of the therapy, although it is carried out as psychotherapy by the group and of the group, including its conductor, is the individual. As such, the group-analytic group has no specific task to perform (Foulkes, 1975); it meets to help its members analyse and make conscious the unconscious motives of their basic inner conflict, as seen in their associations, which are intermingled in the group with the associations of other patients in the form of free-floating discussion. Then, the unconscious meaning of the dynamics developed in the group is interpreted as representing the reactivation of each patient's stages of development and morbid behavioural patterns as they first occurred in their families. The patient is actively engaged in the interpretative work, as is the group as a whole. The group and the therapist represent a mother and father figure, respectively, on the transference level. Also of great relevance is the quality of the communication established through the matrix, conceived as the ideational counterpart of all communicational networks developed in the group in which the individual is the sole nodal point. Similarly relevant are some specific factors and phenomena that develop in the group, particularly multiple mirroring among the members, or between the members and the group or the conductor, that serve as a means of reconstituting deficits at the level of primary narcissism and resonance by which each member responds to communication according to his/her fixations in some stages of their development. The members sit in a circle with a table in the middle, together with the conductor, who facilitates the communication process and the development of group dynamics through his/her non-intrusive and non-censuring stance (Foulkes, 1964; Foulkes & Anthony, 1957).

In contrast, a symphonic orchestra is a real-life task group that meets frequently to prepare and present music to an audience (Foulkes & Anthony, 1957). The orchestra evolved from that of the baroque period, which was based on polyphonic and contrapuntal music, through the orchestra of the classical period, which was strictly founded on the homophonic genre, to that of the romantic and contemporary post-romantic or neo-classical period, in which tonal and atonal music coexist. The baroque orchestra of the late seventeenth century, which was mainly based on a nucleus of string instruments and the harpsichord that played the Basso Continuo, was modified in the mid-eighteenth century by the Mannheim school, leading to the omission of the Basso Continuo and its replacement by two oboes and two horns. During this period, the various instrumental groups were, for the first time, placed on a stage in front of a conductor The use of the piano instead of the harpsichord or clavichord led the Mannheim school to invent and impose the colours of musical dynamics (*crescendo–diminuendo*) and rhythm (*accelerando–rallentando*). At the end of the eighteenth century the use of wood instruments was extended and led to the classical orchestra of Haydn, Mozart, and Beethoven, which, unlike that of the baroque period, required a conductor. From the romantic period until the late nineteenth and early twentieth century, the full spectrum of brass and percussion instruments was adopted, especially by Wagner. The number of musicians in the orchestra, from baroque to classical and from there to the romantic period, increased progressively from thirty or thirty five to fifty or seventy and from there to eighty or ninety members, or, sometimes, many more. During the modern post-romantic or post-classical period, orchestras became much smaller. However, works of classical music continue to be performed by larger orchestras (Bekker, 1963).

It follows that a symphonic orchestra cannot, by nature, be compared with a group-analytic group. If we want to find similarities, they would be to some extent between an orchestra and a large group (de Maré et al., 1991). The evolution of an orchestra of the baroque period to one of the classical period resembles the transformation of a closed *noblesse* system into a democratic community (Bekker, 1963), which is closer especially to the idea of a large group and, by extension, to that of a group-analytic group. Undoubtedly, like the members of a group-analytic group, the musicians in an orchestra, at least a classical or romantic orchestra, cannot exhibit all the communicational patterns involved in a performance unless the conductor is present to function as the third factor between each member separately and the group as a whole, thereby initiating the beginning of the group and facilitating its evolution. Furthermore, many group-specific factors and phenomena or dynamics as described by Foulkes (1964), especially multiple mirroring and resonance between the musicians in the group and between the group and the conductor, function as vehicles and necessary prerequisites for the music to be executed as successfully as possible through interpersonal and transpersonal relationships (Wittry, 2007). Finally, as will be seen later, whereas the group-analytic group evolves towards its therapeutic goals, according to the culture imposed on the group by the personality of the group analyst, how the orchestra performs will depend on the degree to which it is influenced by the conductor's approach to his score. However, more than a symphonic orchestra, the group-analytic group resembles a chamber group, such as an octet or, in its optimal form, a trio-sonata of the baroque period, the difference being, unlike both these musical groups, which use an informal conductor (usually the first violin leader or the musician playing the harpsichord), the group-analytic group, like a classical or romantic orchestra, uses a professional conductor (Berlioz, 1902; Wagner, 1887).

Yet, even in the form of a chamber orchestra, the evolution of the group-analytic group presents a number of similarities with the evolution of many musical pieces and their execution in symphonic music. These similarities will be considered as the musical features of the group-analytic process, and will refer not only to elements such as form, rhythm (mainly tempo), dynamics, melody, harmony, timbre, and texture, which are common to both music and human speech, but also to the total architecture on the basis of which the group-analytic process usually evolves, which resembles the polyphonic structure of a baroque fugue or the structure of a sonata form. In this sense, any group session is a performance in itself, the main difference being that there have been no rehearsals. Moreover, group-analytic performances have no ostensible audience, although it could be argued that patients inevitably perform (or exhibit their new, healthier behaviours to others) in the same way that members of an orchestra exhibit their new enriched world as both musicians and individuals as a result of their interaction with other musicians and the conductor. The study of all these elements is the object of the last part of the present paper.

The need for a conductor

What are the reasons why a group-analytic group needs a therapist to act as a conductor and how do they resemble the reasons why an orchestra needs a conductor? An orchestra is a large group of expert musicians playing different families of instruments, and divided into sub-groups whose task is to execute musical masterpieces accurately and artistically (either all together or in parts), usually very complex, rhythmically or harmonically, before a well-informed, demanding audience. In this sense, an orchestra has to deal with a series of complicated factors such as the right tone, the balance between instruments with a different sound and dynamic, intonation, tonality, rhythm, and the correct interpretation of the score (articulation, styling, phrasing, and dynamics), the latter usually indicated by the composer but in a manner open to subjective approaches. The issue is much more difficult in the execution of operas or symphonic pieces which include vocal parts performed by either singers or choruses. To keep it all together in a co-ordinated way, a conductor is needed. It is he who, as an expert among experts, but also an equal among his peers, assumes the role of persuading the members of the orchestra to trust him and follow him in his interpretation of the particular piece of music. In addition, the conductor has the technical ability to conduct and communicate the music without speaking, while standing on the podium playing a pantomime with his whole body, his eyes, and especially his hands, which addresses rhythm as well as indicating melodic flow, colours, and dynamics (Botstein, 2010; Meier, 2009; Wittry, 2007). "The conductor is a kind of sculptor whose element is time instead of marble" (Bernstein, 1955).

In addition to his technical skills on the manifest conscious level, the conductor represents for the members of the orchestra a father (or mother) figure for latent transference on the unconscious level (Wittry, 2007). If the musicians in the orchestra do not trust him as a father figure for his pre-eminent musical knowledge (Berlioz, 1902) and leadership, based on respect and trust rather than on his position (Wittry, 2007), and, above all, for his love of real human fraternity rather than himself (Wagner, 1887), why should they follow him and play for him? Any morbidity engendered by the experience of the interactions and dynamics between the conductor as omnipotent primordial leader/father and the members of the orchestra as immature children is either suppressed or sublimated by being channelled into the only divine entity unanimously recognised by the musicians, which is the music. According to Freud (1912–1913) and Foulkes (1964), the conductor remains in essence a "dead"/symbolic father because the higher symbolic meaning of the music with which he identifies has replaced all speech on his part. The conductor is openly "alive" solely by giving instructions behind the scene during rehearsals. During the performance, he is only phenomenally active and in the position of a "live" father (by cueing entrances, holding fermata, etc.); in fact he is conducting the orchestra from the position of a "dead" father. It is through this position that the archaic leadership (sometimes tyranny) that was exhibited during rehearsals is transformed into leadership in the sense of servant leadership, meaning that he is used by the orchestra as an instrument, while he, too, uses the orchestra as an instrument (Wis, 2007). This is done by trying to keep the orchestra in a state of constant tension to produce refined sound, by avoiding the extravagant gestures that represent omnipotent archaic leadership. The conductor likewise helps musicians to become autonomous players and decision makers. The ultimate goal, however, unlike group analysis, is for the ensemble to develop beautiful sound and to perform successfully. The paradigms of ideal conductors, in the sense that they represent a "dead" rather than a "live" father, are abundant. Leaving aside the first great conductors, such as Hans von Bülow and Gustav Mahler, who, according to the sources, were more authoritarian/"live" fathers than "dead" fathers in the sense of servant leadership, suffice it here to refer to modern conductors such as Arturo Toscanini, Karl Böhm, Georg Solti, Herbert von Karajan, Dimitri Mitropoulos, and Leonard Bernstein, or, nowadays, Riccardo Muti, Simon Rattle, Valery Gergiev, and Gustavo Dudamel (although they all make extensive use of hand or body movements and facial expressions, indicating strong leadership) or to Claudio Abbado, Daniel Barenboim, and Zubin Mehta, who conduct an orchestra with the greater subtlety and serenity generated by their smooth, minimalist hand/body gestures and facial expressions in a manner achieved solely by Richard Strauss among the earlier maestros.

The role of conductor of the group as Foulkes (1948, 1964) described it, is reminiscent of the maestro's position in reverse. Unlike the maestro, the group analyst, despite being silent for long periods, is presented from the beginning of the group as an active "live" father and continues to be "alive", as an authority figure who possesses the legislative power of speech as well as the power of expression through body language and gestures, as long as the group lasts, and especially when the group, whatever its level of maturity, requires it.

This automatically ascribes to the group analyst the position of primal omnipotent father, and of transference figure on the unconscious latent level. This happens only so that the group analyst can progressively lead the members to understand "by default" that their need for dependence on a leader is precisely the source of their symptoms (Foulkes, 1964, p. 54). This is the reason why, on the manifest level of current intercommunications and dynamics at every session, the group analyst simultaneously participates from the position of "dead" father by trying to conduct the group in the way a maestro conducts an orchestra. By avoiding identification with the role of the "leader *of* the group" that the group projects on him, the conductor essentially registers himself in the rank of "dead" father or "leader *in* the group" (Foulkes, 1964, p. 61, my italics). By trying to keep silent in most cases, he conducts the group through his non-verbal communication with its members, by following in full mindfulness the deeper unconscious inner voice of each member separately and of the group as a whole. He mainly communicates his agreement or disagreement with attitudes and aspects, or marks the possible desire of a patient to speak or to pause through his discreet, smooth facial expressions or body language. He may ask questions or make connections with some members' accounts or interpret behaviours. He avoids suggesting solutions to their problems immediately, but, rather, leaves the patients to take an active part in group communications and to behave in the here-and-now of the group-analytic situation with no thought of attempting interpretation. The conductor facilitates group intercommunication by analysing or interpreting the group process, in terms of a servant leadership, by using the group as an instrument and, at the same time, allowing himself to be led and used as "an instrument of the group" (Foulkes, 1964, p. 57). Thus, he "digs his own grave", hoping that the idea of the group analyst as a leader who maintains the infantile neurosis of the patients will progressively decline, while the group itself will be identified as a figure who has real strength and helps patients to become better adjusted to reality and to communicate with others in the "community" as socially autonomous and independent beings in a truly "democratic way" (Foulkes, 1964, pp. 62–64). Unlike the orchestra, the ultimate target here is the therapy of the individual, the group being only a means to achieve this end.

To describe the simultaneous empowerment of the group and the fading idea of the group therapist as a leader/"live" father, Foulkes

(1964, p. 59) makes metaphorical use of the simultaneous and continuous execution of the dynamics of a "crescendo" and "decrescendo" (or *diminuendo*) move in an asymmetrical way, which, in real music, is rare or exceptional (Huron, 1990; Todd, 1992). As long as the group progresses towards maturity, the power of the therapist as leader diminishes (*diminuendo*) and the power of the group is reinforced (*crescendo*) in a constant interplay. This resembles the way in which, in an orchestra, some instruments cease progressively to play (not necessarily in a *diminuendo* but as fading of the sound) while others enter playing in either a real (expressive) *crescendo* (empowerment of the sound) or an inner (intensive) *crescendo* engendered by the phrasing as a tendency of the notes of an ascending scale to reach their target (Scherchen, 1953). At the end, the orchestra, usually as a whole, will conclude with a real *crescendo*, combined with an *allegro* or *presto* tempo indicating the ultimate triumph of the music itself as expressed by the orchestra and the fading out of the maestro through his assimilation into it. In the same way, the patients' therapy will conclude, session by session, with a *crescendo* by which the internalisation of the group as mother figure has achieved its highest level as real inner strength (in contrast with the power of the leader being in *diminuendo*), together with which the internalisation of the conductor's strength as "dead"/symbolic father is signalled.

In sum, the act of conducting a group-analytic group and the act of conducting an orchestra meet at the point where the absolute and servant leadership are continuously negotiated in the hope that the latter will prevail and achieve the replacement of the "live" father by the "dead" father. This ideal, common in music and group analysis, is provided by western societies in the context of modern liberalism and democracy. The efforts of some orchestras in Russia or Europe to perform without a conductor as leaderless groups (Botstein, 2010), as well the efforts of some analysts to conduct leaderless groups in therapeutic settings (Bion, 1946, 1961) have both been proved, so far, fruitless and utopian.

Interpreting the score and interpreting the group-analytic processes

Given the similarities and analogies between the art of conducting an orchestra and that of conducting a group-analytic group, it might be expected that the ways in which the analyst and the group interpret group communication, behaviour, and dynamics would present significant analogies with the ways in which a conductor and an orchestra interpret a score, especially in terms of tempo and dynamics. But it is not only in baroque music that there are no indications of tempo or dynamics; in music from the classical or romantic period as well, in which full instructions are provided, no musician and no conductor can find the true tempo or achieve the real dynamic of a piece (Meier, 2009; Wagner, 1887). For a composition to be performed successfully, much depends on the way the conductor, with his culture and insight, represents the perfect sound of the piece as a whole, as it was first performed in the composer's mind. Similarly, the way in which a group-analytic group evolves towards its therapeutic aim likewise depends on the equally subjective way in which the group analyst/conductor presents his or her interpretations of group processes and the culture that is imposed on the group by the conductor's personality.

Group processes and communications do not, of course, follow a score, although human interactions based on speech articulation in the group-analytic group express an unwritten score that is produced instantaneously in an improvised way. Instrumental music maintains an inherent relationship not only with vocal music (songs), but also with the sound of the human voice and everyday speech which emanates from the voice by imitating it (Gregg, 2002). Contemporary psychological and neuroscientific research has shown that manipulation of the temporal structure in music and speech share common neuro-anatomical resources in the brain (Abrams et al., 2010). Research has also verified that the musical intervals in the chromatic scale that is widely used in both western diatonic and eastern pentatonic tonal music are embedded as fundamental features in the vocal prosody of everyday vocalisations (Ross et al., 2007; Schwartz et al., 2003). An innate preference, strictly related to the activity of specific brain areas, for consonant rather than dissonant intervals for the octave has been found (Schwartz et al., 2003). The same is true of preference for consonant rather than dissonant chords. Researchers (Ross et al., 2007) have also raised the question of whether the varying emotional impact of major and minor musical scales is derived from variations in the predominant intervals in human vocalisations that express enjoyment or sadness, respectively, and whether a deeper psychological need is hidden under the importance of the established tendency of western tonal harmony to return necessarily to a tonal anchor and to finish with the tonic after the melody has traversed different chord grades (Schenker, 1906; Westergaard, 1975). Music has likewise been widely regarded as a language, and musical symbols/notes, like linguistic symbols/words, are similar conventional abstract signs organised into the patterns of a musical text whose formal structure is similar to that of language (Hrushovski, 1981). In any event, a group-analytic group and an orchestra share a common substratum, melody, which is an inherent element of everyday human speech and prosody (Wennerstrom, 2001). The human voice was the first primordial instrument (Titze, 2008; Ware, 2001) and, as Wagner (1887) persists in saying, it is impossible for a conductor and an orchestra to find the right tempo and the right phrasing and dynamics of a musical piece unless both continuously sing the music to be played.

The difficult task then emerges for group conductors, especially if they are also musicians, to find the precise ways in which a group-analytic group works like an orchestra and to schedule and orientate their analytic and interpretative stance accordingly. Foulkes (1948, 1964) maintained that group-analytic sessions develop in specific musical keys under the influence of the conductor's culture. This alone implies that the group analyst/conductor cannot simply be a significant note (the tonic) between other notes by not imposing the tempo of the group, as Wotton (2013a) argues. The group situation, as we shall see, tends to evolve in ways that resemble atonal music. Wagner (1887) correctly insisted that a successful musical performance depends totally on the degree to which the conductor has conceived and imposed the right tempo and modulations on the music to be performed. Similarly, one could say that constant regulation of the tempo is of extreme importance for a successful evolution of the group-analytic group. Unconscious mental processes are, in themselves, "*timeless*" (Freud, 1915e, p. 187, original italics), so their smooth and effective expression through speech and dynamics in the group's real time is crucially dependent on the ways in which the tempo of the group is manipulated. By combining the views of Foulkes and Wagner, we support the notion that the task of the group analyst as conductor is, above all, to properly schedule the instrumentation of the group-analytic group and to understand and impose the correct tempo or modulations of tempo to be followed in every group session.

Instrumentation and tempo, together with the fine tuning of every member or instrument of the group or orchestra, and then of the group as a whole, leading to fine intonation, constitute the cornerstone of every group-analytic session or performance. It is by properly using tempo, instrumentation, and tuning in the session, as linked with the conductor's views and personality, that the group-analytic culture of the group (Foulkes, 1948, 1964) is established. Correct instrumentation depends on the selection of appropriate patients, generally conceived as an ideal mixture of personalities with both active/higher voices and passive/lower voices. Fine tuning of the group/orchestra is linked with another basic element common to music and speech: pitch. In a typical group-analytic group, which resembles a chorus rather than an orchestra, not only are the high-pitched voices of women and the low-pitched voices of men intermingled, but very high notes and very low notes rapidly interchange with each other and pitches either change gradually in small steps (conjunct), as usually happens in classical music, or jump up and down in large intervals (disjunct), as in baroque music, especially in Bach, thus forming the contour of a wide-range octave (Caplin, 1998; Maunder, 2004).

Things become much more difficult if we consider that the above situation is only an expression on the conscious surface level of the members' and the group's "inner" unconscious speech and of related conflicts that come to the fore through group dynamics and resonance phenomena (Thygesen, 2008). Unlike the orchestra, which must be fine-tuned at least an hour before the performance begins (Scherchen, 1953), the group and the conductor should tune themselves in an instantaneous and highly improvised way (Foulkes, 1990; Wotton, 2013a). Our experience indicates that the tuning of the members of the group/orchestra with their personal inner world, with each other, with the group as a whole, and with the group analyst/conductor takes place just a few minutes before the latter enters the group. The group, once gathered, resembles an orchestra whose members are either tuned in or not tuned in to an intermingled consonant and mainly dissonant murmuring. It is up to the conductor, before entering the group, to find a way to listen to every member's voice, tone, pitch, and dynamic as expressing the general mood, mentality, and dynamics of the group at the moment of the group-analytic situation, and to fine-tune himself to it. For the conductor to be fine-tuned to a group in which dissonance, rather than consonance, prevails sounds like a paradox. We must, however, bear in mind that, unlike an orchestra, the group is not present to perform in full harmony. Its purpose is to develop in a smoothly dissonant rather than consonant manner, since dissonance is conceived as better expressing unconscious conflicts and a sign of the group's maturity (Davies & Richards, 2010); the conductor's aim is to achieve a harmonic result and therapeutic effect at the end of every session.

Despite his/her fine-tuning with the group, the conductor, unlike the conductor of an orchestra, cannot preconceive the issues that will arise in any group session or the group tempo and dynamics that will develop, because of the improvised nature of the situation. This is why he/she is advised always to enter the group by following a tempo that is initially rather *lento* to *adagio*, through his/her thoughtful and deeply reflective attitude, as expressed by slow body movement and receptive silence. Before the conductor enters, the group's tempo is sometimes *andante* to *allegro* or *allegretto* or, on the contrary *adagio*, *lento*, or *largo*, depending on whether the mood of the group reflects cheer or sadness. In order for the group to transform conventional conversations into free-floating discussion, the group-analyst/conductor is advised to set a *lento* pace. This can either be fine-tuned with the group's sadness as expressed through its *lento*, or function as a meaningful container of the group's joy as expressed in *allegro* forms. Progressively, the *lento* can be transformed into *largo*, *adagio*, or *andante* in an *accelerando*, or it may return to the initial *lento* in a *rallentando* or *ritardando*, depending on the evolution of the group-analytic situation. It is in this sense that the conductor follows the tempo of the group without imposing his own tempo on it.

Regarding the conductor's interpretative and analytic stance, it is of extreme importance for him/her to lead the group in the way an ideal conductor would lead an orchestra, with the minimal gestures or facial expressions and the least possible speech. The more subtle his verbal and non-verbal expressions are, the less intrusive he becomes, with the result that the group is left alone to perform freely. The mean dynamic of a group's speech, like the mean dynamic of an orchestra's playing, is *mezzoforte*, which is embroidered by instances of *piano/pianissimo* and *forte/fortissimo* on different levels, *crescendo* and *decrescendo*. As all these are improvised, the group conductor, unlike the conductor of the orchestra, does not prescribe or cue them, although he can direct them unconsciously (through his/her countertransference feelings) or consciously (depending on the needs of the members and group). The same is true of the "entrance" of the members' voices/instruments. Unlike the orchestra, each member is called upon to contribute to group communication when and if they want; as in an orchestra, the conductor can selectively cue some entrances verbally or non-verbally, or stop and prevent others.

Another important issue on which the conductor must concentrate is the rhythm and timbre of the members' speech (Powers & Trevarthen, 2009). Every word spoken in the group, like every note heard in the orchestra, is pronounced with specific power, duration, volume, colour, character, emotional charge, and tension. Each sound remains the same while its qualities keep changing according to how it intermingles and combines with other sounds in strict dependence on innate human musicality (Malloch & Trevarthen, 2009; Scherchen, 1953). The conductor must listen for the dissonances in the whole free-floating discussion, since they reflect the members' inner conflicts and, by interpreting them himself or permitting the group to interpret them, favours the smoothness of the phrasing and lends the discussion a more consonant melodic and harmonic contour. The main difficulty here is that group members, unlike the members of the orchestra or soloists in a concert, because of resonance phenomena, due either to their regression or psychopathology, enter the discussion/performance not as partial groups of instruments/voices or as solo voices in harmony with the group, but in a narcissistic way, as soloists in the context of a vocal melody which has no specific rhythm or is interwoven with different rhythms superimposed on each other. The texture of the group-analytic melody is a complex issue since, unlike polyphonic simultaneity as expressed by improvising music in music therapy groups (Davies & Richards, 2010), it more closely resembles early polyphonic melodies in the sense of simple separate monophonic melodies that succeed one other, rather than mature polyphonic melodies (the voices of the group enter successively and contrapuntally, as in polyphony, but are not developed in parallel) (Butterfield, 1997; Fallows, 1997; van der Werf, 1997) or homophonic melodies (it is doubtful whether voices that are sometimes heard in parallel form specific chords (Schenker, 1954). Despite this, the conductor must always try to answer questions, such as whether the sounds occur at regular and constant time intervals, or regarding the measures of which each rhythm consists (Wotton, 2013a). Unlike the conductor of an orchestra, he must not beat a rhythm; yet, he must notice whether pauses occur suddenly after a frantic flourish of speech or the words end slowly in a natural break, and whether pauses with a long duration, from one to ten or more minutes (which, unlike a musical score, are customary in the group-analytic situation) have any significant value. Similarly, on the level of timbre, the conductor must notice whether the members' speech sounds rough and hard, cold or warm, intrusive or reflective, sonorous or not, or whether some sounds are more accentuated or sustained as *legato* or *staccato*, etc. As in music, the balance between the *legato* and *staccato* vocalisation by group members is crucial for a successful sound to be produced (not so brilliant and defensive, and not so deep and intrusive) (Scherchen, 1953). The conductor of the group must find the ideal balance by interpreting the unconscious conflict underlying each member's articulation and by encouraging other members to speak in a more s*taccato* or *legato* voice, depending on their specific needs.

The conductor must be aware that, regarding melody and scale, the group is not like an orchestra, but more like a chorus with an antiphonal effect that combines features from baroque, classical, romantic, and modern styles. Some members use longer, usually unpaired, phrases with regular rhythmic and metric patterns, although rhythmically complex and with few pauses or breaks, as in baroque music (Buelow, 2004; Maunder, 2004); others use short phrases usually in contrasting or successive pairing with an entirely different rhythm that is determined by the rhythm itself rather than by beat or measure as in classical music. Others use longer phrases with excessive melodic chromaticism, leading to expressive melodic peaks with freer rhythmic layers that undermine the beat through the use of *rubato* and *syncopation*, as in romantic music (Collaer, 1961; Dahlhaus, 1989); yet others are more disjointed with wide leaps and changes of direction that seem to expand to modal or whole-tone scales or have no rhythm or beat at all, or with a strong rhythm but asymmetric metre (modern music). Harmonic motion, which is assumed to be expressed by the conductor's interventions, mainly in a calm voice, is slow with few chord changes, in the guise of a basso supporting the melody produced by the group, as in classical music (Caplin, 1998), especially when the group is in the depressive position (Klein, 1946). Usually, though, when the group is in either the oral stage or the paranoid–

schizoid position (Klein, 1946), the conductor's bass line is forced by group interactions to move around a lot, leading to the more rapid harmonic changes and movement of baroque music (Maunder, 2004). In either case, the harmony seems to be ambiguous and sometimes more complex chords (seventh or even ninth) are used by either the conductor or some members that are more dissonant than in baroque or classical music (romantic feature). During the period in which a member is preparing to bid farewell to the group, a minor key is often used by the group or the conductor, to express the group's depressive position (Klein, 1946). The conductor can also use a minor key to reduce the anxiety of the group and some members, as expressed in the paranoid–schizoid position by favouring their entrance into the depressive position. In most other cases, the group seems to be in major keys. However, the sense of being in a key is often weakened, while modulations of remote keys and chromatic modulations become frequent, with the clear distinction between major and minor being blurred, as in romantic music. In most cases, as in modern music, when tonality breaks down, bitonality, or even atonality, is employed with dissonance (frequent use of altered chords) that undermines any feeling of a leading tonic or a tonic centre (Dahlhaus, 1989).

Finally, as in modern music, the overall form of group session performances seems like the expansion of a central idea or conflict as presented by a member or members of the group in a circle whose radius expands as each member contributes to the free-floating discussion with a high degree of unpredictability (Collaer, 1961). The absence of any clear-cut distinction of long movements, clear phrases and form-defining pauses or key relationships is reminiscent of romantic music (Dahlhaus, 1989). By contrast, sometimes one or two themes are presented by some members as the main entrance of voices, and when these voices arrive at a cadence and make a pause, other voices are successively added, sometimes separately and sometimes simultaneously, contributing to the discussion of the themes in a way that resembles the *stretti* of a fugue in baroque music. Then, other issues of secondary importance are discussed by the group, similar to the episodes of a fugue, and then, towards the end of the session, the main theme tends to be repeated, as in a fugue (Mann, 1965; Walker, 2000). Discussion is continuous within movements, with long phrases and few breaks at cadence points. Interestingly, when such a situation develops, the themes discussed are treated superficially rather than profoundly, on the border between the paranoid–schizoid position and the depressive position, so there is a weak change of key usually ranging between the major and minor state of the same scale, as in baroque music. Ordinarily, the group evolves on the basis of the deep elaboration of one or two interrelated themes in a constant negotiation between the paranoid–schizoid and the depressive position (Bion, 1992). The theme or themes are clearly stated from the beginning, in distinct phrase breaks, and phrases are balanced in a specific key and somewhat discussed during the first movement of the group session. A second movement follows, clearly differentiated from the first, during which themes tend to be repeated in a non-tonic key with the members contributing to the discussion of the themes through their own related experiences. The third movement then comes along to end the session by restating the theme or themes in the tonic. In such cases, we could perhaps draw some similarities between the development of a group-analytic session and the development of a three-form sonata in either pre-classic or classical music.

A clinical vignette

The group-analytic group, a session of which will be presented here, is one of the four oldest heterogeneous outpatient groups conducted by me; it has been running continuously twice a week from 1998 to the present. As we have seen in some of the previous chapters, over these years many members have successively completed their therapy and new members have joined the group. Last year, at the session described here, the group consisted of four men (Andreas, Leonidas, Panagiotis, and Petros), and five women (Joanna, Stavroula, Penelope, Alexia, and Helen), all of whose psychopathology is mainly neurotic, with a few members showing signs of regression to borderline personality disorder states, plus the conductor. Five members, three men and two women, entered this group after having completed two years of therapy in two different closed groups. The session described here was the antepenultimate one before the group stopped for a month's summer vacation in July 2014. All members are present and one of them, Joanna, is preparing to announce her farewell to the group after the holidays. Interestingly, in this session, the members have taken their places in the group by sitting in twos or threes according to their previous membership in this group or to their first closed group. The whole situation reminds one of an orchestra with three sections of different instruments, and the conductor is sitting between Joanna and Stavroula, who are its oldest members (in a sense, the leaders of the first violins) and have been in this group since the beginning.

The whole tone of the group as it was "heard" by the conductor before entering the room is on a low-to-medium pitch, with the members discussing various themes while different voices successively enter the discussion in a baroque musical way in a key ranging between major and minor scales and in a tempo ranging from *adagio* to *andante*. The mood of the group is rather one of anxiety and sadness in the depressive position, perhaps because the members will be separated from the group during the vacation and because of Joanna's pre-announcement of her departure.

The conductor enters and sits down with slow body movements, after which there is a one-minute pause, indicating a general mood of reflection and melancholy. After that the tempo begins in *lento* with Stavroula stating the first theme of the group. Stavroula, a forty-nine-year-old unmarried businesswoman, after the previous group session, paid the two months' fees she owed, and on this occasion raised the issue that, after paying for her therapy, she usually feels emotionally closer to her dead father, as represented by the conductor, and that the distance from her mother, as represented by the group, has grown. Unlike other times, she speaks for about five minutes at a low pitch and in a rather minor key, following the imposed tempo. There is a thirty-second pause and Joanna enters the discussion by presenting the group's second theme, strictly related to the first, which had resonated with her. Joanna, a thirty-five-year-old mathematician, also unmarried, has not yet managed to accept and fully come to terms with the death of her father, which occurred suddenly ten years earlier. It is this largely unprocessed mourning for her father's death, together with a very conflictual relationship with her mother, which creates difficulties for Joanna in her relationship with men. Joanna talks for fifteen minutes in a louder pitch (about one fifth above the voice pitch of Stavroula), in a rather *andante* tempo and an atonal scale, or sometimes a major scale which imperceptibly only touches the intervals of a minor scale (thus indicating how difficult mourning is for her). She says that her mother, unlike her father, has never supported her and that her mother's identification with her husband was less than that of Joanna with her father. She differentiates her mother from the group, which has supported her, but finds that the conductor is not so good for her because, unlike her father, he does not satisfy her every capricious whim. Stavroula said that she understands Joanna. A two-minute pause followed, signifying a deeper anxiety and anger in the group like an impending storm. The other members listened, and the conductor nodded his head with comprehension and acceptance, in accordance with the evident oral-stage needs of the members and the group, thus closing the first movement of the session.

The second movement was marked by the elaboration of both themes and began at a somewhat *andante* to *allegretto* tempo and on the paranoid–schizoid position level, mainly in major scales, by Penelope, a thirty-nine-year-old married teacher, who raised the question about the meaning of the conversation between the two older members. Penelope had lost her father just ten days earlier, and tried to keep cool by avoiding mourning. The themes that were raised resonated heavily with her and, in this sense, she implied that Joanna, in particular, ought to have resolved these problems or should be able to refer to them in an uncomplaining tone. After that Penelope, as well as the other women in the group, remained silent throughout the second movement. Andreas, an unmarried twenty-nine-year-old who is completing his engineering degree, stated that he also fails to understand Joanna's complaints about her mother. The pitch of his voice is higher, sometimes leading from *forte* to *fortissimo* and *crescendo*, which is evidently linked with his pain at his own mother's death some months earlier. Joanna continues to speak by defending her views and was frequently interrupted by Andreas, who, by being in a strong resonance position, also defended his position. Stavroula often intervened by saying that she had no intention of provoking a confrontation with Andreas. Sometimes, the three voices were intermingled, each in its melodic evolution and each upon the other, as in a fugue. Leonidas, Petros, and Panagiotis, in a *decrescendo* voice, stated that Joanna's complaints represent one of her last attempts to renegotiate her central conflicts through a regression that is legitimate. The conductor intervened in a somewhat *andante* tempo. He said that this was a very important moment, especially because the group had an opportunity to hear two older members restating their conflicts to the group and for them to present these conflicts from another, more thoughtful, perspective, like the two leading violins in an orchestra.

The intervention of Helen marked the transition of the group to its third movement, which lasted for the remaining twenty minutes in an *adagio* to *lento* tempo, marking the group's return to the depressive position and to its initially prevailing minor tonality. Helen, a twenty-nine-year-old married psychologist, asked, in a *pianissimo* way, what was the reason why the women in the group, including herself, remained silent throughout the above conversation. Stavroula intervened *forte* by saying that the silence of the other women, as mother figures in the group, indicated their disapproval of Joanna's stance, which re-enacted the stance of Joanna's own mother. The women left the conductor/father to assume the role of mother in the group by showing acceptance of Joanna's attitude. This intervention led to a release of the underlying tension in the group on a paranoid–schizoid position level which would have prevented the group from terminating the session in a meaningful way in the depressive position, and a thirty-second pause followed, indicating temporary relaxation. Then, Penelope, in a *fortissimo* way, defended herself by saying that she just wanted Joanna to speak in a more mature way. Joanna replied, now more emotionally and very *piano*, that she understood Penelope's feelings towards her, and she does not equate her with her mother. Alexia, in a *pianissimo*, said that she had remained silent because she felt the way she had frequently felt as a child listening to her parents' adult conversations. The men in the group in one voice stated that they understood Joanna's position. The conductor, following the group's *lento*, said that the group itself had interpreted the situation. He added, very *piano*, that the women in the group do not necessarily represent mother figures since the major mother figure remains the group, in which the real strength lies. Stavroula, acting now in the role of the conductor, recapitulated the situation by drawing a link between her initial statement about her feeling of being closer to the conductor/father when she pays her therapy fees and Joanna's ambivalence (to which Joanna had referred previously in the session as a secondary issue). Joanna had initially decided to pay the therapy fees she owed for two months but later thought it would better to pay one month first (as had happened after the previous group session) but finally decided to pay the other in the days to come. This implied, on an unconscious level, that, had Joanna thought of paying for two months at the same time, she would be closer to the conductor and to a more unified representation of the conductor and the group as a whole. The group agreed that there was a hidden competition between the two women as to which of them was closer to the conductor/father; however, it stressed that the main problem was that some members cannot decide whether the conductor is a "dead" or "live" father, with the result that they cannot mourn the death of their own father.

The cyclical evolution of the tempo of this group in three movements was strongly reminiscent of the evolution more of a French overture (slow–quick–slow movement) rather than of an Italian symphony (quick–slow–quick movement) of pre-classical music (Maunder, 2004) or of a classical symphony (which is not always the case, since a reverse group evolution can often happen), while its three-part content (exposition of two themes, elaboration, and recapitulation of them) resembled the structure of a sonata form, which usually constitutes the first movement of a classical symphony (Caplin, 1998; Newman, 1963; Rosen, 1980). In any event, the group concluded by augmenting its strength in a *crescendo* way parallel to the conductor's *diminuendo*.

Conclusions and final remarks

The above analysis indicates that Foulkes' (1964, 1990) comparison between the art of conducting a group-analytic group and the art of conducting an orchestra is more than just a metaphor. These arts are similar in that they are based on the idea of a conductor conceived as a symbolic or "dead" father who follows the principles of servant leadership. Both the conductor of the group and the maestro fade away as long as they either produce from the orchestra the highest harmony and melody as an instrumental expression of the human voice, or extract the melodic and harmonic texture of human speech as developed in the free-floating discussion of the group-analytic situation. Interpretations of group communications and dynamics that are made mainly by the group can benefit from considering group speech as an improvised score. The group evolves like a pre-classical overture or symphony in tempo and like a sonata form in content, in the context of chamber music or a baroque orchestra, rather than a symphonic orchestra, and with different tonality and intonation modifications that are closer to romantic and modern rather than classical music. Conducting it by imposing, above all, the right tempo, as in an orchestra (Wagner, 1887), can contribute decisively to making group psychotherapy function more smoothly and perhaps more effectively as both an art and a science by helping the members to keep finding flexible ways of negotiating between the paranoid–schizoid position and the depressive position (Bion, 1992; Klein, 1946). Since this is one of the first studies to investigate systematically the role of the conductor of the group in conjunction with the latter's music, melodic texture, and evolution, the subject would clearly benefit from further investigation.

EPILOGUE

This book has endeavoured above all to investigate and substantiate certain ideas that are focused mainly on the mothering role of the group-analytic group and the role of the father as expressed by the group conductor, on the basis of which a fairly systematic theory and meta-theory of group analysis, as first devised and proposed by Foulkes (1948, 1964, 1975, 1990), and then by Foulkes and Anthony (1957), can be developed. Although group analysis has evolved as a broad spectrum of analytic activity representing a rich reservoir of experience, it has not yet developed a solid theoretical foundation, on the basis of which the above material can be reliably assessed on both the scientific and clinical level. Without such a theory, the future of group analysis, which is largely based on processes of multi-fragmentation in almost every domain, looks decidedly gloomy in this postmodern world. Of great relevance here was our effort to explore the central ideas of psychoanalysis as formulated by Freud, Lacan, Klein, and Bion in correlation with the philosophy of Kant and the anthropological views of Lévi-Strauss in particular, by absorbing them into group-analytic theory and technique.

On these premises, our main target, covered in Part I, consisted of re-establishing the idea of the pre-oedipal circle, or maternity as expressed mainly by group analysis, and the idea of the oedipal triangle or paternity, as principally provided by psychoanalysis, on a new epistemological model that would smoothly combine both perspectives in a more integrated way than has been achieved to date. In the first chapter, we studied the ways in which, within the limits of this model—unlike those of Freud, Bion, and Foulkes—psychoanalysis and group analysis, or, in mathematical terms, the triangle (oedipal situation) and the circle (pre-oedipal situation), instead of one prevailing over the other in a malignant symbiosis, are conceived as two autonomous entities, each of which was produced through the inherent unfolding of the other, so that they touch each other externally rather than internally, as a benign symbiosis. In Chapter Two, the effort has been made to supplement the new proposed model by considering the role of father and mother as parts of a kaleidoscope rather than as triangle and circle, respectively. Paternity and maternity, or psychoanalysis and group analysis, ceased to be registered on the triangle and circle, respectively, that represent static schemata and are conceived in terms of a mental and psychological kaleidoscope that combines both circular and triangular dimensions in a flexible way. The function of father (triangle) and mother (circle) as symbolic, imaginary, and real father and/or mother (following Lacan's views) are conceived in their kaleidoscopic dimension as autonomous and interchangeable positions, "languages" or "mythemes" that rotate continuously and freely in a dynamic way founded on the "reverse symmetry" of the parental functions as expressed by Lévi-Strauss (1958, 1973). It is our hope that these ideas will be further explored and extended, in co-ordination with recent advances in group analysis and psychoanalysis, with a view to building a more solid body of group-analytic theory.

The attempt to initiate the process of building a group-analytic theory and meta-theory was assisted in Part II by the systematic investigation of some of the basic phenomena on which group-analytic psychotherapy is based and can best reveal its clinical and theoretical efficacy. In its first chapter, we explored the way in which the group manages the money that is its members' payment for their therapy, conceived as indicating their path to maturity by re-experiencing the pre-oedipal phase (payment used as a means of favouring the members' fusion with the mother group) and the oedipal phase (payment as an expression of the members' identification with the qualities of father in terms of servant leadership as expressed by the conductor as a leader in the group, not of the group) during their therapy and as the group evolves as a whole. In the two next chapters we investigated the way in which group-analytic psychotherapy approaches and restores projection and projective identification and related group phenomena conceived as the cornerstones of human communication and social activity, such as envy and scapegoating, respectively, in groups. Their manifestation was explained as being due to malignant mirroring and a distorted symbiosis syndrome together with unprocessed aggressiveness and unresolved destructiveness towards the group conceived mainly as the "good" aspect of the mothering object. In the following chapter, we endeavoured to shed light on the phenomenon of early termination by investigating the ways in which the group can lead to a successful ending of therapy, or at least to the management of early termination processes as performed by people with borderline personality disorder. The deep symbiotic needs of such people, due to their introjection of a mothering object partially conceived as "dead" (Bion, 1992), are difficult for the group to meet, with the result that, in these cases, analysands are unable to complete their therapy. In the last chapter of this part, the process of a normal ending in group-analytic psychotherapy was also studied. Although its meaning in psychoanalysis and psychotherapy remains inconclusive, it was linked with patients' capacity to re-experience an inverted oedipal normally, and to resolve the Oedipus complex adequately by selecting and deciding on the right timing of their farewell.

Part III was dedicated to group analysis as applied to the treatment of major psychic disorders such as eating disorders and psychosis, in which, especially in psychosis, the object has been introjected as thoroughly "bad" (Klein, 1935, 1946) or "dead" (Bion, 1992). The treatment of anorexia nervosa, bulimia nervosa, and depression in schizophrenia through group analysis was explored in particular in the two respective chapters and proved to be effective. The crucial phenomenon of the inability of patients with psychosis to dream, especially patients who hear voices, was also systematically investigated in another chapter, and the ways in which dreaming proper in these patients can be reconstituted through group-analytic psychotherapy were verified. The contribution of the group-analytic group to helping people who suffer from psychosis to reconstruct their lost ability to dream was studied with particular interest in the last chapter of

Part II, using relevant clinical material and citing recent neuropsychological research.

Notwithstanding the above, and following the discussion initiated in the Introduction, it might be said that there are at least two serious reasons why reservations could be expressed as to whether group analysis, even if it is considered to be founded on a relatively solid epistemological, theoretical, and meta-theoretical substratum, constitutes a science in the strict sense of the term. Both reasons necessitated the writing of Part IV of the book. The first reason has to do with a problem shared with the social sciences in general. It is this: even if group-analytic clinical and theoretical parameters could be attested and measured using observational and experimentally quantifiable methods, the two cornerstones of scientific verification, its results are constantly undermined by the fact that the group-analytic situation is essentially a social domain, strictly linked with broader socio-political and historical factors that largely determine the human mind and self in a way that is always open to subjectivity. In order to achieve some balance between strict positivism and social science, a chapter was devoted to investigating the ways in which phenomena of the social unconscious become intermingled with the history and practice of group analysis, especially in the context of postmodern Western societies today. This was explored specifically in the evolution of human desire leading to despair due to the tendency imposed by postmodern capitalism to over-consumption, which leads to a hallucinatory aspect of desire as being linked with the immediate fulfilment of needs and the demand for love and, thus, in fact "deadens" it by reifying people and human relationships. Group analysis, which is founded on the idea of the development of relationships based primarily on the foundation matrix, within the limits of a democratic community according to Foulkes (1990), has proved to be a strong antidote to the devouring dragon that is the international matrix of postmodern communication.

The second reason concerns the very nature of group analysis. On the other side of the scientific spectrum, whether it is conceived as positivist or social, group analysis presents strong similarities with certain arts, especially music. The relationship of group analysis to music is an inherent one and most intriguing. This is because the group-analytic process is based on all the turns, pitches, and tonalities of human speech, man's primordial musical instrument. As Wagner (1887) maintained, music follows human speech, not the other way round. This is why Foulkes (1964) drew a strong analogy between the group conceived as an orchestra and its conductor considered as a maestro. The similarities and differences between music and group analysis were systematically investigated in the last chapter of Part IV, which also closes this book. By examining rich clinical material, in close connection with the inherent musicality in the group, this study has raised the question of whether group analysis should be considered and practised more as an art than a science, or at least as an activity that combines these two major human activities. Can these two domains be combined in the context of group analysis, and if so, how, and to what extent? Odd though it may sound, this is as crucial as the question about the scientific foundations of group analysis, which is why this book has tried to provide some material to stimulate discussion. In any event, the hope is that, through the future investigation of the ways in which group analysis and music or other artistic processes overlap, group-analytic theory, meta-theory, and treatment cannot fail to derive great benefit and enrichment.

REFERENCES

Abrams, D. A., Bhatara, A., Ryali, S., Balaban, E., Levitin, D. J., & Menon, V. (2010). Decoding temporal structure in music and speech relies on shared brain resources but elicits different fine-scale spatial patterns. *Cerebral Cortex*, 21(7): 1507–1518.

Agazarian, Y. M., & Peters, R. (1981). *The Visible and Invisible Group: Two Perspectives on Group Psychotherapy and Group Process*. London: Routledge & Kegan Paul [reprinted London: Karnac, 2004].

Agmon, S., & Schneider, S. (1998). The first stages in the development of a small group: a psychoanalytic understanding. *Group Analysis*, 31(2): 131–156.

Agraval, H. R., Gunderson, J., Holmes, B. M., & Lyons-Ruth, K. (2004). Attachment studies with borderline patients: a review. *Harvard Review of Psychiatry*, 12(2): 94–104.

Allport, G. W. (1954). *The Nature of Prejudice*. Reading, MA: Addison-Wesley.

American Psychiatric Association (1994). *Diagnostic and Statistical Manual of Mental Disorders (DSM-IV)* (4th edn). Washington, DC: American Psychiatric Association.

Ancona, L., & Mangiarotti, A. (1999). The couple in group therapy as a source of hate. *Group Analysis*, 32(4): 547–558.

Anderson, D. A., Williamson, D. A., Duchmann, E. G., Gleaves, D. G., & Barbin, J. M. (1999). Development and validation of a multifactorial treatment outcome measure for eating disorders. *Assessment*, 6(1): 7–20.

Andreasen, N. C., Flaum, M., & Arndt, S. (1992). The comprehensive assessment of symptoms and history (CASH). An instrument for assessing diagnosis and psychopathology. *Archives of General Psychiatry*, 49(8): 615–623.

Anzieu, D. (1984)(1975). *The Group and the Unconscious*, B. Kilborne (Trans.). London: Routledge & Kegan Paul. First published in French as: *Le Group et l' Inconscient. L' imaginaire groupal*. Paris: Dunod, 1975.

Anzieu, D. (1989)(1974). *The Skin Ego*, C. Turner (Trans.). New Haven, CT: Yale University Press. First published in French as: *Le Moi-Peau*. Paris: Dunod, 1974.

Barenboim, D. (2008). *Everything is Connected: The Power of Music*. London: Weidenfeld & Nicolson.

Barth, F. D. (2001). Money as a tool for negotiating separatedness and connectedness in the therapeutic relationship. *Clinical Social Work Journal*, 29(1): 79–93.

Bekker, P. (1963). *The Orchestra*. New York: Norton.

Bentall, R. P., Haddock, G., & Slade, P. D. (1994). Cognitive behaviour therapy for persistent auditory hallucinations: from theory to therapy. *Behaviour Therapy*, 25(1): 51–66.

Bergmann, M. S. (1997). Termination: the Achilles heel of psychoanalytic technique. *Psychoanalytic Psychology*, 14(2): 163–174.

Berlioz, H. (1902). *The Orchestral Conductor. Theory of His Art*. New York: C. Fischer [reprinted Oxford: Benediction Classics, 2011].

Bernard, H. S., & Drob, S. L. (1989). Premature termination: a clinical study. *Group*, 13(1): 11–22.

Bernstein, D., & Fink, L. (1998). *The Childhood Trauma Questionnaire: A Retrospective Self Report*. San Antonio, TX: Psychological Corporation and Harcourt Brace.

Bernstein, L. (1955). The art of conducting (CBS, 12/4/55), *Omnibus*. http://www.youtube.com/watch?v=KrILZgv_0oQ.

Bion, W. R. (1946). The leaderless group project. *Bulletin of the Menninger Clinic*, 10(3): 77–81.

Bion, W. R. (1961). *Experiences in Groups and Other Papers*. London: Tavistock [reprinted London: Brunner-Routledge, 2000].

Bion, W. R. (1962). *Learning from Experience*. Heinemann [reprinted London: Karnac, 1991].

Bion, W. R. (1963). *Elements of Psycho-Analysis*. London: Heinemann [reprinted London: Karnac, 1989].

Bion, W. R. (1967). *Second Thoughts*. London: Heinemann [reprinted London: Karnac, 1993].

Bion, W. R. (1970). *Attention and Interpretation*. London: Tavistock [reprinted London: Karnac, 1993].

Bion, W. R. (1992). *Cogitations*. London: Karnac [reprinted London: Karnac, 1994].

Birchwood, M., Iqbal, Z., Chadwick, P., & Trower, P. (2000). Cognitive approach to depression and suicidal thinking in psychosis: 1. Ontogeny of post-psychotic depression. *British Journal of Psychiatry*, 177(6): 516–521.

Borneman, E. (1976). *The Psychoanalysis of Money*. New York: Urizen.

Botstein, L. (2010). The art of conducting music. http://bigthink.com/videos/the-art-of-conducting-music.

Bridger, H. (1985). Northfield revisited. In: M. Pines (Ed.), *Bion and Group Psychotherapy* (pp. 87–107). London: Routledge & Kegan Paul [reprinted London: Jessica Kingsley, 2000].

Brown, D. G. (1994). Self development through subjective interaction: a fresh look at 'ego training in action'. In: D. Brown & L. Zinkin (Eds.), *The Psyche and the Social World: Developments in Group-Analytic Theory* (pp. 80–98). London: Routledge.

Brown, D. G. (2001). A contribution to the understanding of the social unconscious. *Group Analysis*, 34(1): 29–38.

Bruch, H. (1970). Psychotherapy in primary anorexia nervosa. *Journal of Nervous and Mental Disease*, 150(1): 51–67.

Bruch, H. (1978). *The Golden Cage: The Enigma of Anorexia Nervosa*. Cambridge, MA: Harvard University Press.

Buelow, G. J. (2004). *A History of Baroque Music*. Bloomington, IN: Indiana University Press.

Butterfield, A. (1997). Monophonic song: questions of category. In: T. Knighton & D. Fallows (Eds.), *Companion to Medieval and Renaissance Music* (pp. 104–106). Berkeley, CA: University of California Press.

Caparrós, N. (1999). Splitting and disavowal in group psychotherapy of psychosis. In: V. L. Schermer & M. Pines (Eds.), *Group Psychotherapy of the Psychoses. Concepts, Interventions and Contexts* (pp. 83–96). London: Jessica Kingsley.

Caplin, W. E. (1998). *Classical Form: A Theory of Formal Functions for the Instrumental Music of Haydn, Mozart, and Beethoven*. New York: Oxford University Press.

Carlyle, T. (1841). *On Heroes, Hero-Worship, and the Heroic in History*. London: J. Fraser [reprinted Berkeley, CA: University of California Press, 1993].

Casper, R. C. (1998). Depression and eating disorders. *Journal of Depression and Anxiety, 8*(Suppl. 1): 96–104.
Chadwick, P., & Birchwood, M. (1994). The omnipotence of voices. A cognitive approach to auditory hallucinations. *British Journal of Psychiatry, 164*(2): 190–201.
Chadwick, P., Lees, S., & Birchwood, M. (2000). The revised beliefs about voices questionnaire (BAVQ-R). *British Journal of Psychiatry, 177*(3): 229–232.
Chazan, R. (1999). The group as therapist for psychotic and borderline personalities. In: V. L. Schermer & M. Pines (Eds.), *Group Psychotherapy of the Psychoses. Concepts, Interventions and Contexts* (pp. 200–220). London: Jessica Kingsley.
Cohn, H. W. (1993). Matrix and intersubjectivity: phenomenological aspects of group analysis. *Group Analysis, 26*(4): 481–486.
Coker, S., Vize, C., Wade, T., & Cooper, P. J. (1993). Patients with bulimia nervosa who fail to engage in cognitive behavioural therapy. *International Journal of Eating Disorders, 13*(1): 35–40.
Collaer, P. (1961). *A History of Modern Music*, S. Abeles (Trans.). New York: World.
Conlon, I. (1991). The effect of gender on the role of the female group conductor. *Group Analysis, 24*(2): 187–200.
Cooper, P. J., Taylor, M. J., Cooper, Z., & Fairburn, C. G. (1987). The development and validation of the body shape questionnaire. *International Journal of Eating Disorders, 6*(4): 485–494.
Cornwell, G. (1967). Scapegoating: a study in family dynamics. *American Journal of Nursing, 67*(9): 1862–1867.
Crick, F., & Mitchison, G. (1983). The function of dream sleep. *Nature, 304*(5992): 111–114.
Dahlhaus, C. (1989). *Between Romanticism and Modernism: Four Studies in the Music of the Later Nineteenth Century*, M. Whittall (Trans.). Berkeley, CA: University of California Press.
Dalal, F. (1998). *Taking the Group Seriously. Towards a Post-Foulkesian Group Analytic Theory*. London: Jessica Kingsley.
Dalenberg, C. (2000). *Countertransference and the Treatment of Trauma*. Washington, DC: American Psychological Association.
Davies, A., & Richards, E. (2010). Making links between group analysis and group music therapy. *Group, 34*(1): 21–35.
De Maré, P. (1983). Michael Foulkes and the Northfield experiment. In: M. Pines (Ed.), *The Evolution of Group Analysis* (pp. 218–231). Routledge & Kegan Paul [reprinted London: Jessica Kingsley, 2000].

De Maré, P., Piper, R., & Thompson, S. (1991). *Koinonia. From Hate through Dialogue, to Culture in the Large Group*. London: Karnac.

De Zulueta, F., & Mark, P. (2000). Attachment and contained splitting: a combined approach of group and individual therapy to the treatment of patients suffering from borderline personality disorder. *Group Analysis*, 33(4): 486–500.

Dellaverson, V. (1997). The desomatizing selfobject transference: analysis of an eating disorder. *Clinical Social Work Journal*, 25(1): 107–119.

Dement, W., Zarcone, V. P. Jr, Ferguson, J., Cohen, H., Pivik, T., & Barchas, J. (1969). Some parallel findings in schizophrenic patients and serotonin depleted cats. In: S. Sankar (Ed.), *Schizophrenia: Current Concepts and Research* (pp. 775–811). Hicksville, NY: PJD.

Dimen, M. (1994). Money, love and hate: contradiction and paradox in psychoanalysis. *Psychoanalytic Dialogues*, 4(1): 69–100.

Einsink, B. (1994). Trauma: a study of child abuse and hallucinations. In: M. Romme & S. Escher (Eds.), *Accepting Voices* (pp. 165–171). London: Mind.

Engels, E. (2001). Ego training in action in culture and history. *Group Analysis*, 34(1): 55–64.

Fairburn, C. G., & Cooper, Z. (1993). The eating disorder examination. In: C. G. Fairburn & G. T. Wilson (Eds.), *Binge Eating: Nature, Assessment, and Treatment* (12th edn) (pp. 317–360). New York: Guilford Press.

Fairburn, C. G., Cooper, Z., & Cooper, P. J. (1986). The clinical features and maintenance of bulimia nervosa. In: K. D. Brownell & J. P. Foreyt (Eds.), *Handbook of Eating Disorders: Physiology, Psychology and Treatment of Obesity, Anorexia and Bulimia* (pp. 389–404). New York: Basic Books.

Fallows, D. (1997). Polyphonic song. In: T. Knighton & D. Fallows (Eds.), *Companion to Medieval and Renaissance Music* (pp. 123–126). Berkeley, CA: University of California Press.

Farber, B. A., Lippert, R. A., & Nevas, D. B. (1995). The therapist as attachment figure. *Psychotherapy: Theory, Research, Practice, Training*, 32(2): 204–212.

Farrell, E. (1995). *Lost for Words: The Psychoanalysis of Anorexia and Bulimia*. London: Process Press.

Feinberg, I. (1982–1983). Schizophrenia: caused by a fault in programmed synaptic elimination during adolescence? *Journal of Psychiatric Research*, 17(4): 319–334.

Feldman, E., & De Paola, H. (1994). An investigation into the psychoanalytic concept of envy. *International Journal of Psychoanalysis*, 75(2): 217–234.

Fletcher, P. C., McKenna, P. J., Frith, C. D., Grasby, P. M., Friston, K. J., & Dolan, R. J. (1998). Brain activations in schizophrenia during a graded memory task studied with functional neuroimaging. *Archives of General Psychiatry*, 55(11): 1001–1008.

Foguel, B. S. (1994). The group experienced as mother: early psychic structures in analytic groups. *Group Analysis*, 27(3): 265–285.

Fombonne, E. (1995). Anorexia nervosa: no evidence of an increase. *British Journal of Psychiatry*, 166(4): 462–471.

Foulkes, S. H. (1948). *Introduction to Group Analytic Psychotherapy. Studies in the Social Integration of Individuals and Groups*. London: Heinemann [reprinted London: Karnac, 2005].

Foulkes, S. H. (1964). *Therapeutic Group Analysis*. London: Allen & Unwin [reprinted London: Karnac, 2002].

Foulkes, S. H. (1975). *Group Analytic Psychotherapy. Method and Principles*. London: Gordon & Breach [reprinted London: Maresfield Library, 1986].

Foulkes, S. H. (1990). *Selected Papers. Psychoanalysis and Group Analysis*. London: Karnac.

Foulkes, S. H., & Anthony, E. J. (1957). *Group Psychotherapy. The Psychoanalytic Approach*. Harmondsworth: Penguin Books [reprinted London: Karnac, 2003].

Freud, S. (1900a). The Interpretation of Dreams. *S. E.*; 4–5. London: Hogarth.

Freud, S. (1905d). Three Essays on the Theory of Sexuality. *S. E.*, 7: 123–243. London: Hogarth.

Freud, S. (1908b). Character analysis and anal erotism. *S. E.*, 9: 167–175. London: Hogarth.

Freud, S. (1911c). Psycho-analytic notes on an autobiographical account of a case of paranoia (dementia paranoides). *S. E.*, 12: 2–82. London: Hogarth.

Freud, S. (1912–1913). Totem and Taboo. *S. E.*, 13: vii–162. London: Hogarth.

Freud, S. (1914c). On narcissism: an introduction. *S. E.*, 14: 67–107. London: Hogarth.

Freud, S. (1915c). Instincts and their vicissitudes. *S. E.*, 14: 109–140. London: Hogarth.

Freud, S. (1915d). Repression. *S. E.*, 14: 141–158. London: Hogarth.

Freud, S. (1915e). The unconscious. *S. E.*, 14: 159–215. London: Hogarth.

Freud, S. (1916–1917). Introductory Lectures on Psycho-Analysis. *S. E.*, 15–16. London: Hogarth.

Freud, S. (1917c). On transformations of instinct as exemplified in anal erotism. *S. E.*, 17: 125–133.

Freud, S. (1917d). A metapsychological supplement to the theory of dreams. *S. E., 14*: 217–235. London: Hogarth.

Freud, S. (1918b). *From the History of an Infantile Neurosis. S. E., 17*: 1–122. London: Hogarth.

Freud, S. (1920g). *Beyond the Pleasure Principle. S. E., 18*: 1–64. London: Hogarth.

Freud, S. (1921c). *Group Psychology and the Analysis of the Ego. S. E., 18*: 65–143. London: Hogarth.

Freud, S. (1923b). *The Ego and the Id. S. E., 19*: 1–66. London: Hogarth.

Freud, S. (1923e). The infantile genital organisation (an interpolation into the theory of sexuality). *S. E., 19*: 139–145. London: Hogarth.

Freud, S. (1924d). The dissolution of the Oedipus complex. *S. E., 19*: 171–179. London: Hogarth.

Freud, S. (1924e). The loss of reality in neurosis and psychosis. *S. E., 19*: 181–187. London: Hogarth.

Freud, S. (1926d). *Inhibitions, Symptoms and Anxiety. S. E., 20*: 75–175. London: Hogarth.

Freud, S. (1930a). *Civilization and its Discontents. S. E., 21*: 57–145. London: Hogarth.

Freud, S. (1933a). *New Introductory Lectures on Psycho-analysis. S. E., 22*. London: Hogarth.

Freud, S. (1937c). Analysis terminable and interminable. *S. E., 23*: 209–253. London: Hogarth.

Freud, S. (1940a). *An Outline of Psycho-analysis. S. E., 23*: 139–207. London: Hogarth.

Friedman, R. (2000). The interpersonal containment of dreams in group psychotherapy: a contribution to the work with dreams in a group. *Group Analysis, 33*(2): 221–233.

Frith, C. D. (1987). The positive and negative symptoms of schizophrenia reflect impairments in the perception and initiation of action. *Psychological Medicine, 17*(3): 631–648.

Fromm-Reichman, F. (1950). *Principles of Intensive Psychotherapy*. Chicago, IL: University of Chicago Press.

Gabbard, G. O. (2004). *Long-term Psychodynamic Psychotherapy: A Basic Text*. Washington, DC: American Psychiatric Publishing.

Gabbard, G. O., & Wilkinson, S. M. (1994). *Management of Countertransference with Borderline Patients*. Washington, DC: American Psychiatric Press.

Garner, D. M. (1991). *Eating Disorder Inventory-2 Manual*. Odessa, FL: Psychological Assessment Resources.

Garner, D. M., & Garfinkel, P. E. (1979). The eating disorders test: an index of the symptoms of anorexia nervosa. *Psychological Medicine*, 9(2): 273–279.

Garner, D. M., & Garfinkel, P. E. (1980). Socio-cultural factors in the development of anorexia nervosa. *Psychological Medicine*, 10(4): 647–656.

Geist, R. A. (1989). Self psychological reflections on the origins of eating disorders. *Journal of American Academy of Psychoanalysis*, 17(1): 5–27.

Gemmill, G. (1989). The dynamics of scapegoating in small groups. *Small Group Research*, 20(4): 406–418.

Glick, P. (2005). Choice of scapegoats. In: J. F. Dovidio, P. Glick, & L. A. Budman (Eds.), *On the Nature of Prejudice. Fifty Years after Allport* (pp. 244–261). Malden, MA: Blackwell.

Glick, P., & Fiske, S. T. (2001). Ambivalent stereotypes as legitimazing ideologies: differentiating paternalistic and envious prejudice. In: J. T. Jost & B. Major (Eds.), *The Psychology of Legitimacy: Ideology, Justice, and Intergroup Relations* (pp. 278–306). Cambridge: Cambridge University Press.

Gold, B. (1999). An ethnic disorder—the challenge that eating disorders patients offer group analysts. *Group Analysis*, 32(1): 7–20.

Gonzalez de Chavez, M. (2009). Group psychotherapy and schizophrenia. In: Y. O. Alanen, M. Gonzalez de Chavez, A.-L. S. Silver, & B. Martindale (Eds.), *Psychotherapeutic Approaches to Schizophrenic Psychoses. Past, Present and Future* (pp. 251–266). London: Routledge.

Gottesmann, C. (2006). The dreaming sleep stage: a new neurobiological model of schizophrenia? *Neuroscience*, 140(4): 1105–1115.

Gould, L. N. (1949). Auditory hallucinations and sub-vocal speech: objective study in a case of schizophrenia. *Journal of Nervous and Mental Disease*, 109(5): 418–427.

Green, A. (1996). *On Private Madness*. London: Karnac.

Green, M. F., & Kinsbourne, M. (1990). Subvocal activity and auditory hallucinations: clues for behavioral treatments? *Schizophrenia Bulletin*, 16(4): 617–625.

Gregg, J. (2002). Vocal development and articulation in speech and song. *Journal of Singing*, 58(5): 431–438.

Haddock, G., McCarron, J., Tarrier, N., & Faragher, E. B. (1999). Scales to measure dimensions of hallucinations and delusions: the psychotic symptom rating scales (PSYRATS*). Psychological Medicine*, 29(4): 879–889.

Hafsi, M. (1998). Experimental inquiry into the psychodynamics of the relationship between the group's dominant basic assumption type and scapegoating. *Psychologia: An International Journal of Psychology in the Orient*, 41(4): 272–284.

Harper-Giuffre, H., & McKenzie, K. R. (1992). *Group Psychotherapy for Eating Disorders*. Washington, DC: American Psychiatric Press.

Heesacker, R., & Neimeyer, G. (1990). Assessing object relations and social cognitive correlates of eating disorders. *Journal of Counseling Psychology*, 37(4): 419–426.

Hegel, G. W. F. (1977). *Phenomenology of Spirit*, A. V. Miller (Trans.). Oxford: Clarendon Press.

Herron, W. G., & Welt, S. R. (1994). *Money Matters: The Fee in Psychotherapy and Psychoanalysis*. New York: Guilford Press.

Hinshelwood, R. D. (1999). How Foulkesian was Bion? *Group Analysis*, 32(4): 469–488.

Hobsbawm, E. (1994). *Age of Extremes. The Short Twentieth Century 1914–1991*. London: Michael Joseph.

Hobson, A. (2004). A model of madness? Dream consciousness: our understanding of the neurobiology of sleep offers insight into abnormalities in the waking brain. *Nature*, 430(6995): 21.

Hoffman, R. E. (1986). Verbal hallucinations and language production processes in schizophrenia. *Behavioural and Brain Sciences*, 9(3): 503–517.

Hoffman, R. E., & Dobscha, S. K. (1989). Critical pruning and the development of schizophrenia: a computer model. *Schizophrenia Bulletin*, 15(3): 477–490.

Holmes, J. (1997). "Too early, too late": endings in psychotherapy—an attachment perspective. *British Journal of Psychotherapy*, 14(2): 159–171.

Hopfield, J. J., Feinstein, D. I., & Palmer, R. G. (1983). "Unlearning" has a stabilizing effect in collective memories. *Nature*, 304(5992): 158–159.

Hopper, E. (1981). *Social Mobility. A Study of Social Control and Insatiability*. Oxford: Basil Blackwell.

Hopper, E. (1997). Traumatic experience in the unconscious life of groups: a fourth basic assumption. *Group Analysis*, 30(4): 439–470.

Hopper, E. (2001). The social unconscious: theoretical considerations. *Group Analysis*, 34(1): 9–27.

Hopper, E., & Weyman, A. (1975). A sociological view of large groups. In: L. Kreeger (Ed.), *The Large Group. Dynamics and Therapy* (pp. 159–189). London: Karnac.

Horne, A. (1992). Control and leadership in group psychotherapy. *Group Analysis*, 25(2): 195–205.

Horwitz, L. (1983). Projective identification in dyads and groups. *International Journal of Group Psychotherapy*, 33(3): 259–278.

Horwitz, L. (1987). Indication for group psychotherapy with borderline and narcissistic patients. *Bulletin of the Menninger Clinic, 51*(3): 248–260.

Horwitz, L. (2000). Narcissistic leadership in psychotherapy groups. *International Journal of Group Psychotherapy, 50*(2): 219–235.

Hrushovski, B. (1981). The structure of semiotic objects: a three-dimensional model. In: W. Steiner (Ed.), *The Sign in Music and Literature* (pp. 11–25). Austin, TX: University of Texas Press.

Hudson, I., Ritchie, S., Brennan, C., & Sutton-Smith, D. (1999). Consuming passions: group for women with eating problems. *Group Analysis, 32*(1): 37–51.

Hulse, W. C. (1958). Psychotherapy with ambulatory schizophrenic patients in mixed analytic groups. *Archives of Neurology & Psychiatry, 79*(6): 681–687.

Hummelen, J. W. (1994). Psychotic decompensation during group psychotherapy: early recognition and treatment. *Group Analysis, 27*(4): 433–440.

Huron, D. (1990). Crescendo/diminuendo asymmetries in Beethoven's piano sonatas. *Music Perception, 7*(4): 395–402.

Jameson, F. (1991). *Post-modernism, or, the Cultural Logic of Late Capitalism*. London: Verso.

Johns, L. C., & McGuire, P. K. (1999). Verbal self-monitoring and auditory hallucinations in schizophrenia. *The Lancet, 353*(9151: 6 Feb): 469–470.

Juranville, A. (1984). *Lacan et la Philosophie*. Paris: Presses Universitaires de France.

Kahn, L. S. (1980). The dynamics of scapegoating: the expulsion of evil. *Psychotherapy: Theory, Research & Practice, 17*(1): 79–84.

Kanas, N. (1986). Group therapy with schizophrenics: a review of controlled studies. *International Journal of Group Psychotherapy, 36*(3): 339–351.

Kant, I. (2004)[1783]. *Prolegomena to Any Future Metaphysics. That Will Be Able to Come Forward as Science. With Selections from the Critique of Pure Reason*, G. Hatfield (Trans.). Cambridge: Cambridge University Press.

Karterud, S. (1998). The group self, empathy, intersubjectivity and hermeneutics: a group analytic perspective. In: I. N. H. Harwood & M. Pines (Eds.), *Self Experiences in Group: Intersubjectivity and Self Psychological Pathways to Human Understanding* (pp. 83–98). London: Jessica Kingsley.

Kauff, P. F. (1977). The termination process: its relation to the separation–individuation phase of development. *International Journal of Group Psychotherapy, 27*(1): 3–18.

Kelly, P. H. (1998). Defective inhibition of dream event memory formation: a hypothesized mechanism in the onset and progression of symptoms of schizophrenia. *Brain Research Bulletin, 46*(3): 189–197.

Kendell, R. E., & Brockington, I. F. (1980). The identification of disease entities and the relationship between schizophrenic and affective psychoses. *British Journal of Psychiatry, 137*(4): 324–331.

Kernberg, O. F. (1975). *Borderline Conditions and Pathological Narcissism.* New York: Jason Aronson.

Klein, M. (1923). Early analysis. In: *Love, Guilt and Reparation and Other Works 1921–1945* (2nd edn) (pp. 77–105). London: Vintage, 1998.

Klein, M. (1928). Early stages of the Oedipus conflict. In: *Love, Guilt and Reparation and Other Works 1921–1945* (2nd edn) (pp. 186–198). London: Vintage, 1998.

Klein, M. (1935). A contribution to the psychogenesis of manic-depressive states. In: Love, Guilt and *Reparation and Other Works: 1921–1945* (2nd edn) (pp. 262–289). London: Vintage, 1998.

Klein, M. (1936). Weaning. In: M. Klein, *Love, Guilt and Reparation and Other Works 1921–1945* (2nd edn) (pp. 290–305). London: Vintage, 1998.

Klein, M. (1937). Love, guilt and reparation. In: *Love, Guilt and Reparation and Other Works 1921–1945* (2nd edn) (pp. 306–343). London: Vintage, 1998.

Klein, M. (1940). Mourning and its relation to manic-depressive states. In: *Love, Guilt and Reparation and Other Works: 1921–1945* (2nd edn) (pp. 344–369). London: Vintage, 1998.

Klein, M. (1945). The Oedipus complex in the light of early anxieties. In: M. Klein, *Love, Guilt and Reparation and Other Works 1921–1945* (2nd edn) (pp. 370–419). London: Vintage, 1998.

Klein, M. (1946). Notes on some schizoid mechanisms. In: *Envy and Gratitude and Other Works 1946–1963* (2nd edn) (pp. 1–24). London: Vintage, 1997.

Klein, M. (1950). On the criteria for the termination of a psycho-analysis. In: *Envy and Gratitude and Other Works 1946–1963* (2nd edn) (pp. 43–47). London: Vintage, 1997.

Klein, M. (1952). On observing the behaviour of young infants. In: *Envy and Gratitude and Other Works 1946–1963* (2nd edn) (pp. 94–121). London: Vintage, 1997.

Klein, M. (1955). On identification. In: *Envy and Gratitude and Other Works 1946–1963* (2nd edn) (pp. 141–175). London: Vintage.

Klein, M. (1957). Envy and gratitude. In: *Envy and Gratitude and Other Works 1946–1963* (2nd edn) (pp. 176–235). London: Vintage, 1997.

Klein, M. (1960). A note on depression in the schizophrenic. In: *Envy and Gratitude and Other Works 1946–1963* (2nd edn) (pp. 264–267). London: Vintage, 1997.
Koelsch, S. (2012). *Brain and Music.* Oxford: Wiley-Blackwell.
Kohon, G. (Ed.) (1999). *The Dead Mother: The Work of André Green.* London: Routledge.
Kohut, H. (1971). *The Analysis of the Self.* New York: International Universities Press.
Koukis, A. (2004). Το όνειρο στην Ομαδική Ανάλυση [*Dreams in Group Analysis*]. Athens: Savalas.
Koukis, A. (2009). Η παρακμή της Πατρότητας [*The Decline of Paternity*]. Athens: Savalas.
Kretsch, R., Goren, Y., & Wasserman, A. (1987). Change patterns of borderline patients in individual and group therapy. *International Journal of Group Psychotherapy, 37*(1): 95–112.
Krueger, D. (1986). *The Last Taboo: Money as Symbol and Reality in Psychotherapy and Psychoanalysis.* New York: Brunner-Mazel.
Lacan, J. (1988). *The Seminar of Jacques Lacan. Book II. The Ego in Freud's Theory and in the Technique of Psychoanalysis 1954–1955,* S. Tomaselli (Trans.). Cambridge: Cambridge University Press.
Lacan, J. (1993). *The Psychoses. The Seminar of Jacques Lacan. Book III, 1955–1956,* R. Grigg (Trans.). New York: Norton.
Lacan, J. (1994). *Le Séminaire. Livre IV. La relation d'objet.* Paris: Seuil.
Lacan, J. (1998a). *The Seminar XX, Encore: On Feminine Sexuality, the Limits of Love and Knowledge,* B. Fink (Trans.). New York: Norton.
Lacan, J. (1998b). *Le Séminaire. Livre V. Les formations de l'inconscient.* Paris: Seuil.
Lacan, J. (2004). *Le Séminaire. Livre X: L'Angoise.* Paris: Seuil.
Lacan, J. (2006a). The mirror-stage as formative of the I as revealed in psychoanalytic experience. In: *Ecrits: The First Complete Edition in English* (pp. 75–81), B. Fink (Trans.). New York: Norton.
Lacan, J. (2006b). The subversion of the subject and the dialectic of desire in Freudian unconscious. In: *Ecrits: The First Complete Edition in English* (pp. 671–721), B. Fink (Trans.). New York: Norton.
Lacan, J. (2006c). *Le Séminaire. Livre XVI: D'un Autre à l'autre.* Paris: Seuil.
Lake, C. R. (2008). Disorders of thought are severe mood disorders: the selective attention defect in mania challenges the Kraepelinian dichotomy—a review. *Schizophrenia Bulletin, 34*(1): 109–117.
Lawrence, R., Bradshaw, T., & Mairs, H. (2006). Group cognitive behavioural therapy for schizophrenia: a systematic review of the literature. *Journal of Psychiatric and Mental Health Nursing, 13*(6): 673–681.

Lawrence, W. G., & Biran, H. (2002). The complementarity of social dreaming and therapeutic dreaming. In: C. Neri, M. Pines, & Friedman, R. (Eds.), *Dreams in Group Psychotherapy* (pp. 220–232). London: Jessica Kingsley.

Laxenaire, M. (1983). Group analytic psychotherapy according to Foulkes and psychoanalysis according to Lacan. In: M. Pines (Ed.), *The Evolution of Group Analysis* (pp. 167–182). London: Routledge & Kegan Paul [reprinted London: Jessica Kingsley, 2000].

Le Bon, G. (2002). *The Crowd: A Study of the Popular Mind*. New York: Dover.

Lear, T. (1985). The inspiring role of the group conductor. *Group Analysis*, 18(2): 150–154.

Leudar, I., Thomas, P., McNally, D., & Glinski, A. (1997). What voices can do with words: pragmatics of verbal hallucinations. *Psychological Medicine*, 27(4): 885–898.

Leung, N., Thomas, G., & Waller, G. (2000). The relationship between parental bonding and core beliefs in anorexic and bulimic women. *British Journal of Clinical Psychology*, 39(2): 205–213.

Lévi-Strauss, C. (1958). Anthropologie structural. Paris: Plon [*Structural Anthropology. Volume I*, C. Jacobson & B. G. Schoepf (Trans.). New York: Basic Books, 1963].

Lévi-Strauss, C. (1962). La pensée sauvage. Paris: Plon [*The Savage Mind*. Chicago, IL: University of Chicago Press, 1966].

Lévi-Strauss, C. (1976) (1973). *Structural Anthropology. Volume II*, M. Layton (Trans.). New York: Basic Books.

Lo Verso, G. (1996). Towards a group-analytic epistemology. *Group Analysis*, 29(4): 474–484.

Lo Verso, G., & Profita, G. (1991). The group-analytic model of the functioning of the inner world. *Group Analysis*, 24(4): 425–436.

Lofton, P., Daughterty, C., & Mayerson, P. (1983). Combined group and individual treatment for the borderline patient. *Group*, 7(3): 21–26.

Lyndon, P. (1994). The leader and the scapegoat: a dependency group study. *Group Analysis*, 27(1): 95–104.

Maar, V. (1989). Attempts at grasping the self during the termination phase of group-analytic psychotherapy. *Group Analysis*, 22(1): 99–104.

Mahler, M., Pine, F., & Bergman, A. (1975). *The Psychological Birth of the Human Infant: Symbiosis and Individuation*. New York: Basic Books.

Mahler, M. S. (1968). *On Human Symbiosis and the Vicissitudes of Individuation. Vol I: Infantile Psychosis*. New York: International Universities Press.

Maizels, N. (1985). Self-envy, the womb and the nature of goodness. A reappraisal of the death instinct. *International Journal of Psychoanalysis, 66*(2): 185–192.

Malloch, S., & Trevarthen, C. (2009). Musicality: communicating the vitality and interests of life. In: S. Malloch & C. Trevarthen (Eds.), *Communicative Musicality: Exploring the Basis of Human Relationship* (pp. 1–11). Oxford: Oxford University Press.

Mandel, E. (1978). *Late Capitalism*. London: Verso.

Mann, A. (1965). *The Study of Fugue*. New York: Norton.

Mannheim, K. (1985). *Ideologie und Utopie*. Frankfurt: Klostermann.

Marcuse, H. (1964). *One Dimensional Man. Studies in the Ideology of Advanced Industrial Society*. London: Routledge & Kegan Paul.

Martean, L. (2014). The triangle and the eye inside the circle: dyadic and triadic dynamics in the group. *Group Analysis, 47*(1): 42–61.

Marx, K. (1906). *Capital: A Critique of Political Economy, Vol. I. The Process of Capitalist Production*. Chicago, IL: Charles H. Kerr.

Matte-Blanco, I. (1975). *The Unconscious as Infinite Sets: An Essay in Bio-logic*. London: Duckworth.

Maunder, C. R. F. (2004). *The Scoring of Baroque Concertos*. Woodbridge: Boydell Press.

McKisack, C., & Waller, G. (1996). Why is attendance variable at groups for women with bulimia nervosa? The role of eating psychopathology and other characteristics. *International Journal of Eating Disorders, 20*(2): 205–209.

Meier, G. (2009). *The Score, the Orchestra, and the Conductor*. Oxford: Oxford University Press.

Meyer, C., Leung, N., Feary, R., & Mann, B. (2001). Core beliefs and bulimic symptomatology in non-eating-disordered women: the mediating role of borderline characteristics. *International Journal of Eating Disorders, 30*(4): 434–440.

Mikkelsen, E. J., & Gutheil, T. G. (1979). Stages of forced termination: uses of the death metaphor. *Psychiatric Quarterly, 51*(1): 15–27.

Milders, C. F. A. (1994). Kernberg's object-relations theory and the group psychotherapy of psychosis. *Group Analysis, 27*(4): 419–432.

Mosse, G. L. (1999). *The Fascist Revolution. Toward a General Theory of Fascism*. New York: H. Fertig.

Myers, C. (2008). Show me the money: (the "problem of") the therapist's desire, subjectivity, and relationship to the fee. *Contemporary Psychoanalysis, 44*(1): 118–140.

Newman, W. S. (1963). *The Sonata in the Classic Era*. Chapel Hill, NC: University of Carolina Press.

Nitsun, M. (2006). *The Group as an Object of Desire: Exploring Sexuality in Group Therapy*. London: Routledge.
Nitzgen, D. (1999). From demand to desire: what do we offer when we offer group-analytic training? *Group Analysis*, 32(2): 227–239.
Nitzgen, D. (2001). Training in democracy—democracy in training. Notes on group analysis and democracy. *Group Analysis*, 34(3): 331–347.
Ormay, T. (2012). *The Social Nature of Persons: One Person is No Person*. London: Karnac.
Palazzoli, M. S. (1978). *Self-starvation: From Individual to Family Therapy in the Treatment of Anorexia Nervosa*. New York: Jason Aronson.
Peternel, F. (1991). The ending of a psychotherapy group. *Group Analysis*, 24(2):159–169.
Pines, M. (1984). Mirroring in group analysis as a developmental and therapeutic process. In: T. E. Lear (Ed.), *Spheres of Group Analysis* (pp. 119–137). London: Group-Analytic Society.
Pisani, R. A. (2014). A comparison between the art of conducting in group analysis and the art of conducting an orchestra. *Group-Analytic Contexts*, 64(1): 33–45.
Powell, A. (1983). The music of the group: a musical enquiry into group-analytic psychotherapy. *Group Analysis*, 16(1), 3–19.
Powell, A. (1991). Matrix, mind and matter: from the internal to the eternal. *Group Analysis*, 24(3): 299–322.
Powers, N., & Trevarthen, C. (2009). Voices of shared emotion and meaning: young infants and their mothers in Scotland and Japan. In: S. Malloch & C. Trevarthen (Eds.), *Communicative Musicality: Exploring the Basis of Human Companionship* (pp. 209–240). Oxford: Oxford University Press.
Prodgers, A. (1990). The dual nature of the group as mother: the urobonic container. *Group Analysis*, 23(1): 17–30.
Racker, H. (1968). *Transference and Countertransference*. New York: International Universities Press.
Read, J., & Argyle, N. (1999). Hallucinations, delusions, and thought disorder among adult psychiatric inpatients with a history of child abuse. *Psychiatric Services*, 50(11): 1467–1472.
Rizzolatti, G., & Craighero, L. (2004). The mirror-neuron system. *Annual Review of Neuroscience*, 27: 169–192.
Robbins, M. (1982). Narcissistic personality as a symbiotic character disorder. *International Journal of Psychoanalysis*, 63(4): 457–473.
Romme, M. A., & Escher, S. (1989). Hearing voices. *Schizophrenia Bulletin*, 15(2): 209–216.

Rorty, M. (1994). Childhood sexual, physical and psychological abuse in bulimia nervosa. *American Journal of Psychiatry*, 151(8): 1122–1126.

Rosen, C. (1980). *Sonata Forms*. New York: Norton.

Ross, D., Choi, J., & Purves, D. (2007). Musical intervals in speech. *PNAS*, 104(23): 9852–9857.

Ryle, A., & Golynkina, K. (2000). Effectiveness of time-limited cognitive and analytic therapy for borderline personality disorder: factors associated with outcome. *British Journal of Medical Psychology*, 73(2): 197–210.

Sandison, R. A. (1991). The psychotic patient and psychotic conflict in group analysis. *Group Analysis*, 24(1): 73–83.

Sandison, R. A. (1994). Working with schizophrenics individually and in groups: understanding the psychotic process. *Group Analysis*, 27(4): 393–406.

Scarone, S., Manzone, M. L., Gambini, O., Kantzas, I., Limosani, I., D'Agostino, A., & Hobson, J. A. (2008). The dream as a model for psychosis: an experimental approach using bizarreness as a cognitive marker. *Schizophrenia Bulletin*, 34(3): 515–522.

Scheidlinger, S. (1982). On scapegoating in group psychotherapy. *International Journal of Group Psychotherapy*, 32(2): 131–143.

Schenker, H. (1954). *Harmony*, E. M. Borgese (Trans.). Chicago, IL: University of Chicago Press.

Scherchen, H. (1953). *Lehrbuch des Dirigierens*. Mainz: B. Schott's Sohne.

Schermer, V. L. (2013). Mirror neurons: their implications for group psychotherapy. In: S. P. Gantt & B. Badenoch (Eds.), *The Interpersonal Neurobiology of Group Psychotherapy and Group Process* (pp. 25–49). London: Karnac.

Schermer, V. L., & Pines, M. (Eds.) (1999). *Group Psychotherapy of the Psychoses. Concepts, Interventions and Contexts*. London: Jessica Kingsley.

Schlesinger, H. J. (2014). *Endings & Beginnings. On Terminating Psychotherapy and Psychoanalysis*. New York: Routledge.

Scholz, R. (2003). The foundation matrix—a useful fiction. *Group Analysis*, 36(4): 548–554.

Schreter, R. K. (1980–1981). Treating the untreatable: a group experience with somaticizing borderline patients. *International Journal of Psychiatry in Medicine*, 10(3): 205–215.

Schulte, P. (2000). Holding in mind: intersubjectivity, subject relations and the group. *Group Analysis*, 33(4): 530–544.

Schwartz, D. A., Howe, C. Q., & Purves, D. (2003). The statistical structure of human speech sounds predicts musical intervals. *Journal of Neuroscience*, 23(18): 7160–7168.

Searles, H. F. (1965). *Collected Papers on Schizophrenia and Related Subjects.* London: Hogarth [reprinted London: Karnac, 1986].

Segercrantz, U. (2006). Treating bulimics in groups. *Group Analysis, 39*(2): 257–271.

Sengun, S. (2001). Migration as a transitional space and group analysis. *Group Analysis, 34*(1): 65–78.

Shedler, J. (2010). The efficacy of psychodynamic psychotherapy. *American Psychologist, 65*(2): 98–109.

Silver, C. B. (2007). Womb envy: loss and the grief of the maternal body. *Psychoanalytic Review, 94*(3): 409–430.

Simpson, K. (2002). Anorexia nervosa and culture. *Journal of Psychiatric and Mental Health Nursing, 9*(1): 65–71.

Siris, G. (1991). Diagnosis of secondary depression in schizophrenia: implications for DSM-IV. *Schizophrenia Bulletin, 17*(1): 75–98.

Skodol, A. E., Buckley, P., & Charles, E. (1983). Is there a characteristic pattern to the treatment history of clinic outpatients with borderline personality? *Journal of Nervous and Mental Disease, 171*(7): 405–410.

Skolnick, M. R. (1998). Schizophrenia from a group perspective. In: P. T. Bion, F. Borgogno, & S. A. Merciali (Eds.), *Bion's Legacy to Groups* (pp. 69–82). London: Karnac.

Skolnick, M. R. (1999). Psychosis from a group perspective. In: V. L. Schermer & M. Pines (Eds.), *Group Psychotherapy of the Psychoses. Concepts, Interventions and Contexts* (pp. 43–82). London: Jessica Kingsley.

Skynner, R. (1974). The large group in training. In: L. Kreeger (Ed.), *The Large Group* (pp. 227–251). London: Constable.

Sluming, V., Barrick, T., Howard, M., Cezayirli, E., Mayes, A., & Roberts, N. (2002). Voxel-based morphometry reveals increased gray matter density in Broca's area in male symphony orchestra musicians. *Neuroimage, 17*(3): 1613–1622.

Smith, J. (1999). Five questions about group therapy in long-term schizophrenia. *Group Analysis, 32*(4): 515–524.

Springer, T., & Silk, E. R. (1996). A review of inpatient group therapy for borderline personality disorder. *Harvard Review of Psychiatry, 3*(5): 268–278.

Stacey, R. (2000). Reflexivity, self-organisation and emergence in the group matrix. *Group Analysis, 33*(4): 501–514.

Stacey, R. (2001). What can it mean to say that the individual is social through and through? *Group Analysis, 34*(4): 457–471.

Steel, Z., Jones, J., Adcock, S., Clancy, R., Bridgford-West, L., & Austin, J. (2000). Why the high rate of dropout from individualized cognitive–behaviour therapy for bulimia nervosa? *International Journal of Eating Disorders*, 28(2): 209–214.

Strich, S. (1983). Music and the patterns of human interactions. *Group Analysis*, 16(1): 20–26.

Taylor, M. A. (1992). Are schizophrenia and affective disorder related? A selective literature review. *American Journal of Psychiatry*, 149(2): 22–32.

Thelen, M. H., Farmer, J., Wonderlich, S., & Smith, M. (1991). A revision of the bulimia test: the BULIT-R. *Psychological Assessment: A Journal of Consulting and Clinical Psychology*, 3(1): 119–124.

Thomas, K. (1996). The defensive self: a psychodynamic perspective. In: R. Stevens (Ed.), *Understanding the Self*. London: Sage with the Open University Press.

Thompson-Brenner, H., Glass, S., & Westen, D. (2003). A multidimensional meta-analysis of psychotherapy for bulimia nervosa. *Clinical Psychology: Science and Practice*, 10(3): 269–287.

Thornton, C., & Russell, J. (1997). Obsessive compulsive comorbidity in the dieting disorders. *International Journal of Eating Disorders*, 21(1): 83–87.

Thygesen, B. (2008). No music without resonance—without resonance no group. *Group Analysis*, 41(1): 63–83.

Titze, I. R. (2008). The human instrument. *Scientific American*, 298(1): 94–101.

Todd, N. P. M. (1992). The dynamics of dynamics: a model of musical expression. *Journal of the Acoustical Society of America*, 91(6): 3540–3550.

Trist, E. (1985). Working with Bion in the 1940s: the group decade. In: M. Pines (Ed.), *Bion and Group Psychotherapy* (pp. 1–46). London: Routledge & Kegan Paul [reprinted London: Jessica Kingsley, 2000].

Urlić, I. (1999). The therapist's role in the group treatment of psychotic patients and outpatients. A Foulkesian perspective. In: V. L. Schermer & M. Pines (Eds.), *Group Psychotherapy of Psychoses. Concepts, Interventions and Contexts* (pp. 148–180). London: Jessica Kingsley.

Valbak, K. (2001). Good outcome for bulimic patients in long-term group analysis: a single-group study. *European Eating Disorders Review*, 9(1): 19–32.

Valbak, K. (2003). Specialized psychotherapeutic group analysis: how do we make group analysis suitable for "non-suitable" patients? *Group Analysis*, 36(1): 73–86.

van der Werf, H. (1997). Early western polyphony. In: T. Knighton & D. Fallows (Eds.), *Companion to Medieval and Renaissance Music* (pp. 107–113). Berkeley, CA: University of California Press.

Vogel, E. F., & Bell, N. W. (1960). The emotionally disturbed child as a family scapegoat. *Psychoanalytic Review*, 47(2): 21–42.

Wagner, R. (1887). *On Conducting. A Treatise on Style in the Execution of Classical Music*, E. Dannreuther (Trans.). London: William Reeves.

Walker, P. M. (2000). *Theories of Fugue from the Age of Josquin to the Age of Bach*. New York: University of Rochester Press.

Waller, G. (1992). Sexual abuse and the severity of bulimic symptoms. *British Journal of Psychiatry*, 161(1): 90–93.

Waller, G. (1997). Drop-out and failure to engage in individual outpatient cognitive behavioural therapy for bulimia disorders. *International Journal of Eating Disorders*, 22(1): 35–41.

Wardi, D. (1989). The termination phase in the group process. *Group Analysis*, 22(1): 87–98.

Ware, C. (2001). From speech to singing: the voice as a single instrument. *Opera Journal*, 34(3): 66–68.

Weber, M. (1930). *The Protestant Ethic and the Spirit of Capitalism*, T. Parsons (Trans.). London: Allen & Unwin.

Weegmann, M. (2001). Working intersubjectively: what does it mean for theory and therapy? *Group Analysis*, 34(4): 515–530.

Weinberg, H. (2007). So what is this social unconscious anyway? *Group Analysis*, 40(3): 307–322.

Weinberg, H., & Toder, M. (2004). The hall of mirrors in small, large and virtual groups. *Group Analysis*, 37(4): 492–507.

Wennerstrom, A. (2001). *The Music of Everyday Speech: Prosody and Discourse Analysis*. New York: Oxford University Press.

Westergaard, P. (1975). *An Introduction to Tonal Theory*. New York: Norton.

Weston, M. D. (1999). Anorexia as a symbol of an empty matrix dominated by the dragon mother. *Group Analysis*, 32(1): 71–85.

Wilke, G. (2014). *The Art of Group Analysis in Organisations. The Use of Intuitive and Experiential Knowledge*. London: Karnac.

Willis, S. (1999). Group analysis and eating disorders. *Group Analysis*, 32(1): 21–35.

Wing, J. K., Cooper, J. E., & Sartorius, N. (1974). *The Measurement and Classification of Psychiatric Symptoms*. Cambridge: Cambridge University Press.

Winnicott, D. W. (1971). *Playing and Reality*. Harmondsworth: Penguin.

Winnicott, D. W. (1976). *The Maturational Processes and the Facilitating Environment: Studies in the Theory of Emotional Development*. London: Hogarth.

Winship, G. (2003). The democratic origins of the term 'group analysis': Karl Mannheim's 'third way' for psychoanalysis and social science. *Group Analysis*, 36(1): 37–51.

Wis, M. R. (2007). *The Conductor as Leader. Principles of Leadership Applied to Life on the Podium*. Chicago, IL: GIA.

Wittry, D. (2007). *Beyond the Baton. What Every Conductor Needs to Know*. Oxford: Oxford University Press.

Wolberg, L. (1954). *The Technique of Psychotherapy*. New York: Grune & Stratton.

Wooster, E. G. (1998). The resolution of envy through jealousy. *Group Analysis*, 31(3): 327–340.

Wotton, L. (2013a). Between the notes: a musical understanding of change in group analysis. *Group Analysis*, 46(1): 48–60.

Wotton, L. (2013b). Concerto for group analysis. *Group Analysis*, 46(4): 386–394.

Yalom, I. D. (1970). *The Theory and Practice of Group Psychotherapy*. New York: Basic Books.

Zarcone, V. P. Jr, Azumi, K., Dement, W., Gulevitc, G., Kraemer, H., & Pivik, T. (1975). REM phase deprivation and schizophrenia II. *Archives of General Psychiatry*, 32(11): 1431–1436.

Zender, J. (1991). Projective identification in group psychotherapy. *Group Analysis*, 24(2): 117–128.

Zerbe, K. J. (1992). Eating disorders in the 1990s: clinical challenges and treatment implications. *Bulletin of the Menninger Clinic*, 56(2): 167–187.

Zinkin, L. (1983). Malignant mirroring. *Group Analysis*, 26(2): 113–126.

Žižek, S. (1989). *The Sublime Object of Ideology* (eighth impression). London: Verso.

Žižek, S. (2006). *The Universal Exception: Selected Writings, Volume Two*. London: Continuum.

INDEX

a priori, 8, 11, 16, 20
   analytic judgment, 6, 8, 10
   synthetic judgment, 6–8, 10–11
Abrams, D. A., 208
abuse, 121, 143
   sexual, 155, 157, 159, 161
accelerando, 202, 211
acting out, 67–68, 72, 84, 86–87, 90, 100, 145
adagio, 211, 216, 218
Adcock, S., 123, 134
addiction, 185, 196
Agazarian, Y. M., 78–79, 84, 87
aggression, 79, 91–92, 223
Agmon, S., 78–79, 84, 87
Agraval, H. R., 96
allegretto, 211, 217
allegro, 207, 211
Allport, G. W., 77
ambivalence, 28, 104, 218
American Psychiatric Association, 121, 126, 155
Ancona, L., 141
andante, 211, 216–217
Anderson, D. A., 127
Andreasen, N. C., 155
anger, 84–85, 101, 117, 136, 141–143, 146–147, 160, 217

anorexia, 122, 124–125, 130–131, 134, 143–144
   nervosa, xvi, 121–126, 131–133, 223
Anthony, E. J., xv, 3, 10, 12, 24, 67, 128, 133, 138–140, 192–193, 201, 221
antinomies, 7, 10, 13–14
anxiety, xvii, 69, 78, 81, 91, 93, 95, 105, 136, 214, 216–217
   castration, 159–160
   depressive, 96, 136
   paranoid, 129, 159, 169
   persecutory, 96, 128, 132, 159
   psychotic, xvii, 193
Anzieu, D., 99, 101
archetype, xii, 40, 43, 191 *see also*: father, mother
Argyle, N., 154
Arndt, S., 155
articulation, 40, 71, 172, 204, 208, 213
associations, 48, 93, 104, 201 *see also*: free association
atonal(ity), 202, 209, 214, 216
attachment, 54, 95, 128
attack(s), 68, 72–73, 75, 90, 103, 159, 164
   on linking, 19, 72, 102
   on the mother, 70
   panic, 125, 156, 169
   sadistic, 17, 91, 150

Austin, J., 123, 134
authority, 21, 32, 193, 198
　conductor's/father's, 11, 21, 50, 198
　figure, 205
　friendly, 32–33
　issue phase, 79, 87
autonomy, xv, 7, 22, 42, 53, 121, 145,
　192, 197, 205–206, 222
axis
　diagnosis in, 126
　imaginary, 41
　manic, 91
　metaphoric/symbolic, 41
　metonymic/imaginary, 41
　paradigmatic, 179
　real, 41
　symbolic, 41
Azumi, K., 172

Bach, J. S., 210
Balaban, E., 208
Barbin, J. M., 127
Barchas, J., 172
Barenboim, D., 200, 205
Barrick, T., 200
Barth, F. D., 47–48
basic assumption, 18, 29, 191 *see also*:
　group, group phases, leader
　dependence, 29, 51, 191
　　and fight–flight, 53–54, 84, 87, 191
　pairing, 87, 191
Basso Continuo, 202
Beethoven, L. van, 202
behaviour(al), 42, 66, 70–71, 84, 91, 93,
　97–99, 101–104, 122, 127, 142–143,
　150, 206, 208 *see also*: therapy
　bulimic, 134
　elements, 126, 200
　healthy, 137, 203
　mother's, 88
　pattern, 82, 201
Bekker, P., 202
beliefs about voices questionnaire-1
　(BAVQ-1), 155
Bell, N. W., 78
Bentall, R. P., 140

bereavement, 159, 185
Bergman, A., 98–99, 106, 122, 133
Bergmann, M. S., 96
Berlioz, H., xvii, 203–204
Bernard, H. S., 98
Bernstein, D., 155
Bernstein, L., 204–205
Bhatara, A., 208
binge-eating, 127, 129
Bion, W. R. (*passim*)
　alpha-elements, 15–18, 29–31, 50,
　　55, 97, 101, 103, 112, 165
　beta-elements, 15, 17–18, 29–31, 50,
　　55, 97, 101, 103, 112, 165
　cited works, xv–xvi, 3, 6, 8, 15–22,
　　24, 29–30, 39, 41, 49–51, 53–55,
　　64–69, 72, 74–75, 78–80, 82–84,
　　87, 89, 91, 97, 108–109, 111–112,
　　118, 122, 132–133, 136–137, 141,
　　145, 148, 150–152, 157–158, 161,
　　164–167, 171, 181, 191, 195, 198,
　　207, 215, 220, 223
Biran, H., 153
Birchwood, M., 131, 140, 150, 155
body mass index (BMI), 126
body shape questionnaire (BSQ), 127
Böhm, K., 205
bond(s), 26, 99, 128, 130, 143, 146, 178
　emotional, 84, 90
　libidinal, 21, 26
　maternal, 25, 106
　mothering, 99
Borneman, E., 47–48
Botstein, L., 204, 207
Bradshaw, T., 150
breast, 17, 22, 41, 49–53, 61, 63–64, 68,
　136–137, 140, 164, 178, 185, 187
　see also: envy, group, mother, self
　as real, 41, 108, 164–165, 172, 187
　"bad", 29, 178
　"dead", 29, 152
　"good", 50, 63, 137, 178
　/penis, 19, 29, 41, 63
Brennan, C., 123
Bridger, H., 30
Bridgford-West, L., 123, 134

Brockington, I. F., 135
Brown, D. G., 4–5, 25
Bruch, H., 122
Buckley, P., 97
Buelow, G. J., 213
bulimia, 134, 143 *see also*: behaviour
  nervosa, xvi, 121–126, 130–133, 223
Bulimia Test-Revised (BULIT-R), 126
Bülow, H. von, 205
Butterfield, A., 212

cadence, 214
Caparrós, N., 51, 53–54, 66, 125
capitalism, 184
  consumer, xvii, 187, 196–197
  industrial, 183–184
  modern, 197
  postmodern, xvii, 224
Caplin, W. E., 210, 213
Carlyle, T., 189
case
  acute, 125
  history, 83, 86
  individual, 124, 134
Casper, R. C., 121
castration, 12, 64, 160, 180, 183, 195
  see also: anxiety
  non-, 108
  symbolic, 12–13, 33, 37–40, 108–109, 113, 116–117, 179–180, 187, 195–196
  traumatic (unsymbolised), 36
category(ies), xviii, 8, 187
cause, 9, 38–39, 41–42, 65, 66, 100, 117, 181, 188
Cezayirli, E., 200
Chadwick, P., 131, 140, 150, 155
Charles, E., 97
Chazan, R., 138, 139
childhood trauma questionnaire (CTQ), 155
Choi, J., 208
chord(s), 208–209, 212–214
circle, xv, 12, 14–16, 20–22, 37, 42, 201, 214, 222 *see also*: groupishness, oedipal, therapeutic

and the triangle, xv, 16–17, 20, 42, 222
vicious, 10, 183, 197
clan, 6, 25–26, 28
Clancy, R., 123, 134
clinical vignettes
  Alexander, 125, 128–129
  Alexia, 215, 218
  Alexis, 58–60
  Andreas, 215, 217
  Angela, 57–60
  Angeliki, 80, 82–90, 92–93
  Anita, 156, 160
  Anna, 125–131
  Antonis, 125, 128–129, 131
  Aphrodite, 80, 82, 85
  Betty, 59, 61
  Christos, 168
  Dimitra, 125–131
  Evangelos, 57, 59–60
  Fotini, 125, 128–129
  Gabriella, 125, 128–129
  George, 143–148, 154–155, 157, 159–160, 167–171
  Georgia, 143
  Grigoris, 58–60
  Helen, 215, 218
  Helena, 143–144, 146
  Helka, 80, 82–85, 89, 92
  Hilary, 92
  Irene, 70–71
  Jane, 102–103
  Jim, 168
  Joanna, 215–218
  John, 143
  Kate, 154–155, 157, 160
  Katerina, 80–93
  Katy, 92
  Konstantin, 115–116
  Kosmas, 116–117
  Kostas, 154–155, 157, 160
  Leonidas, 215, 217
  Lila, 156–157, 159–160
  Maria, 114–115
  Maria-Helena, 169–171
  Mary, 143–144, 146

250   INDEX

Michael, 156–157, 159–160
Natalia, 57, 60
Nikos, 141–148, 154–155, 157–158, 160
Panagiotis, 215, 217
Panos, 156, 159–160
Penelope, 215, 217–218
Peter, 125, 128–129
Petros, 215, 217
Socrates, 125, 128–129, 131
Sofia, 154–155, 157, 159–160, 167–171
Stavros, 89–90, 92
Stavroula, 215–218
Stella, 69
Stylianos, 102–105
Vassilis, 80, 82–83, 86–88, 89–90, 92
Virginia, 59–60
Voula, 72–75
Cohen, H., 172
Cohn, H. W., 4–5
Coker, S., 134
Collaer, P., 213–214
combined parents, 18, 20–21, 65, 68, 70, 141, 167
commodity, 181–182, 184–186
communication(s), 17, 19, 50, 69, 111, 144, 148, 152–153, 164–165, 170, 185, 192, 198, 201–202, 208, 223–224
  group, 152, 165, 206, 208, 212, 219
  inter-, 8, 10, 127, 132–133, 139–140, 156, 192, 206
  interpersonal and transpersonal, 34, 198
  verbal, xii
  non-, 128, 206
community, 34, 182, 189, 192, 194, 198, 206
  democratic, 32, 34, 202, 224
comprehensive assessment of symptoms and history (CASH), 155
concept, xvi, 6–7, 10, 12, 16, 19–20, 25, 27, 30–31, 33, 35–37, 53, 61, 77, 109, 166, 177–178, 185, 189, 191, 193, 196, 198

conductor (*passim*) *see also*:
    authority, countertransference, group, identification, imago, internalisation, intervention, need, relationship, representation, thinking
  as a father, 52, 61, 117, 204, 219, 221
  as a significant note, 200
  as intellectual leader, 55, 113, 115
  as leader, 14
  competition with the, 56
  considered as a maestro, 225
  exclusively as a mother, 130
  ideal, 205, 211
  informal, 203
  modern, 205
  of an orchestra, 55, 191, 211, 213
  professional, 203
  the role of, 114, 205, 218, 220
conflict(ual), xii, 4, 33, 40–42, 57, 68, 77, 79, 81, 84, 91–92, 99, 105, 114, 147, 159, 186, 190, 195, 197, 210, 214, 216–218 *see also*: unconscious
  family, 10, 78
  inner, 97, 201, 212
  oedipal/Oedipus, 10–11, 14, 33
confrontation, 50, 84, 113, 116–117, 158, 217
  between father and son, 82, 117
  with the therapist, 115
Conlon, I., 23
conscious(ness), 5–6, 18, 40, 66–67, 72, 74, 110, 152, 181, 201, 212 *see also*: unconscious
  level, 181, 204, 210
  pre-, 150, 153, 161
  self-, 113, 118, 181
  social, 110, 112–113, 115–118
consumption
  ceaseless, 185
  conspicuous, 197
  over-, 185, 195–196, 224
container, 8, 10, 15–17, 19–20, 22, 31, 90, 103, 122, 132, 167, 211 *see also*: group, matrix
  function as, 64, 101

contemporaneity, 38–39, 41–42
content, xvii–xviii, 152, 158–159, 169, 181, 219
  manifest, 152, 158
  of a dream, 152, 158–159, 172
contour, 210
  harmonic, 212
Cooper, J. E., 149
Cooper, P. J., 123, 127, 134
Cooper, Z., 123, 126–127
Cornwell, G., 78
countertransference, 98, 107–108
  see also: transference
  conductor's, 79–80
  feelings, 122, 212
Craighero, L., 172
crescendo, 32, 35, 93, 202, 207, 211, 217, 219
Crick, F., 172
culture, 35, 38, 49, 51, 56, 81, 83, 188–189, 203, 208–209
  analytic, 153, 191, 210
  evolution of, 38, 40

D'Agostino, A., 172
Dahlhaus, C., 213–214
Dalal, F., xv, 4–5, 25
Dalenberg, C., 98, 108
Daughterty, C., 100
Davies, A., 200, 211–212
De Maré, P., xvii, 24, 49, 51, 190, 202
De Paola, H., 63, 65
De Zulueta, F., 100
death, 19, 73, 91, 96, 104, 114, 116, 147, 159, 216–217, 219
  instinct, 65, 72–74, 91–92
  symbolic, 11, 32, 35, 54, 61, 108, 112, 116, 160, 164, 170
decline, xvii, 142, 177, 181, 206
decrescendo, 32, 35, 93, 207, 211, 217
defence, 68, 70, 150
  mechanism(s), 65–66, 70, 78, 150, 190–191
Dellaverson, V., 123
delusion(al), 35, 74, 154, 171

demand, 72, 113, 137, 180–184, 187–189, 191, 194–195, 197
  for love, 38, 178, 180, 182, 184–185, 187, 189, 194–195, 197–198, 224
  for the breast, 41, 187
Dement, W., 172
dependence, 18, 55, 78–79, 84, 95, 100, 157, 190, 197, 212 *see also*: basic assumption, fear
  counter-, 79, 84, 87
  malignant, 67, 69
  need, 33, 97, 157, 206
  on a divinity, 18, 29
  on a leader, 24
  on the group, 55, 157
  on the mother, 33, 55
depression, 80, 121, 125–127, 129, 134–137, 142–143, 145, 147–148, 156 *see also*: symptom
  and borderline personality disorder, 125, 134
  and obsessive compulsive disorder, 121, 125, 156
  in schizophrenia, xvi, 140, 223
  severe, 127, 152, 155
  syndrome, 135, 137
depressive position, 15–16, 19, 21, 29–31, 54–55, 61, 66–67, 70, 73, 78–79, 87, 96–97, 103, 105, 109, 122, 124, 129, 132–133, 136–137, 141, 145, 147–148, 151–152, 157–159, 164–167, 170, 213–216, 218, 220
deprivation, 12, 36, 41, 83, 103, 145, 186, 196
desire *see also*: mother, oedipal, representation
  and despair, 182
  "deadening" of, xvii
  degeneration of, 197
  dialectic of, xvii
  distortion of, 186
  evolution of human, 224
  familiarisation with, 195
  for imaginary recognition, 188
  for relatedness, 182

for the arrival of a new member, 89
for the Other's desire, 180
for the parent, 177
hallucinated, 152
incestuous, 82
mature, 36
members', 186
memory and, 65, 172
of the group, 39
of the Other/Phallus, 179–180
psychotic dimension of, 195
roots of, 177–178
despair, xvii, 142, 182–184, 186, 194, 224
destruction, 18, 65, 183–184 *see also*: imaginary, symbolic
destructiveness, 65, 91, 223
development(al), xi, xvi, 14, 51, 70, 95, 110, 114, 118, 122, 127, 130, 156, 179, 185–186, 188, 190, 192, 198, 201, 215, 224
level of, 55
mature, 18
mental, 42, 136
of hallucinations, 154
of neurosis, 183
of psychoanalysis, 177
of social consciousness, 115
patient's, 64
personal, 145
phase of, 21, 61
separation–individuation, 54
psychic, 65, 67
psychosocial, 95
social, 194
stage of, 64, 201
anal–sadistic, 48
oral–sadistic, 78
therapeutic, xvi
Diagnostic and Statistical Manual of Mental Disorders (DSM-IV), 126, 155
differentiation, 4, 24, 48, 70, 122, 130, 132
Dimen, M., 47–48
diminuendo, 202, 207, 219

disjunct, 5, 38, 210
disorder, 136 *see also*: eating disorders
affective, 135
schizo-, 149, 154–155, 161, 188
obsessive–compulsive, 121, 125, 156
personality
borderline, xvi, 13, 72, 96–102, 105–107, 116, 121, 123, 125–126, 131, 134, 148, 156, 215, 223
compulsive–neurotic, 115
narcissistic, 66, 96, 99, 116
paranoid, 67
psychic, 223
dissonance, 211–212, 214
Dobscha, S. K., 172
Dolan, R. J., 172
dream(ing) (*passim*) *see also*: content, symbolic
ability to, xvi, 151, 153–154, 157, 161, 163, 166–167, 171, 223
evolution of, 164
group, 152, 156, 158–160, 165–166, 169, 172
in psychosis, xviii, 163, 171–172
individual, 152, 172
memory, 172
neurotic, 157–159, 161, 173
normal, 152, 158, 173
psychotic, 151, 164–165, 169, 171–173
reconstitution of, xviii, 153, 171
screen, 165
telling, 154
the nucleus of, 171
-work-alpha, 164–165
Drob, S. L., 98
drop(ping)-out, 68–69, 75, 78, 80, 87–88, 91–92, 96–98, 100–101, 106–107, 123, 126, 130, 132, 134
Duchmann, E. G., 127
Dudamel, G., 205
dynamics, 157, 165, 201, 203–204, 206–209, 211, 219, *see also*: family, oedipal
group, xi, 68, 98, 130, 156, 192, 201, 202, 209–210

eating attitudes test (EAT), 126
eating disorder examination (EDE), 126
eating disorder inventory-2 (EDI-2), 127
    symptom checklist (EDI-SC), 127
eating disorders, 122, 124, 126, 132–133, 139, 223 *see also*: anorexia, bulimia, symptoms
    group analysis, xvi, 123, 133
effect, 18, 35, 38–39, 41–42, 74, 116, 150, 200, 211, 213
efficient generation mechanism (EGM), 149
ego, xvi, 9, 26–28, 65, 75, 101, 150, 188, 190 *see also*: leadership
    alteration of the, 64–68, 72
    ideal, 6–9, 26–27, 32, 34, 36, 41, 109–112, 114, 118, 190–191, 197
    super-, 27–28, 32–34, 79, 93, 109–110, 112, 118, 150, 154, 158
        archaic, 83, 85, 118
        mothering, 165
        murderous, 137, 152
Einsink, B., 154
ending(s)
    complete psychoanalytic, 111
    early, 93, 96–98, 106, 113
    ideal, 109
    in group analysis, 96, 117, 223
    mature, 106
Engels, E., 81
enjoyment, 12, 21, 184, 208
envy (*passim*) *see also*: penis
    breast, 52, 63–64, 68, 70
    emergence of, 64, 73
    foundations of, 65–66
    in people with psychosis, 66
    manifestations of, 66, 71–72
    object of, 63
    of knowledge, 18, 21
    of the opposite sex, 111
    origins of, 64
    phenomenon of, 63, 67–68
epistemological model, xv, 4, 8, 14, 17, 222

Eros, 177–178
    and Thanatos, 65
Escher, S., 149
exogamy, 7–8, 26, 28, 38–39, 41
experience, xvi, 8–9, 37, 49, 54, 56, 66, 75, 90, 92, 95, 99, 106, 109, 118, 123–125, 127–126, 128–130, 133, 135, 138, 144–145, 148, 153, 156–159, 168, 181, 198, 204, 210, 215, 221, 223
    biological, 10–11, 14
    clinical, 3, 8, 95, 98, 107
    emotional, 170, 172
    fragmentary, 99, 165
    normal, 54–56, 99
    sensory, 15, 21, 31
    sensual, 164, 171

factor(ial), 5, 24, 30–31. 37, 57, 65–66, 79, 98–99, 105, 107–108, 121, 123, 127, 133, 153, 165–167, 172, 183, 201–202, 204, 224
    contributing, 143, 184
    group-
        analytic, xvi, 124, 139
        specific, 153, 192, 202
        therapeutic, 151, 154
Fairburn, C. G., 123, 126–127
Fallows, D., 212
family, 6, 10, 26, 28, 49, 59, 72, 74, 78, 86, 102–103, 137, 141–142, 177, 197 *see also*: group
    conflict, 10, 78
    level, 22, 29
    primary, 34, 78, 155
fantasy, 65, 74, 86, 90, 169–170, 185
    see also: object, unconscious
    archaic, 15, 17, 114
    of returning to the womb, 64–65
    of the "anal child", 81
    of the primal father, 110
    of the primal scene, 15, 80, 163–169, 171, 173
    primary, 168
Faragher, E. B., 155
Farber, B. A., 95

INDEX

farewell, 71, 74–75, 103, 105–106, 131, 147, 214–215, 223
   one-session, 131, 133
   prepare, 71, 125, 131, 133–134, 159
   successful, 118, 156, 168
Farmer, J., 126
Farrell, E., 122
father (*passim*) *see also*: authority, conductor, confrontation, fantasy, figure, function, identification, imago, internalisation, leader, Name-of-the-Father, need, oedipal, penis, representation, therapist
   archaic, 9, 21, 40, 48, 50, 52, 112, 152
   archetype, 40
   as intellectual leader, 27
   castrating, 48–50
   "dead", 9–10, 26–27, 29, 32, 34, 36–37, 48–49, 74, 114–115, 117, 204–207, 219
   genuine symbolic, 49, 55
   good/symbolic, 190
   imaginary, 9–10, 12, 36–37, 186, 189–190, 194
   killing of the, 18–19, 26, 32, 35
   "living", 9, 13, 26, 29, 35–36, 48–49, 114–115, 117, 205–207, 219
   of the primal horde, 9, 50, 54–55
   primal, 8–13, 21–22, 26, 28, 30, 32–38, 40–41, 50, 55–56, 110–111, 206
   real, 36, 222
   symbolic, 9, 36–37, 40, 42, 48–52, 55, 61, 109, 122, 133, 179, 186–187, 189–190, 198, 204, 207
   the ideal of the, 8
fatherhood, 26, 179
   ontology and anthropology of, 25
fear
   of being sexually abused, 159
   of dependency, 100
   of earthquakes, 114
   of incest, 85
   of regression, 144
   of the arrival of a new member, 90

Feary, R., 121
Feinberg, I., 172
Feinstein, D. I., 172
Feldman, E., 63, 65
femininity, 39–40, 91
Ferguson, J., 172
fight, 18, 29, 58, 113, 150 *see also*: basic assumption
   –flight, 31, 53–54, 79, 84, 87, 191
   phase, 79, 84, 87
figure *see also*: authority, transference
   active, 115
   directive, 166
   father, 50, 52, 61, 75, 95, 99, 101, 104, 117, 130, 152, 161, 201, 204
   female, 73, 112, 118
   imaginary, 110
   male, 112
   maternal, 81, 192
   mother, 58, 61, 75, 83, 93, 110, 130, 141, 148, 204, 207, 218
   mothering, 116, 154
   omnipotent, 54
   parental, 48, 113, 117, 194
   paternal, 78–79, 102, 195
   persecutory, 159
   therapeutic, 141
financial, 57–59, 101, 187, 196–197
Fink, L., 155
first violin, 203, 216
Fiske, S. T., 77
fixation(s), 13, 65, 82, 100, 107, 110, 115–117, 118, 122, 188, 197, 201 *see also*: oedipal
   homosexual, 109, 113
   in the oral-sadistic stage, 168
   on interpersonal relations, 193
   on the group, 79, 115–116
   on the mother, 115, 180
Flaum, M., 155
Fletcher, P. C., 172
flight, 18, 29, 79, 84 *see also*: fight
Foguel, B. S., 23, 139, 195
Fombonne, E., 121
forte, 211, 217–218
   mezzo-, 211

fortissimo, 211, 217–218
Foulkes, S. H., xi, xv, xvii, 3–7, 9–16,
    23–25, 27, 30, 32–36, 38–39, 41,
    50, 55, 64, 67, 78–79, 93, 97, 101,
    109–112, 114, 118, 123–126, 128,
    131–133, 138–141, 148, 151–153,
    157, 159, 165–166, 171, 173,
    190–193, 198–202, 204–206,
    209–210, 219, 221–222, 224–225
fragmentation
  multi-, 221
  of mirroring, 193
  of the imaginary, 193
  of the self-image, 187, 193–194
  of the symbolic, 193
  of thought, 194
Frankfurt School, 24
free association, 105, 154
free-floating discussion, xvii, 153,
    211, 214, 219
Freud, S. (*passim*)
  cited works, 4, 6–10, 13, 24, 26–27,
      40–41, 48–51, 53–55, 61–65, 73,
      75, 96, 110–111, 113, 136, 148,
      150–153, 157, 160–161,
      163–164, 171, 177–178, 181,
      186, 188, 190, 197, 204, 209
Friedman, R., 169
Friston, K. J., 172
Frith, C. D., 150, 172
Fromm-Reichman, F., 95, 98, 108
frustration, xii, 11, 51, 79, 97, 101,
    108–109, 116–117, 136, 140, 145,
    147, 182–183, 194–195
fugue, 203, 214, 217
function (*passim*) see also: container,
    money
  alpha-, 31
  direct, 24
  good enough, 140
  maternal, xv, 14, 16, 23, 40, 42–44
  of groups, xv, 23, 25, 111, 169
  of primitive thought, 38
  of the (primal) father, 12, 22, 36–37,
      222
    /leader/therapist, 36

  of the imago, 24
  of the mother, 22
  oral–sadistic stage, 19
  parental, xv, 222
  paternal, 4, 14, 23, 39, 42–44, 194
  propositional, 43
fusion, 13, 33, 50, 52–53, 61, 99, 101,
    116, 123, 132, 179, 190–191, 222
  see also: money
  phenomena, 128
  with the archaic mother, 33

Gabbard, G. O., 98, 108, 123
Gambini, O., 172
Garfinkel, P. E., 121, 126
Garner, D. M., 121, 126–127
Geist, R. A., 122
Gemmill, G., 78
genitality, 72, 82–84, 87, 89, 91–92
Gergiev, V., 205
gift, 22, 55–56, 60–61, 103, 147 see also:
    money
Glass, S., 123
Gleaves, D. G., 127
Glick, P., 77
Glinski, A., 149
global assessment of functioning
    scale (GAF), 126
globalisation, 187, 191, 193
God, 7, 28, 128, 143, 152, 155, 157,
    160, 167–169, 179
Gold, B., 123, 132–133
Golynkina, K., 139–140
Gonzalez de Chavez, M., 153
good (the)
  common, 186
  primary, 196
  relational, 197
Goren, Y., 97
Gottesmann, C., 172
Gould, L. N., 149
Grasby, P. M., 172
gratification, xvii, 52, 108, 133, 136,
    182, 185, 197
gratitude, 54, 61, 70, 75
Green, A., 185

Green, M. F., 149–150
Gregg, J., 208
grief, 88, 103, 116, 147, 159
group (*passim*) *see also*:
communication, dependence, desire, dream, dynamics, factor, fixation, function, identification, illusion, individual, internalisation, leader, level/phase/stage, matrix, member, movement, orchestra, process, psychotherapy, relationship, representation, speech, state, symbiosis, tempo, therapist
  analyst, xii–xiii, xvii, 5, 23–24, 138, 140–141, 199, 201, 203, 205–206, 208–211
  and the conductor, 33, 69, 71, 75, 79, 81, 83–84, 89, 92, 103, 115, 157, 160, 203, 206, 210
  as a "cold womb", 86
  as a concerto, 200
  as a mass, 190
  as a mature process, 195
  as a persecutory figure, 159
  as a whole, xvi, 24, 51, 54, 61, 68–71, 73, 78, 82–83, 86, 97, 128–130, 145, 156, 167, 171, 193, 201–202, 206, 210, 219
  as an instrument, 206
  as an internalised object, 52
  as breast, 52–53, 140
  as container, 132, 169
  as equal to a breast, 22
  as "good" and omnipotent, 52
  as initial object, 191
  as mother, 27, 56, 93, 101, 125, 132, 139, 148, 154, 167, 191, 207
  basic, 19, 29, 50–51, 53–55, 112, 190
  basic assumption, 18–19, 29, 31–32, 79, 191
  closed, 215–216
  conceived as a dreaming matrix, 153
  concept of the, 189, 191, 198
  evolution, xvi, 27–28, 31, 34, 51, 124, 129–130, 145, 152, 157, 166, 171, 203, 209, 211, 219
  family, 6, 22, 26, 37, 78, 197
  female elements of the, 117–118
  formation of the, 28, 31, 34
  global(ised), 187, 193, 197
  ideal, 9, 26, 152
    as embodied in the leader, 9
  instrumental, 202
  large, xii, xv, 25, 51, 190, 193, 202, 204
  leaderless, 19, 24, 30–31, 112, 191, 207
  modernist imago of the, 190
  music therapy, 200, 212
  musical, 203, 225
  natural, 7–8, 26, 38, 41
  notion of the, 189
  ontology of the, 165
  partial, 212
  phenomena, 93, 97, 165, 193, 201, 223
  post-totemic, 26
  prehistoric, 26
  primal, 110
  primary, 15, 78
  self-exiled, 26
  small, xv, 27, 78, 190–193, 199–200
  social, 7–8, 26–28, 38, 41, 49
  socio-political, 78
  sub-, 204
  therapist, 70, 112, 123, 132–133, 139, 152, 168, 199, 206
  therapy, 3, 36, 70, 96–97, 121, 125–126, 131–132, 142, 144, 147, 153, 156, 167, 195
  totemic, 6
  treatment, 97, 127, 131, 138
  work, 19, 27, 29–32, 50, 54–55, 112, 191, 209
group analysis/analytic (*passim*)
  see also: antinomies, eating disorders, endings, factor, instrumentation, music, postmodern, psychotherapy

epistemological
  foundation of, 5
  paradigm of, 10
history and practice of, 224
meta-theory of, xi, 3, 221
method, 123–124, 131
model, 19, 123, 151
  epistemological, xv, 4, 6, 14
  modified version of, xvi, 124
paradigm, 4, 10
principles, 25, 124, 153, 200
psychoanalysis, xi–xiii, xv, 4, 6, 10, 20, 34, 110, 222
situation, xvi, 64, 206, 210–211, 213, 219, 224
social dimensions of, 199
technique, 126, 221
group phases
  anal-expulsive, 84, 87
  anal-retentive, 87
  anal-sadistic, 61
  basic assumption, 53–54, 84, 87, 191
  counterdependence, 79, 84, 87
  final, 67, 70
  initial, 11, 13, 168
  intermediate, 20–21, 67
  of bodily and mental images, 13
  oral-dependent, 79, 84
  power: authority issue, 79, 87
groupishness, 6, 12, 15, 24–25, 111
  circle of, 15–16, 19, 37
guilt, 28, 82, 86, 136, 142, 182
Gulevitc, G., 172
Gunderson, J., 96
Gutheil, T. G., 96

Haddock, G., 140, 155
Hafsi, M., 79
hallucination(s), 31, 144, 154, 157, 160
  auditory verbal, 144, 149–150, 153–154, 157, 161
  morbid, 152
  visual
    and auditory, 151
    invisible-, 151, 165

harmony, 38, 42, 44, 141, 203, 209, 211–212, 214, 219
Harper-Giuffre, H., 123
hate, 48, 56, 71, 104, 111, 115, 137
  see also: self
  –love, 28
Haydn, F. J., 202
hearing voices, 149–151, 153–161, 167
Heesacker, R., 130
Hegel, G. W. F., 181
Herron, W. G., 47
hieroglyph, 15, 31
Hinshelwood, R. D., 30, 190
history, xvii, 6, 83, 181, 184, 224
Hobsbawm, E., 189
Hobson, A., 172
Hobson, J. A., 172
Hoffman, R. E., 149, 172
Holmes, B. M., 96
Holmes, J., 95
homosexuality, 48–49, 72, 81, 91, 109, 113, 116, 118, 170 *see also*: sublimation
hope, xviii, 11, 18, 21, 29, 52, 68, 101–102, 104–105, 151–152, 183, 186, 207, 222, 225
Hopfield, J. J., 172
Hopper, E., xvii, 5, 81, 181, 193
horde, 13, 28
  primal, 6, 9, 13, 28, 34, 50, 54–55, 110
  primitive, 9, 25–26, 41
Horne, A., 23
Horwitz, L., 79–80, 97
hospitalisation, 167
Howard, M., 200
Howe, C. Q., 208
Hrushovski, B., 209
Hudson, I., 123
Hulse, W. C., 153
Hummelen, J. W., 99
Huron, D., 207

id, 65, 83, 85, 150
  archaic, 65, 83

identification(s) (*passism*)
  counter-, 70, 117
  distorted, 113, 117
  good enough, 116
  in the sense of incorporation, 116
  with an archaic superego, 83
  with one's own sex, 160
  with the absolute phallus, 185
  with the "bad" aspect of the group, 53
  with the breast, 113
  with the conductor, 61, 109, 116–117
  with the ego ideal, 111
  with the father, 15, 32, 37, 113, 122, 133, 179
  with the group, 52, 133, 169
  with the group therapist, 133
  with the mother, 113, 133
  with the Name-of-the-Father, 180, 198
  with the opposite sex, 111
  with the parent of the same sex, 160
  with the parental figures, 113, 117
  with the paternal ideal, 109
  with the penis, 113
ideogram, 15, 21, 31, 164, 165 *see also*: hieroglyph, primal scene
ideology(ies), 6, 24, 77, 182, 184, 189–191, 197
illusion, 9, 18, 21, 26, 29, 52, 188
  group, 9, 26, 28–29
image(ry), 34, 49–50, 78, 93, 101, 129, 152, 157, 160–161, 164–165, 168, 171–172, 178, 198
  bodily and mental, 13, 34, 139–141
  body, 13, 34, 123–124, 127–128, 132, 193
  fragmented, 152, 165, 193
  maternal and paternal, 81
  of self, 132, 140, 178, 187, 193–194
  of the mother, 34, 101
  of the primal scene, 164
  refined, 157, 164, 172
  visual, 164–165

imaginary
  destruction of the, 184
  fragmentation of the, 193
  overspill of the, 184
  saturation of the, 185
imago(es)
  maternal, 6–7, 16, 23–24, 100, 198
  of the conductor, 109
  of the father, 24, 32, 109
  of the group/mother, 109
  of the leader, 24
  of the subject's desire, 191
  paternal, 6–8, 24
  personal parental, 109
impression(s), 8, 69, 97, 150
impulse, 30, 89, 178
incest(uous), 34, 36, 40, 49, 80–84, 86–87, 90–91, 154 *see also*: fear, transference
incorporation, 52, 64, 96, 110, 116, 125
independence, 55, 95, 190, 197
individual
  and the group, 20, 38, 42, 186
  anti-social psychopathic, 138
  /hero, 189
  outstanding, 24, 29
individualism, 4, 178, 189
individuation, 48, 53, 55, 62, 70 *see also*: separation
insatiability, 181–182, 185
instinct(ual), 5, 65, 178 *see also*: death
  constitutional strength of, 64–65
  libidinal, 21
  life, 65, 73–74, 91–92
  satisfaction of, 21
  substratum, 65–66
instrumentation, 209–210
interaction, 16, 34, 127, 131, 192, 198, 200, 203–204, 208, 214
intercommunication(s), 8, 10, 127, 132–133, 139, 156, 192, 206
intercourse, 74, 81, 85, 184
internalisation
  of the conductor/father, 113
  of the group as mother figure, 207
  of the maternal object, 135
  of the parental couple, 71

Internet, 147–148, 187–188, 197
interpretation, 19, 30–31, 73, 84, 103, 164, 167, 204, 206, 208, 219
interrelation(s), xviii, 5–6, 14, 42, 44, 199–200
intertemporaneity, 38–39, 41–42
intervention, 71, 87, 89, 130, 140, 218
   conductor's, 60, 213
   therapeutic, 150, 156
introjection, xvi, 52, 74, 96, 128, 223
Iqbal, Z., 131, 140, 150

Jameson, F., 185
jealousy, 59, 64, 68, 70, 87, 95
Johns, L. C., 150
Jones, J., 123, 134
Juranville, A., 179–180

Kahn, L. S., 79
kaleidoscope, xv, 42–43, 222
Kanas, N., 153
Kant, I., xv, 5–8, 221
Kantzas, I., 172
Karajan, H. von, 205
Karterud, S., 5, 25
Kauff, P. F., 108
Kelly, P. H., 172
Kendell, R. E., 135
Kernberg, O. F., 96, 99
keys, 209, 214–216
Kinsbourne, M., 149–150
kinship, 12, 26, 28, 37
Klein, M. (*passim*)
   cited works, 14–15, 50–54, 61, 63–65, 67–68, 70, 73–75, 78–79, 81, 84, 87, 91–92, 96, 100, 104–106, 108–111, 113, 122, 132–133, 136, 141, 145, 147–148, 157–158, 161, 164, 171, 178, 182, 191, 198, 213–214, 220, 223
knowledge, 3, 6–8, 18, 21, 25, 204
Koelsch, S., 200
Kohon, G., 185
Kohut, H., 96, 99, 122, 132
Koukis, A., xi–xii, 66, 112, 163, 181
Kraemer, H., 172

Kretsch, R., 97
Krueger, D., 47–48

Lacan, J. (*passim*)
   cited works, 9, 12, 37, 40–41, 44, 55, 108, 122, 178–181, 183, 186, 188, 197–198
Lake, C. R., 135
language, xv, 40, 44, 151, 169, 171, 179, 183, 185, 192, 198, 209, 222
   body, 205–206
largo, 211
Lawrence, R., 150
Lawrence, W. G., 153
Laxenaire, M., 193
Le Bon, G., 189–190
leader *see also*: dependence, therapist
   archaic, 28, 112, 114, 205
   as father, 187, 190
   basic-assumption-group, 18, 29, 191
   in the group, 14, 32, 34–35, 50, 55, 114, 118, 166, 206, 223
   intellectual, 19, 22, 27, 29–31, 41, 55, 112–115, 118, 191
   of the group, 7–9, 13–14, 32, 34–35, 50, 55, 112, 118, 166, 206
   work-group, 29
leadership, 127, 191, 204–205
   as ego ideal, 197
   medical, 30
   military, 190
   paternal, 197
   primal, 25
   profile, 141
   sense of, 113
   servant, 205–207, 219, 223
   strong, 49, 205
Lear, T., 23
leave-taking, 101, 103, 110, 116, 145, 147 *see also*: farewell
Lees, S., 155
legato, 213
lento, 211, 216, 218
Leudar, I., 149
Leung, N., 121, 130

level/phase/stage (*passim*) *see also*:
conscious, development, group
phases, libido, mirror, oedipal,
transference, unconscious
anal, 79, 81
 -sadistic, 48–50, 53–56, 78, 109,
 158, 165
archaic, 9, 13, 35, 96, 123, 127–128,
 139
current, 14, 32, 34–35, 139, 152, 157,
 165, 171
family, 22, 29
first, 83, 126, 168
genital, 49, 54–56, 78, 62, 81, 92, 188
group, 8–9, 14, 18, 34, 109, 125, 153,
 156, 192
imaginary, 9–10, 36, 41, 178, 180,
 183–186, 189, 193, 197
immature, 34, 50
individual, 9, 22, 109, 125, 177, 180
latent, 33–34, 205
manifest, 33–34, 206
mature, 13–14, 126, 152, 166, 193,
 205
neurotic, 12, 116, 166, 196
of images, 124, 139
ontological, 37–38, 165, 171
oral, 49, 54–55, 61, 123–124, 127,
 136, 164, 166, 213, 217
 archaic-, 132
 -aggressive, 79
 -dependent, 79, 84
 -sadistic, 15, 17, 19, 21, 29, 48, 51,
 65, 67, 70, 73, 78–79, 84, 96,
 100, 105, 109, 122, 136–137,
 139–140, 144–145, 150,
 157–158, 164–165, 167–168,
 178, 188
personal, 37, 97, 198
phallic, 48, 62, 158, 165
primary, 11, 13, 34–35
primordial, 13, 34, 50, 165–166, 168,
 171
projective, 34, 50, 123–124, 126–128,
 132, 139
psychotic, 12, 51, 53

reality, 33, 124, 129, 133
secondary, 11, 32, 34, 84, 168
separation-individuation, 53–54,
 108
social, 6, 16, 22, 139, 187, 194,
 197–198
symbolic, 10, 12, 27, 36, 51, 164,
 171, 179, 184, 188, 193, 196
Lévi-Strauss, C., xi, xv, 25, 38–40, 44,
 221–222
Levitin, D. J., 208
liberalism, 6, 198, 207
libido, 21, 49, 177–178, 188 *see also*:
 instinct
Limosani, I., 172
linking, xv, 52, 144 *see also*: attack
 a prototype of, 17, 50, 165
Lippert, R. A., 95
Lo Verso, G., 3–5, 14
Lofton, P., 100
loss, 91–92, 100, 116, 130
Lyndon, P., 23, 79, 83
Lyons-Ruth, K., 96

Maar, V., 108
maestro, xvii, 205–207, 219, 225
Mahler, G., 205
Mahler, M. S., 51, 53–54, 67, 98–99,
 106, 108, 122, 133, 145, 159
Mairs, H., 150
Maizels, N., 64–65
Malloch, S., 212
Mandel, E., 185
Mangiarotti, A., 141
Mann, A., 214
Mann, B., 121
Mannheim, K., 24, 189
Mannheim school, 24, 202
Manzone, M. L., 172
Marcuse, H., 186
Mark, P., 100
Martean, L., 99
Marx, K., 184, 194, 197
masochistic psychopathology, 80
maternity, xv, 7, 30, 35, 37, 39–42, 91,
 101, 103, 221–222

matrix, 10, 32, 34, 35, 50, 111, 124, 167, 192–195, 198, 201, 224
   as a container environment, 128
   dreaming, 151–153, 156–157, 161, 167
   dynamic, 34, 165, 192–193, 195–196
   foundation, 34, 192–196, 198, 224
   globalised, 193, 198
   group, 8, 32, 82, 124, 128, 132–133, 152, 161, 200
Matte-Blanco, I., 38
maturity, 166, 190, 205, 207, 211, 222
Maunder, C. R. F., 210, 213–214, 219
Mayerson, P., 100
Mayes, A., 200
McCarron, J., 155
McGuire, P. K., 150
McKenna, P. J., 172
McKenzie, K. R., 123
McKisack, C., 134
McNally, D., 149
meaning *see also*: unconscious
   continuous search for, 183
   joint, 200
   latent, 152
   symbolic, 180, 196, 205
measure, 82, 114, 126–127, 197, 213, 224
medication, 125–126, 129–131, 137, 142, 146, 154–155, 167
Mehta, Z., 205
Meier, G., 204, 208
melancholy, 104, 216
melody, 203, 209, 212–213, 217, 219–220
member (*passim*)
   group, xviii, 8, 10, 24, 26, 32–35, 61, 67, 71, 73, 82, 110, 113–114, 128, 143–145, 156, 167, 190, 200, 202, 210, 212–214
   neurotic, 58, 128, 147, 156
   new, 59, 68–71, 87, 89–92, 102–103, 144, 154, 159, 167, 201, 215
   of mixed psychopathology, 148
   of the orchestra, 200, 203–204, 210, 212

   psychotic, 58, 129, 138, 154–155
   non-, 158
   with schizophrenia, 139–140, 148, 154
   with severe psychosomatics, 139
memory, 49, 172 *see also*: desire, dream
Menon, V., 208
Messiah, 18, 29, 89
metaphor, xvii, 5, 25, 40–42, 77, 199–200, 207, 219
Meyer, C., 121
Mikkelsen, E. J., 96
Milders, C. F. A., 139
milieu, 74, 192, 196
   therapy, 70, 73, 95, 97, 137
mirror(ing), 13, 92, 100, 113, 127, 129, 133, 140, 144, 150, 153, 168, 170, 172–173, 178, 188, 190, 193, 198 *see also*: fragmentation, need
   benign, 113, 128–129, 144, 156
   hall of, 128, 193–194
   malignant, 67, 75, 81, 85, 88, 100, 113, 126, 128, 140, 144, 193, 223
   multi-, 67, 172
   multiple, 132, 140, 148, 201–202
   mutual, 123, 132
   of the dreaming person, 169
   phenomena, 34, 128, 148, 153, 165
   reactions, 34, 124, 153, 165, 192–194
   stage, 178, 198
Mitchison, G., 172
Mitropoulos, D., 205
money, 47–51, 55–61, 103, 184–185, 222 *see also*: space
   -competitor-investment, 54
   -fusion, 51
   genuine symbolic value of, 48, 55
   -gift, 54
   ideational value of, 184
   role of, xvi, 63
   -semi-fusion, 53
   -semi-separation, 53, 61
   symbolism of, 48–49, 184, 195
Mosse, G. L., 189–190

262   INDEX

mother (*passim*) *see also*: attack, behaviour, bond, conductor, ego, figure, fixation, function, group, identification, image, imago, internalisation, matrix, need, object, oedipal, penis, relationship, representation
  archaic, 8, 28, 32–33, 38, 40, 48, 110
  archetypal, 40, 191
  as a feeding person, 197
  -as-thing, 178–180, 182–183
  breast, 182, 185
  castrating, 48
  "dead", 185
  "death" of the, 19
  desire, 36, 40–41, 179, 188
  devouring, 139, 195, 197
  Dragon, 124, 128, 132, 193
  good enough, 51, 56, 93, 132, 148, 154, 167, 191
  imaginary, 122, 179, 187, 194
  omnipotent, 54, 127
  phallic, 11, 14, 111, 170
  phallus, 36, 41
  primal, 110
  primordial, 49, 164
  symbolic, 61, 179, 198
mourning, 53–54, 63, 91–92, 96, 103, 108, 130, 133, 216–217
movement
  "crescendo", 32, 35
  "decrescendo", 32, 35
  first, 215, 217, 219
  of a classical symphony, 219
  of the group session, 215
  second, 215, 217
  third, 215, 218
Mozart, W. A., 202
multi-factorial assessment of eating disorders symptoms (MAEDS), 127
music
  and group analysis, 207, 225
  and human speech, 203
  atonal, 202, 209, 214, 216
  baroque, xvii, 201–203, 208, 210, 213–216, 219
  classical, xii, xvii, 202–203, 208, 210, 213–215, 219–220
  improvising, 212
  instrumental, 202, 219
  modern, 213–214, 220
  pentatonic, 208
  polyphonic and contrapuntal, 201
  romantic, 201–203, 208, 213–214, 220
  symphonic, 201–204, 220
  temporal structure in, 208
  therapeutic effects of, 200
  tonal, 202, 204, 208–209, 214, 218, 220
  vocal, 204, 208, 212
musicality
  human, 200, 212
  inherent, 225
Muti, R., 205
Myers, C., 47–48
mythemes, xv, 40–41, 43–44, 222

Name-of-the-Father, 36, 40, 44, 122, 179–181, 186, 193, 198 *see also*: id
  foreclosure of the, 180
  "signifier" par excellence, 36
narcissism, 6, 13, 110–111, 118, 140, 144, 148, 150, 188 *see also*: disorder, object, personality, state, symmetry
  pathological, 110, 118
  primary, 34, 188, 198, 201
Nazi Germany/Nazism, 24, 83, 189
need *see also*: dependence, object
  absolute, 196
  and/or demand for love, 182
  devouring, 144
  domination of, 185
  for a conductor, 203–204
  for a "good" breast, 137
  for a primal father, 50
  for food, 185
  for intercommunications, 133
  for mirroring, 133

for the breast as real, 164
for the mother, 178, 188, 197
of the illusion, 9
symbiotic, 58, 106, 223
to devour, 185
negative therapeutic reaction, 66
Neimeyer, G., 130
neuroscientific research, 163, 171–172, 208
neurosis, xvi, 13, 66, 80, 100, 117, 143, 150–152, 156, 159, 161, 165–166, 168, 171, 183 *see also*: transference
infantile, 50, 122, 206
obsessive–compulsive, 187–188
Nevas, D. B., 95
Newman, W. S., 219
nipple, 17, 29, 31
Nitsun, M., 192
Nitzgen, D., 23–24, 27, 35, 192

object (*passim*) *see also*: breast, envy, self
archaic, 40, 49, 136, 140, 150
"bad", 61, 100–101, 104–105, 109, 122–123, 161
commercial, 196
"dead", 64, 66, 69–70, 73–74, 137, 141, 150, 161, 165, 182
erotic, 56, 72
external, 151
fantasy of the, 196
"good", 63, 70, 73, 75, 84, 101, 104, 109, 125, 128
good enough, 71
initial, 191
internal, 73, 137
internalised, 52, 136–137
love, 113, 177
maternal, 20, 49–50, 52, 69, 78, 95–96, 99–100, 102, 104–105, 115–116, 135, 168
mothering, xvi, 64, 66, 70, 74–75, 122, 128, 132–133, 150, 153, 223
omnipotent–idealised, 63, 65
part-, 53–54, 61

partial object/breast, 139
pre-narcissistic state without, 141, 148
real, 15, 108
relations, 96
narcissistic "inner", 34
psychoanalysis and, 131
theory, 131
restoration of the, 68
whole, 137, 139
octave, 208, 210
oedipal, 20, 31, 34, 40, 42, 55, 89, 92, 113, 118, 130, 159, 164, 166, 177–179 *see also*: conflict, primal scene, sociality
complex, 9–10, 36, 73, 96, 99
father, 130
inverted, 48–49, 73–74, 81, 91, 111, 113–115, 118, 223
issues, 123, 130
level, 4, 7–8, 12, 19, 27, 51, 99, 105, 122, 129, 132–133, 157, 159–160, 167, 178–179
myth, 9–10, 14
phase, xvi, 222
post-, 11, 34
pre-, 8, 10, 20, 33–34, 42, 64, 130, 132
circle, 221
level, xv, 4, 7–8, 12, 16, 19, 26, 51, 64, 99, 105, 122, 157, 178
mother, 14, 40, 48, 98
phase, xvi, 222
relations, 5, 37
situation, 96, 222
relations/relationships, 5, 9
situation, xv–xvi, 9, 15–16, 20, 27, 52, 57, 60, 91, 96, 109, 114–117, 133, 140, 164, 222
stage, 11, 64, 103, 109
triangle, xv, 16, 18, 37, 64, 140, 221
Oedipus, 14 *see also*: conflict
complex, 8, 11, 14, 16, 19–20, 27–28, 32, 37, 51, 96, 109, 177–179, 223
myth, 6–16, 18–19, 27
Sphinx, 14, 18

omnipotence, 21, 75, 155
orchestra, 55, 199–204, 206–213, 216, 218–220
   as group, 200, 225
   baroque, xvii, 202, 219
   conducting an, xvii, 191, 199–200, 205–207, 211, 213, 219
   romantic, 202–203
   symphonic, 201–203, 219
Ormay, T., 5
Other, 4, 179–181, 188 *see also*: phallus
over-consumption, 185, 195–196, 224
overture, 219

pairing, 18, 29, 31, 54, 79, 81, 83, 87–90, 108, 191, 213
Palazzoli, M. S., 122
Palmer, R. G., 172
paranoia, 100, 163, 183
paranoid–schizoid position, 15, 17–18, 21, 29, 51, 53, 61, 67, 70, 73, 78, 84, 96, 100, 105, 109, 122, 124, 127–128, 132–133, 136, 141, 145, 150, 152, 157–159, 164–167, 169–170, 214–215, 217–218, 220
parental couple, 71–72, 75, 147–148, 166–167, 171, 198
parental union, 19, 68, 164, 166
paternal ideal, 28, 109, 116
paternity, xv, 7, 10, 25, 30, 33, 35, 41–42, 222
   psychotic-like system of, 10
patient(s)
   borderline, 97, 99–101, 106–108, 169
   neurotic, 13, 108, 125, 153, 157, 164, 169–171, 173
   who hear voices, xvi, 151, 153–154, 158, 161, 223
   with borderline personality, 101, 108, 139, 187
   with neuroses, 131
   with schizophrenia, 136–140, 148, 150–151, 153–155, 161, 188
   or other psychoses, 138

payment, xvi, 48, 51–54, 61, 63, 195, 222
penis, 12, 17, 31, 51, 68, 113, 169–170
   see also: identification
   /breast, 19, 29, 41, 54, 63
   envy, 63–64, 68, 70
   father's or mother's, 157, 168–170
   paternal, 64–65, 168
   possession of the, 36, 41, 186
perception, 8, 50, 151, 179
personality *see also*: disorder
   borderline, 57, 138–139, 187
   narcissistic, 104
   neurotic, 107, 144
   psychotic part of, 57–58, 66, 74, 81, 91, 100, 110
Peternel, F., 108
Peters, R., 78–79, 84, 87
phallus, 12, 36, 41, 179–180, 185–186
   see also: desire, identification, level/phase/stage, mother, pleasure
   imaginary, 41, 180, 186–187
   of the Other, 179–180
   real possessor of the, 41, 186
philosophy, xii–xiii, xv, 5–6, 8, 25, 47, 221
phobia, 114, 125, 156
phonemes, 40, 44
phrasing, 204, 207, 209, 212
pianissimo, 211, 218
Pine, F., 98–99, 106, 122, 133
Pines, M., 138, 140, 193
Piper, R., xvii, 49, 51, 202
Pisani, R. A., 200
pitch, 210, 216–217, 224
Pivik, T., 172
plasticity
   brain, 200
   symbolic and imaginative, 170
pleasure, 21, 69, 103, 128
   phallic, 37
   /presence, 51
   principle, 51
post-ideological trends, 197
post-industrial world, 194

postmodern *see also*: capitalism, society, world
　group-analytic thought, 3, 6
　subject, 195–196
Powell, A., 5, 25, 200
Powers, N., 212
pre-conception, 20, 31
presto, 207
primal horde, 6, 9, 13, 34, 50, 54–55
primal scene *see also*: image, incest
　evolution, 15, 164
　fantasy of the, 166
　in an ideogram, 165
　integration of the fantasy of the, 167
　oedipal fate of the, 166
　parental coitus, 15, 65
　parental couple, 167
　visualise the, 171
　was presented as totally split, 168
process
　analytic, 88, 108
　dreaming, 152, 158, 165, 169, 172
　dynamic, 41–42
　group, 13, 101–102, 105, 152, 193, 206, 208
　　analytic, 51, 53, 57, 158, 203, 207, 224
　mental, 74, 209
　primary, 151
　therapeutic, 105
Prodgers, A., 23, 35
production, 149, 152, 166, 169, 172, 184–185, 196
Profita, G., 4, 14
projection, xvi, 13, 18, 33, 69, 79, 81, 86, 87, 91, 101, 164, 166, 223
projective identification, xvi, 17, 67, 74, 78, 80–81, 84–86, 91–92, 101, 103, 151, 164, 166–167, 170, 223
　destructive, 74, 150, 168
　excessive, 150, 152, 165
prosody, xvii, 208–209
psychoanalytic model, 4, 14
psychology, xii, 24–25, 49, 77, 180
　neuro-, 173

psychosis (*passim*)
　bipolar, 138
　paranoid, 125, 143, 156, 167
psychosomatic *see also*: symptom
　disturbances, 59
　illness, 148, 154
　severe, 139
psychotherapy
　analytic, 113, 123
　group, 15, 27, 47, 99–100, 126, 138, 151, 153, 194, 201, 220
　-analytic, xiv, xvi, 50, 61, 69, 75, 93, 97–98, 106, 113, 117, 123, 132, 134, 137, 161, 222–223
　individual, 69, 72, 99–100, 102, 124–125, 131, 137, 139, 142–143, 154, 167
　psychoanalytic, 122
　psychodynamic, 123
psychotic symptoms rating scale (PSYRATS), 155
purging, 126, 129
Purves, D., 208

Racker, H., 98, 108
rallentando, 202, 211
rapid eye movement (REM) sleep, 172
rapprochement, 54, 99
Rattle, S., 205
Read, J., 154
real
　absolute dominance of the, 184
　imaginary and symbolic, 184
　overflow of, 187
reality
　archaic, 172
　bodily, 178
　contact with, 193
　contradiction by, 183
　internal or external, 139
　principle, 41, 51, 110, 178, 194, 197
　psychic, 38, 137
　social, 38
　ultimate, 31

regression, 13, 33, 35, 52, 65, 67, 75, 78, 96, 103, 107, 122, 128, 144, 148, 185, 187, 195, 212, 215, 217
reification, 184, 194, 197
relatedness, 5, 13, 22, 182–183
relations *see also*: oedipal
  family, 34
  human, 182, 185, 197, 224
  intergenerational, 6
  Internet, 197
  interpersonal, 11, 13, 148, 181, 193
  intersubjective, 6
  love, 50
  sexual, 72–73, 85, 102
  social, 184
  transpersonal, 13, 148, 193
  triangular, 99
  with the breast, 178
  with the opposite sex, 69
relationship(s) *see also*: oedipal
  based on the foundation matrix, 224
  conflictual, 216
  dual, 63
  internal, 54
  interpersonal, 181
  of a unified couple, 20
  of inverse symmetry, 39
  of malignant symbiosis, 20
  of trust and symbiosis, 102
  on a non-verbal level, 84
  phantasmagoric form of, 184
  primal, 65
  psychotic, 152
  symbiotic, 59, 68, 98, 104, 142, 185, 196
  the prototype of, 54
  transpersonal, 24, 111, 140, 203
  with the conductor, 69
  with the father, 69
  with the group, 69, 105
  with the mother, 18, 69, 148
  with the therapist, 101, 103–104
reparation, 111
representation (*passim*) *see also*: thing
  "bad", 78, 84, 104
  female, 37
  "good", 78
  maternal, 14
  of desire, 190
  of self, 78
  of the father, 11, 26, 55
  of the group, 105, 166, 190
  of the group and the conductor, 84, 219
  of the mother, 16, 26, 110, 191
  pre-conscious, 150
repression, 110, 182, 185–186
  failed, 111
resistance, 48, 65, 89, 97, 145
resonance, 153, 156, 165, 201–202
  negative, 85
  phenomena, 210, 212
  position, 217
return of the repressed, 111
revenge, 136, 142
reverie, 31, 167
rhythm, xviii, 202–204, 212–213
Richards, E., 200, 211–212
ritardando, 211
Ritchie, S., 123
Rizzolatti, G., 172
Robbins, M., 99
Roberts, N., 200
Romme, M. A., 149
Rorty, M., 121
Rosen, C., 219
Ross, D., 208
rubato, 213
Russell, J., 121
Ryali, S., 208
Ryle, A., 139–140

sadness, 56, 58, 60–61, 208, 211, 216
Sandison, R. A., 100
Sartorius, N., 149
satisfaction, 21, 110, 127, 182, 185
scale, xvii–xviii, 207–208, 213–217
scapegoat(ing), xvi, 77–81, 83–84, 87, 89, 92–93, 223
Scarone, S., 172
Scheidlinger, S., 80

schema(ta), xv, 8, 11, 42, 130
    cognitive, 150
    phylogenetically inherited, 8, 15
    static, 222
Schenker, H., 209, 212
Scherchen, H., 207, 210, 212–213
Schermer, V. L., 138, 172
schizo-affective disorder, 149,
    154–155, 161, 188
schizophrenia, 66, 100, 125, 135–142,
    148–151, 153–155, 161, 183, 188
    see also: depression
    paranoid, 154–155
Schlesinger, H. J., 95–96, 98, 108
Schneider, S., 78–79, 84, 87
Scholz, R., 192
Schreter, R. K., 97
Schulte, P., 4–5, 25
Schwartz, D. A., 208
score, 203–204, 207–208, 213, 219
Searles, H. F., 136–137
Segercrantz, U., 123, 144
selected fact, 15, 19, 39
self (*passim*) *see also*: conscious,
        group, image, projective
        identification, representation,
        transference
    body, 122
    breast, 51, 53
    fragmented parts of, 151
    -hatred, 21
    -object, 122
        archaic, 123
        bodily, 127–129
        idealised, 123, 127, 132
    other, 54
Sengun, S., 81, 83
separation, 48–50, 53–54, 59, 61,
    70–71, 74, 78, 95, 125, 130, 133
separation–individuation, 54, 67, 99,
    108, 122, 133, 145, 159–160
    phase of the, 53, 133
    sub-phase of the, 53, 122
sexual(ity), 21, 38, 54, 64, 85–86, 88,
    157, 178 *see also*: abuse, anxiety,
        homosexuality, relations
    hetero-, 81

Shedler, J., 123
siblings, 49, 64, 102, 128
signified, 40, 160
signifier *see also*: Name-of-the-Father,
        phallus
    law of the, 179
    of the Other, 179–180
    of the subject's expression, 192
    primordial, 179
Silk, E. R., 97
Silver, C. B., 64–65
Simpson, K., 121
Siris, G., 135
Skodol, A. E., 97
Skolnick, M. R., 125, 151
Skynner, R., 193
Slade, P. D., 140
Sluming, V., 200
Smith, J., 125, 151, 153
Smith, M., 126
sociability, 6, 8, 21
social
    classes, 192
    cognition, 140
    mobility, 181
socialisation, 104, 111, 138
sociality
    a new model of, 19
    for the oedipal situation, 20
    genuine, 22, 110
    of narcissistic origin, 110
    pseudo-, 21, 110
    real, 21, 110
society, 9–10, 15, 21, 26, 35, 40, 44, 77,
    179–183, 185, 187–188, 190, 192,
    194, 196–198
    contemporary, 34, 188
    industrial, 182, 184, 186
    post-, 182
    love for the
    modern, 6, 181
    post-, 181, 196, 224
    western, 189, 196, 207, 224
sociology, xi, 5, 25
Solti, G., 205
sonata, 203, 215, 219

space, xii, 38, 59, 104
    and time, 8, 56
    –time and money, 56
speech, 149, 205, 208–213
    group, 211, 219
        "inner" unconscious, 210
    human, xvii, 203, 209, 219, 224
    inner, 149
    rhythms, xviii
    therapist, 125
splitting, 9, 19, 26, 53, 68, 70, 81, 105, 114, 122, 136, 147, 166, 168
Springer, T., 97
staccato, 213
Stacey, R., 4–5, 25
state(s) *see also*: object, oedipal
    emotional, 48, 66, 71, 159
    family, 177
    fusion, 132, 179, 191
    group formations, 26
    mental, 178
    narcissistic/pre-narcissistic, 141, 148, 197
    nervous, 84
    neurotic, 183
    of confusion, 53
    of demand for love, 178
    of desire, 179
    of immobilisation, 13
    of need and demand, 178, 182, 187, 198
    of real, 187
    of the imaginary, 179
    psychotic, 99, 152, 193, 196
    regressive, 130, 198
Steel, Z., 123, 134
Strauss, R., 205
strength, 10, 26, 64–65, 67, 118, 152, 200, 206–207, 218–219
Strich, S., 200
subjectivity, xviii, 51, 53–54, 224
    inter-, 4, 6, 14, 42, 48, 200
    intra-, 4–5, 78
sublimation, 109, 113, 172
suckling, 50, 61, 63, 140, 164–165, 178, 196
    dialectic of, 49, 147

good enough, 51–52, 54, 164
    uninterrupted, 52
suicide, 18, 104, 137, 155
Sutton-Smith, D., 123
symbiosis, 99, 100–102, 104, 108, 150, 223 *see also*: syndrome
    benign, 20, 22, 100, 222
    malign(ant), xvi, 20, 139, 161, 222
    with the group/mother, 58–59, 70
symbol(ic) (*passim*) *see also*: death, father, fragmentation, therapist, value
    balance between the real, the imaginary and the, 183–184, 186
    "dead", 36–37, 48, 108, 179, 183, 204, 207
    destruction of the, 184
    dream, 169
    inherent in death, 116
    language, 198
    linguistic, 209
    musical, 209
    paternal order, 179–180
    pictorial, 152
    primitive, 43
symmetry, xviii, 38–39, 44, 53
    reverse, xv, 44, 222
symptom(s), 71–72, 105, 107, 115–116, 122, 129, 131–132, 142, 144, 149, 155, 163, 167, 188, 206
    depressive, 141–142, 148
    eating disorder, 127, 134
    psychosomatic, 156, 161
syndrome, 98, 135, 137
    negative-symptom, 142
    of schizophrenia, 142
    post-psychotic depression-like, 142
    secondary depression, 135
    symbiosis, 98
        distorted, 223
        malignant, xvi

Tarrier, N., 155
Taylor, M. A., 135
Taylor, M. J., 127

tempo, 203, 207–211, 216–217, 219–220
termination, 74, 93, 96, 107–108, 134
  abrupt, 196
  early, xvi, 98–99, 223
  of a therapy, 96, 107, 131
  premature, 100, 106
  successful, 96, 109
texture, 203, 212, 219–220
Thelen, M. H., 126
therapeutic
  alliance, 127
  circle, 105
  evolution, 124, 131, 139, 200
  progress, 124, 132, 134
  situation, 34
therapist (*passim*) *see also*: group
  as father, 25, 32, 48, 112, 133
  as leader, 25, 112, 207
  individual, 95
  symbolic death of the, 112
therapy (*passim*) *see also*: group
  cognitive-behavioural, 123, 134, 150
  individual, 70, 72, 104, 125, 129, 132, 139, 143
  psychoanalytic, 47, 110
  violation of the contract, 74
thing *see also*: mother
  encapsulated, 151
  hallucinated and persecuting, 136
  interpretation of, 19, 30
  -presentations, 49
  representations of, 150
  words (as), 151
thinking, xviii, 3, 5, 7, 38, 55–56, 59, 86, 89, 92, 112, 115
  psychoanalytic, 112
  symbolic, 55
  unconscious waking, 18
  Western way of, 38
Thomas, G., 130
Thomas, K., 166
Thomas, P., 149
Thompson, S., xvii, 49, 51, 202

Thompson-Brenner, H., 123
Thornton, C., 121
thought, xi, 5, 14, 25, 38–39, 55–56, 112, 115, 136, 142–143, 149, 151, 156, 177–178, 194, 206, 218
  see also: unconscious
  analytic, 3, 5–6
  psycho-, 6, 36, 64
  in search of a thinker, 112
Thygesen, B., 200, 210
timbre, 203, 212–213
Titze, I. R., 209
Todd, N. P. M., 207
Toder, M., 140, 193
tonality, 204, 209, 214, 218, 220, 224
  see also: music
tonic, 200, 209, 214–215
Toscanini, A., 205
totem(ic), 26, 28 *see also*: group
totemism, 7–8, 26, 28, 38–39, 41
Tower of Babel, 18
tradition, 6, 192, 198
transference, 5, 13, 24, 34–35, 50, 72, 80, 91, 102, 122, 124, 127, 133, 152, 157 *see also*: countertransference
  figure, 206
  latent, 204
  level, 14, 32, 34, 109, 201
  multi-, 67
  negative, 66, 126
  neurosis, 34, 66
  personal, 11, 13
  positive, 74, 109
transposition, 78, 165
  phenomena, 153
trauma(tic), 42, 80, 92, 154, 161, 188, 193–196, 198 *see also*: castration
Trevarthen, C., 212
triangle, xv, 14–16, 19–22, 222
  see also: circle, oedipal
Trist, E., 30
Trower, P., 131, 140, 150
trust, 102, 156, 166, 204
tuning, 210–211

unconscious(ness), xiv, 5–7, 18, 38–41, 67–68, 79, 82, 85, 87, 89, 101, 108, 114, 130, 153, 161, 163, 178–179, 181–182, 187, 206, 209, 212 *see also*: conscious, speech
 collective, xii, 34
 conflict, 211, 213
 "dead", 66
 emotional impulses, 30
 fantasy, 34
 level, 25, 181, 204, 206, 218
 meaning, 201
 motives, 88, 201
 representations, 150
 social, xii, xvii, 5, 7, 81, 181, 193–194, 196–197, 224
 thought, 38, 158
Urlić, I., 99, 126, 138–139

vacation(s), 52–54, 57, 59, 73, 215–216
Valbak, K., 123, 132
value, 14, 16, 27, 89, 92, 110, 142, 148, 164, 181, 184, 192, 213
 symbolic, 49, 52, 55, 147
van der Werf, H., 212
vengefulness, 141, 143
Vize, C., 134
Vogel, E. F., 78
vomiting, 127–128

Wade, T., 134
Wagner, R., xvii, 202–204, 208–209, 220, 224
Walker, P. M., 214
Waller, G., 121, 123, 130, 134
Wardi, D., 96, 109
Ware, C., 209
Wasserman, A., 97

weaning, 49–50, 52, 54, 79, 108, 140, 147, 195
Weber, M., 184
Weegmann, M., 4
Weinberg, H., xvii, 140, 193
Welt, S. R., 47
Wennerstrom, A., 209
Westen, D., 123
Westergaard, P., 209
Weston, M. D., 124, 128, 132, 144
Weyman, A., 193
Wilke, G., 193
Wilkinson, S. M., 98, 108
Williamson, D. A., 127
Willis, S., 123, 132–133
Wing, J. K., 149
Winnicott, D. W., 51, 56, 91, 122, 132, 140, 148
Winship, G., 24
Wis, M. R., 205
Wittry, D., 203–204
Wolberg, L., 108
Wonderlich, S., 126
Wooster, E. G., 64
world, 188, 192–194
 enriched, 203
 inner, 101, 210
 postmodern, xvii, 194, 221
 war, 184
  Second, 189–190, 198
Wotton, L., 200, 209–210, 213

Yalom, I. D., 78–79, 98, 151

Zarcone, V. P. Jr, 172
Zeitgeist, 24, 30
Zender, J., 80
Zerbe, K. J., 122
Zinkin, L., 67, 81, 126, 140, 193
Žižek, S., 183–185